"A witty, concise and delightfully logical guide for the high-tech entrepreneur. Everything you need to know, but not a line more. I'm already recommending it to the faculty, students and business colleagues who are starting companies."

— **Lita Nelsen**
Former Director, Technology Licensing Office
Massachusetts Institute of Technology
Cambridge, Massachusetts

"I wish this book were around when I started my first company. The entrepreneur can learn in one evening's reading what it took me two years of learning-by-doing! I plan on giving a copy to every CEO in our venture fund's portfolio."

— **Gordon B. Baty**
Partner, Zero Stage Capital
Cambridge, Massachusetts

★★★★★ *5 Star Reviews from Amazon.com Readers*

The Best Book on Financial Statements, Period! *Wow, what a great book!* I'm a technical professional and now no longer in the financially confused majority.

— Robert I. Hedges (Burnsville, MN)

Simply the Best! Clearly the first introductory book one should read. This book — a must on every managers shelf — adds value by providing clear and concise definitions and relates them visually to the changing financial statements. A tremendous bang for the buck. *Simply go get it and read it.*

— ClimbHigh

The author has a gift that few experts have. He anticipates all my newbie/beginner stupid questions… As soon as the little voice in my head asks, "But why did they do it this way?" the author gives me the answer. *This book has been of enormous value to me. It is an essential reference for anyone who needs to understand what business finances are about.*

— M. Kramer (United States)

A Masterpiece. Every single financial term is clarified with a layman's language. Moreover, for every single term, there is a very understandable example. Likewise, in every page there is a sheet explaining all the transactions. *I strongly believe that this book is a masterpiece for non-financial managers.*

— a reader

Excellent! I purchased this book for an MBA course and ended up using it more than the assigned text. *The author makes a complicated subject seem like child's play!*

— Bill Holcomb (Cleveland, OH)

Perfect book when first learning... This is a wonderfully clear and concise introduction to the interpretation of financial statements... Read this if you are not a CPA or MBA but must "get a handle" on Balance Sheets, Income Statements and Cash Flow Statements. *This should be the first book you buy.*

— Jack Fossen (Dallas, TX)

Outstanding!! Looking to understand how financial statements work?...then purchase this book—*there's none better.* I am a graduate student nearing the completion of my MBA degree. The author speaks in basic terms about what financial statements mean and how they work. This book puts it all together for the reader.

— Joseph P. Gallagher (Bellinghan, WA)

A very useful book. While the book gets only skin deep on accounting concepts, it does an excellent job in deconstructing how the Income Statement, Statement of Cash Flows, and Balance Sheet are changed. Very few accounting-related books make explicit what happens the way this book does.

— R. Chonchol (Florida)

Want to understand financial statements? I took an accounting class...and I had difficulty interpreting financial statements. So, I gambled and bought this book with a hope to unravel the mystery on financial statements. It really worked! *Overall, the knowledge gained exceeds multiple folds of the time and money invested on this book!*

— Tuan minh Tran

Excellent, buy it!! If you are in the finance business, of any kind, and you are not an accountant, *this book is for you.*

— Richard Gomez (San Diego, CA)

WOW, Incredible. I took an accounting course at University; I now wish that my professor used this book in the course. So easy to understand and with great examples. *Suitable for anyone who wants to learn accounting the fast and easy way.*

— Kavkazy (Toronto, Canada)

Hands down the best resource on financial statements I have ever seen. The content is very clear. I especially enjoyed the section on the fictional AppleSeed company, and its evolving financial statements based on what was happening.

— Paul R. Chitoiu

Great for Everyone! Great book for Everyone from finance manager, non-finance managers or people who just want to understand finance.

— Brian L.

A Definite buy! This book is seriously so good. I've been in the accounting world for 10 years, I have my Accounting degree, and I am a Controller for a small regional company. This book should be required reading in any entry-level accounting class in college.

— The Lamars

This book is special. I'm a CFA and have a MS in Finance and I have never read a book that so beautifully explains financial statement analysis.

— Nick

Excellent to help understand financial statements. I enjoyed reading this book (as much as one could enjoy a book on numbers, that is!). I took accounting a long time ago in college so knew the basics but rough around the edges .

— M. Vigod

The first book for beginners in business. Thomas Ittelson has done what most authors fail to do: explain something to beginners in an understandable way. I cannot say enough good things about this book.

— Brian B.

Finally, a book to really help you understand!. BEST book I've ever read on understanding financials! I have been a solo entrepreneur for years and never really understood the financials and how they interrelate until now!

— Bill Mayer

A joy to read. If you're new to accounting, this book should be your first stop. The explanations are accessible. It's a joy to read.

— Alison DePew

Revised, Updated, & Expanded 3rd Edition

Financial Statements

A Step-by-Step Guide to Understanding and Creating Financial Reports

CAREER PRESS

Revised, Updated, & Expanded 3rd Edition

Financial Statements

A Step-by-Step Guide to Understanding and Creating Financial Reports

Thomas R. Ittelson

Cover design by Ellen Varitimos

Interior Design and Layout by Thomas R. Ittelson

Typeset in NewCenturySchoolbk LT and **Century Gothic**

Career Press, an Imprint of Red Wheel\Weiser
65 Parker Street, Suite 7
Newburyport, MA 01950
www.careerpress.com
www.redwheelweiser.com

Printed in Canada
MAR
10 9 8 7 6 5 4 3 2 1

Library of Congress Cataloging-in-Publication Data

Available upon request.

~

I dedicate this book to my son Alesdair, who has had the good sense to become a nonprofit lawyer and not an accountant. Also, to Cas, scholar and toy designer. A good combination.

~

Acknowledgments

Many people helped make this book a reality. First and foremost, thanks to my family: Mary, Johnny, Bobbi, Darcy, Sara & Tim, Brenden, Bryce and baby Callie for being on my side. at my side

Many people helped make this book possible. My special thanks go to the late Isay Stemp, who first showed me that knowing a little finance and accounting could be fun. Many thanks to my original publisher, Ronald Fry of Career Press, who saw promise in the original version of this book and agreed to publish it now over 20 years ago. With over 200,000 copies in print, we certainly forged a productive partnership. Continued thanks to my current publishers Michael Kerber and Michael Pye at Red Wheel/Weiser for keeping the franchise alive.

My thanks to: Gwen Acton and Paul O'Brian for keeping me (mostly) sane; Stephen J. Potter for calling me from the road; Barbarajo Bockenhauer for her continuing encouragement and heckling; David Reid for sending me laughs; Mary Brinton for being the most brilliant of women; Drs. Leann Canty and Rachel Fawcett for keeping me healthy; Sallie Randolf, Esq. for keeping me out of jail'; Stacia O'Neil for the New Hampshire coast; and Jean-Ann Schulte for caring.

Also, to Barbie and Joe.

Contents

Section A. Financial Statements: Structure & Vocabulary

Much of what passes for complexity in accounting and financial reporting is just specialized vocabulary and simple numeric structures. This section will introduce the words, the basic accounting principles and the structure of the main financial statements.

Accountants have some basic rules upon which all their work in preparing financial statements is based. Who makes these rules? The simple answer is that the "FASB" makes the rules and they are called "GAAP." Got that?

The *Balance Sheet* is one of the two main business financial statements. The other is the *Income Statement*. The *Balance Sheet* states the basic equation of accounting at an instant in time: *What you have minus what you owe is what you're worth.*

The *Income Statement* is one of the two main financial statements of a business. The other one is the *Balance Sheet*. The *Income Statement* gives a significant perspective on the health of the enterprise by showing its profitability.

Where the company gets cash, and where that cash goes. The *Cash Flow Statement* tracks the movement of cash through the business over a defined period of time.

The financial statements are connected; an entry in one may well affect each of the others. This interlocking flow of numbers allows the three statements together to form a cohesive picture of the company's financial position.

- Balance Sheet Connections.
- Sales Cycle.
- Expense Cycle.
- Investment Cycle.
- Asset Purchase and the Depreciation Cycle.

Section B. Transactions:
Exploits of AppleSeed Enterprises, Inc.

With our knowledge of the three main financial statements, we will now draft the books of a hypothetical company, AppleSeed Enterprises, Inc. We will report the common and everyday actions that AppleSeed takes as it goes about its business of making and selling applesauce. Accounting for these "transactions" (T1 through T33 below) is the subject of much of this book. We will describe the Balance Sheet, Income Statement and Cash Flow Statement entries for common and ordinary business actions from selling stock, to shipping product, to paying the owners a dividend.

Welcome to our little business, AppleSeed Enterprises, Inc. Imagine that you are AppleSeed's entrepreneurial chief executive officer (CEO). You also double as treasurer and chief financial officer (CFO).

T1. Sell 150,000 shares of AppleSeed's common stock ($1 par value) for $10 per share.

T2. Pay yourself your first month's salary. Book all payroll-associated fringe benefits and taxes.

T3. Borrow $1 million to buy a building. Terms of this 10 year mortgage are 10% per annum.

T4. Pay $1.5 million for a building to be used for office, manufacturing and warehouse space. Set up a depreciation schedule.

T5. Hire administrative and sales staff. Pay first month's salaries and book fringe benefits and taxes.

T6. Pay employee health, life and disability insurance premiums plus FICA, unemployment and withholding taxes.

Now begins the fun stuff. In a few short weeks we will be producing thousands of cases of the best applesauce the world has ever tasted.

T7. Order $250,000 worth of manufacturing machinery. Pay one-half down.

T8. Receive and install manufacturing machinery. Pay the remaining $125,000 due.

T9. Hire production workers; expense first month's salary and wages.

- Prepare bill of materials and establish labor requirements.

- Set up plant and machinery depreciation schedules.

- Plan monthly production schedule and set standard costs.

T10. Place standing orders for raw materials with suppliers; receive 1 million jar labels.

We're ready to start producing applesauce. The machinery is up and running, the workers are hired, and we are about to receive a supply of raw materials.

T11. Receive two months' supply of raw materials.

T12. Start up production. Pay workers and supervisor for the month.

T13. Book depreciation and other manufacturing overhead costs for the month.

T14. Pay for the labels received in Transaction 10 in Chapter 7.

T15. Finish manufacturing 19,500 cases of applesauce and move them into finished goods inventory.

T16. Scrap 500 cases' worth of work-in-process inventory.

- Manufacturing variances: what can go wrong, what can go right and how to account for both.

T17. Pay for the two months' supply of raw materials received in Transaction 11 above.

T18. Manufacture another month's supply of applesauce.

Section C. Financial Statements: Construction & Analysis

Here are some of the details of constructing and analyzing a company's financial statements, and also some of the ways of fudging them.

Journals and ledgers are where accountants scribble transaction entries. A journal is a book (or computer memory) in which all financial events are recorded in chronological order. A ledger is a book of accounts. An account is simply any grouping of like-items that we want to keep track of.

- Cash Ledger.
- Accounts Payable Ledger.
- Accrued Expenses.
- Accounts Receivable Ledger.

Often in judging the financial condition of an enterprise, it is not so much the absolute amount of sales, costs, expenses and assets that are important, but rather the relationships between them.

- Common Size Statements:
  — Income Statement,
  — Balance Sheet.
- Liquidity Ratios:
  — Current Ratio,
  — Quick Ratio.
- Asset Management Ratios:
  — Inventory Turn,
  — Asset Turn,
  — Receivable Days.
- Profitability Ratios:
  — Return on Assets,
  — Return on Equity,
  — Return on Sales,
  — Gross Margin.

- Leverage Ratios:
  — Debt-to-Equity,
  — Debt Ratio.
- Industry and Company Comparisons.

Various alternative accounting policies and procedures are completely legal and widely used but may result in significant differences in the values reported on a company's financial statements. Conservative? Aggressive? Some people would call this chapter's topic "creative accounting."

"Cooking the books" means intentionally hiding or distorting the real financial performance or financial condition of a company. Cooking is most often accomplished by incorrectly and fraudulently moving Balance Sheet items onto the Income Statements and vice versa. Outright lying is also a favorite technique.

Section D. Business Expansion: Strategy, Risk & Capital

"The numbers" are just a single tool—albeit a very useful one — to use with other management tools (and common sense) in deciding how to invest capital for expansion. But remember: A strategically unsound business expansion is very seldom financially sound ... regardless of what the numbers say. *Think strategy first.* This section is all about planning the future and raising capital.

How to expand? Why expand? Why stick our necks out? What strategies should we employ to help us meet our goals? What are our goals anyway? Think through AppleSeed's mission, vision, goals, strategies, actions and tactics. The Board of Directors wants to see our strategic plan!

- Mission, Vision & Goals ... a hierarchy of destinations.
- Strategies, Actions & Tactics ... a hierarchy of ways to get there.

Section E. Making Good Capital Investment Decisions

Capital investment decisions are among the most important that a company's management can make. Often capital is a company's scarcest resource and using capital well is essential for success. The chief determinant of what a company will become is the investments it makes today. Capital budgeting decisions require analyzing business cash flows spanning years. Accounting for the "time value of money" is essential in these analyses.

Would you rather I give you $1,000 today or in five years? Most everyone intuitively knows that a "bird in the hand is worth two in the bush." Now you understand the "time value of money." The rest is details.

- Present Value (PV).
- Future Value (FV).
- Interest and Interest Rates.
- Discounting and Discount Rates.
- Computing Discounted Values.
- Present Value Table.

We are going to invest cash now with high hopes of a large future return. But will the anticipated payback be enough to cover our initial investment? Further, would any of our alternative projects provide us with a better financial return? Net Present Value (NPV) computations are the "gold standard" for capital budgeting. NPV and Internal Rate of Return (IRR) are the two mainstays of investment valuation.

- Net Present Value (NPV).
- Internal Rate of Return (IRR).
- Cash Flow Forecasting for NPV and IRR Analysis.
- Other Capital Budgeting Techniques: ROI, Payback Period, Real Options and Monte Carlo Analysis.

Let's apply all that we have learned about capital budgeting and select the best business expansion course for AppleSeed. After all, the kids are getting older and will graduate soon; maybe one will want to join the business?

- Make vs. Buy Decision for AppleSeed's Business Expansion.
- Forecasting Cash Flows.
- NPV & IRR Analysis of AppleSeed's Expansion Alternatives.
- Business Combination Accounting.

T33. Chips-R-Us joins the AppleSeed happy family of companies!

∼

Crooked investment promoters, speculative investment bubbles waiting to pop and even outright business fraud in high places have been with us for centuries. There are many ways to lose money. Some of the most infamous are discussed in this chapter. Congress recently passed far-reaching legislation to stop these shenanigans — the Sarbanes-Oxley Act — requiring that business bosses certify their company's financial statements are correct under penalty of going to jail and paying big fines. *Don't you feel much safer?*

- Ponzi Schemes and Pyramids.
- Bubbles: Tulips, Technology Stocks and U.S. Houses.
- Garden-Variety Frauds.

In financial calculations spanning time, currency value can be looked at from two different perspectives. It's important when doing historical analysis or making financial projections to understand these two views of value. In "nominal dollars" a McDonald's Big Mac only cost 50¢ 30 years ago, and it costs $5.30 today. Prices tend to increase over time primarily due to inflation. Sometimes it is useful to look at values (i.e., "real dollars") of goods in the past (or expected values in the future) rather than what they actually cost way back when in nominal dollars.

Nonprofit accounting has a different focus than its for-profit cousin. Profit is less important (no taxes to collect) but demonstrating how charitable donations are spent in furtherance of public mission is of great importance. Revenue generation, cost & expense reporting, and management controls are documented for all (i.e., the public and the government) to see. Much of for-profit and nonprofit accounting and financial statements are the same. Here we describe the major differences.

Accountants prefer to use a *Statement of Changes in Financial Position* in the formal reporting of cash flow. This statement is likened to a "bridge" between the *Balance Sheet* at the start of a period and the *Balance Sheet* at the end of a period. This bridging format specifically shows the asset, liability, and equity accounts that change to provide cash and the accounts that use cash.

Back in the olden days when systematic accounting and statement presentation was first developed, the monks would write down each and every transaction as they occurred. The concept of *debits* and *credits* was invented to structure: (a) the layout of accounting journal and ledger books for everyone to understand, (b) to aid the monks in classifying and recording transactions properly, and (c) to catch manual transcribing errors. Today we use computers.

Preface

The first two editions of this book have sold over 200,000 copies. Not as many books as would be expected for a best-selling novel or a famous (or infamous) politician's memoir, but that is a lot for an accounting text.

To keep the book timely, we have updated and expanded this new 3rd edition. I've gotten older and wiser in the 20 years since the 1st edition was published, and I've tried to add some of that wisdom to this new edition.

The text has been reformatted with *spot color* for emphasis and clarity. The layout is more attractive and modern. Tables and charts have been updated and new material added.

Of particular interest is the addition of a discussion of pricing theory. Pricing is more than just guessing, trial and error, or following an old rule of thumb. This section introduces profit maximization pricing theory based on use of price-volume curves. AppleSeed Enterprises, Inc.'s applesauce price deliberations are described.

～

Two new appendixes have been added at the back of the book:

Appendix C. Nonprofit Accounting
—Nonprofit accounting has a different focus than its for-profit cousin. Profit is less important (no taxes to collect) but demonstrating how charitable donations are spent in furtherance of public mission is of great importance. Revenue generation and cost & expense reporting is of interest too. It is documented and available for all (i.e., the public and the government) to see.

Appendix E. Debits and Credits
— Back in the olden days when systematic accounting and statement presentation was first developed, the monks would write down each and every transaction as they occurred. The concept of *debits* and *credits* was invented to structure: (a) the layout of accounting journal and ledger books for everyone to understand, (b) to aid the monks in classifying and recording transactions properly, and (c) to catch manual transcribing errors. Today we use computers and I have not used the debit and credit concepts in this book (they are confusing for non-financial managers). However, since accountants still rely on this double entry system when they discuss the company's books and financial statements, it is good for you to have a basic understanding of what they mean.

Also added at the end of the Index are suggestions for further reading. The internet revolution has made relevant accounting and finance information easily accessible at all levels. In this section we have listed the best sources for more details for topics introduced in this basic text. On-line exploring can be fun and informative.

Enjoy the read. If you have questions or comments, please contact me. I'll be happy to hear from you. My contact information is in *About the Author*.

Thomas Ittelson
Cambridge, Massachusetts

Preface to the 2nd Edition:

If the first edition of this book was an entrepreneurial business, it would be a huge success. Now over 100,000 copies of *Financial Statements: A Step-by-Step Guide to Understanding and Creating Financial Reports* are in press and helping non-financial managers and students of accounting and finance cope with the "numbers of business."

With this new revised second edition, we have expanded the book into five sections from the original three. Many readers of the first edition wanted to better understand making capital investment decision, the focus of our two new sections.

Capital is often a company's scarcest resource and using capital wisely is essential for success. The chief determinant of what a company will become in the future is the capital investments it makes today. So in this new edition, we will use the financial analysis techniques of net present value (NPV) and internal rate of return (IRR) to make investment decisions.

Preface to the 1st Edition:

We needed to hire an accountant to keep the books at our venture-capital backed, high-technology startup of which I was a founder and CEO. I interviewed a young woman — just out of school — for the job and asked her why she wanted to become an accountant. Her answer was a surprise to all of us,

"Because accounting is so symmetrical, so logical, so beautiful and it always comes out right," she said.

We hired her on the spot, thinking it would be fun to have "almost-a-poet" keeping our books. She worked out fine.

I hope you take away from this book a part of what my young accountant saw. Knowing a little accounting and financial reporting can be very satisfying. Yes, it does all come out right at the end and there is real beauty and poetry in its structure.

~

But, let's discuss perhaps the real reason you've bought and are now reading this book. My bet is that it has to do with power. You want the power you see associated with knowing how numbers flow in business

Be it poetry or power, this accounting and financial reporting stuff is not rocket science. You've learned all the math required to master accounting by the end of the fourth grade — mostly addition and subtraction with a bit of multiplication and division thrown in to keep it lively. The specialized vocabulary, on the other hand, can be confusing. You will need to learn the accounting definitions of revenue, income, cost, and expense. You'll also need to understand the structure and appreciate the purpose of the three major numeric statements that describe a company's financial condition.

Here's a hint: Watch where the money flows; watch where goods and services go. Documenting these movements of cash and product is all that financial statements do. It is no more complicated than that. Everything else is details.

But why is it all so boring, you ask? Well, it's only boring if you do not understand it. Yes, the day-to-day repetitive accounting tasks are boring. However, how to finance and extract cash from the actions of the enterprise is not boring at all. It is the essence of business and the generation of wealth.

Not boring at all.

Introduction

Many non-financial managers have an accounting phobia ... a financial vertigo that limits their effectiveness. If you think "inventory turn" means rotating stock on the shelf, and that "accrual" has something to do with the Wicked Witch of the West, then this book is for you.

Financial Statements: A Step-by-Step Guide to Understanding and Creating Financial Reports is designed for those business professionals: (a) who know very little about accounting and financial statements, but feel they should, and those (b) who need to know a little more, but for whom the normal accounting and financial reporting texts are mysterious and unenlightening. In fact, the above two categories make up the majority of all people in business. You are by no means alone.

Financial Statements: A Step-by-Step Guide to Understanding and Creating Financial Reports is a transaction-based, business training tool with clarifying and straightforward, real-life examples of how financial statements are built and how they interact to present a true financial picture of the enterprise.

We will not get bogged down in details that get in the way of conceptual understanding. Just as it is not necessary to know how the microchips in your computer work to multiply a few numbers, it's not necessary to be a CPA (Certified Public Accountant) to have a working knowledge of the "accounting model of the enterprise."

~

Transactions This book describes a sequence of "transactions" of our sample company, AppleSeed Enterprises, Inc., as it goes about making and selling delicious applesauce. We will sell stock to raise money, buy machinery to make our product, and then satisfy our customers by shipping wholesome applesauce. We'll get paid and we will hope to make a profit. Then we will expand the business.

Each step along the way will generate account "postings" on AppleSeed's books. We'll discuss each transaction to get a hands-on feel for how a company's financial statements are constructed. We'll learn how to report using the three main financial statements of a business — the

---

"Accounting is a language, a means of communicating among all the segments of the business community. It assumes a reference base called the accounting model of the enterprise. While other models of the enterprise are possible, this accounting model is the accepted form, and is likely to be for some time.

"If you don't speak the language of accounting or feel intuitively comfortable with the accounting model, you will be at a severe disadvantage in the business world. Accounting is a fundamental tool of the trade."

Gordon B. Baty
Entrepreneurship, Prentice Hall, Englewood Cliffs, NJ, 1990

Balance Sheet, Income Statement and *Cash Flow Statement* — for these common business dealings:

1. selling stock
2. borrowing money
3. receiving orders
4. shipping goods
5. invoicing customers
6. receiving payments
7. paying sales commissions
8. writing off bad debts
9. prepaying expenses
10. ordering equipment
11. paying deposits
12. receiving raw materials
13. scrapping damaged product
14. paying suppliers
15. booking manufacturing variances
16. depreciating fixed assets
17. valuing inventory
18. hiring staff and paying salary, wages and payroll taxes
19. computing profit
20. paying income taxes
21. issuing dividends
22. acquiring a business
23. and more ...

By the end of this book, you'll know your way around the finances of our applesauce-making company, AppleSeed Enterprises, Inc.

Goals My goal in writing this book is to help people in business master the basics of accounting and financial reporting. This book is especially directed at all those managers, scientists, salespeople who should know how a *Balance Sheet, Income Statement*, and *Cash Flow Statement* work ... but don't. Your goal here is to gain knowledge of accounting and finance to assist you in your business dealings. You want the power that comes from understanding financial manipulations. You must know how the score is kept in business. You recognize, as Gordon Baty says that you must "feel intuitively comfortable with the accounting model" to succeed in business.

~

This book is divided into five main sections, each with a specific teaching objective:

Section A. Financial Statements: Structure & Vocabulary will introduce the three main financial statements of the enterprise and define the special vocabulary that is necessary to understand the books and to converse with accountants.

Section B. Transactions: Exploits of AppleSeed Enterprises, Inc. will take us through 31 business transactions, showing how to report the financial impact of each on the *Balance Sheet, Income Statement*, and *Cash Flow Statement* of AppleSeed Enterprises.

Section C. Financial Statements: Construction & Analysis will subject the financial statement of our sample company to a rigorous analysis using common ratio analysis techniques. Then finally we will touch on how to "cook the books," why someone would want to, and how to detect financial fraud.

"... even if it's boring and dull and soon to be forgotten, continue to learn double-entry bookkeeping. People think I'm joking, but I'm not. You should love the mathematics of business."

Kenneth H. Olsen
Entrepreneurial founder of Digital Equipment Corporation

Section D. Business Expansion: Strategy, Risk & Capital will describe the strategic decisions that a fledgling company must make when it expands. We will answer the question, "Where will we get the money, and how much will it cost?"

Then in **Section E. Making Good Capital Investment Decisions** we will analyze business expansion alternatives and select the best using sophisticated net present value (NPV) techniques.

Then, the **Appendices** will be fun. We will discuss: (a) business fraud and speculative bubbles, (b) the value difference between having a dollar today and a dollar tomorrow, (c) the differences between accounting methods for traditional for-profit companies and for non-profit organizations and finally (d) the medieval concept of debits and credits.

~

With your newly acquired understanding of the structure and flow of money in business, you will appreciate these important business quandaries:

- How an enterprise can be rapidly growing, highly profitable and out of money all at the same time and why this state of affairs is fairly common.

- Why working capital is so very important and which management actions lead to more, which lead to less.

- The difference between cash in the bank and profit on the bottom line and how the two are interrelated.

- When in the course of business affairs, a negative cash flow is a sign of good things happening and when it's a sign of impending catastrophe.

- Limits of common costing systems and when to apply (and, more importantly, when to ignore) the accountant's definition of cost.

- Why a development investment made today must return a much greater sum to the coffers of the company in later years.

- How discounts drop right to the bottom line as lost profits and why they are so very dangerous to a company's financial health.

- How risk is different than uncertainty and which is worse.

- Why a dollar in your pocket today can be worth a lot more than a dollar received tomorrow.

- The necessity (and limitation) of forecasting cash flows over time when making capital investment decisions.

- When to use NPV analysis and when to use IRR and why it is important in capital investment decision making.

To be effective in business, you must understand accounting and financial reporting. Don't become an accountant but do "speak the language" and become intuitively comfortable with the accounting model of the enterprise.

Read on.

Section A.
Financial Statement
Structure and Vocabulary

About This Section

This book is written for people who need to use financial statements in their work but have no formal training in accounting and financial reporting. Don't feel bad if you fall into this category. My guess is that 95 percent of all non-financial managers are financially illiterate when it comes to understanding the company's books. Let's proceed toward some enlightenment.

~

This section is about financial statement structure and about the specialized vocabulary of financial reporting. We will learn both together. It's easier that way. Much of what passes as complexity in accounting and financial reporting is just: (a) specialized (and sometimes counterintuitive) vocabulary, and (b) basically simple reporting structure that gets confusing only in the details.

Vocabulary In accounting, some important words may have meanings that are different from what you would think as a non-financial person.

The box below shows some of this confusing vocabulary. It is absolutely essential to use these words correctly when discussing financial statements. You'll just have to learn them. It's really not that much, but it is important. Examples:

1. *Sales* and *revenue* are synonymous and mean the "top line" of the *Income Statement,* the money that comes in from customers.

2. *Profits, earnings* and *income* are all synonymous and mean the "bottom line," or what is left over from revenue after all the costs and expenses spent in generating that revenue are subtracted.

   Note that *revenue* and *income* have different meanings. *Revenue* is the "top line" and *income* is the "bottom line" of the *Income Statement*.

3. *Costs* are money (mostly for materials and labor) spent making a product. *Expenses* are money spent to develop it, sell it, account for it and manage this whole making and selling process.

Sales and **revenue** mean the same thing.
Profit, earnings and **income** mean the same thing.
Now, **revenue** and **income** do not mean the same thing.

Costs are different from **expenses**.
Expenses are different from **expenditures**.

Sales are different from **orders**, but are the same
as **shipments**.

Profits are different from **cash**.
Solvency is different from **profitability**.

---

4. Both *costs* and *expenses* become *expenditures* when money is actually sent to vendors to pay for them.

5. *Orders* are placed by customers and signify a request for the future delivery of products.

   Orders do not have an impact on any of the financial statements in any way until the products are actually shipped. At this point these shipments become *sales*. The words *shipments* and *sales* are synonymous.

6 *Solvency* means having enough money in the bank to pay your bills. *Profitability* means that your sales are greater than your *costs* and *expenses*.

   You can be profitable and insolvent at the same time. You are making money but still do not have enough cash to pay your bills.

Financial Statements Once you understand the specialized accounting vocabulary, you can appreciate financial statement structure. In the following three chapters, we will learn both together: the three main financial statements: the *Bal-ance Sheet*, the *Income Statement* and the *Cash Flow Statement*. To end the section, we will discuss how these three statements interact and when changing a number in one necessitates changing a number in another.

Chapter 1 will lay some ground rules for financial reporting — starting points and assumptions that accounting professionals require to let them make sense of a company's books. In Chapter 2, we will discuss the *Balance Sheet* — what you own and what you owe. Then in Chapter 3 comes the *Income Statement* reporting on the enterprise's product selling activities and whether there is any money left over after all these operations are done and accounted for.

The last statement, but often the most important in the short term, is the *Cash Flow Statement* discussed in Chapter 4. Look at this statement as a simple check register with deposits being cash-in and any payments cash-out.

Chapter 5 will put all three financial statements together and shows how they work in concert to give a true picture of the enterprise's financial health.

Chapter 1.
Twelve Basic Principles

Accountants have some basic rules and assumptions upon which rest all their work in preparing financial statements. These accounting rules and assumptions dictate what financial items to measure and when and how to measure them. By the end of this discussion, you will see how necessary these rules and assumptions are to accounting and financial reporting.

So, here are the 12 very important accounting principles:

1. accounting entity
2. going concern
3. measurement
4. units of measure
5. historical cost
6. materiality
7. estimates and judgments
8. consistency
9. conservatism
10. periodicity
11. substance over form
12. accrual basis of presentation.

These rules and assumptions define and qualify all that accountants do and all that financial reporting reports. We will deal with each in turn.

1. Accounting Entity The accounting entity is the business unit (regardless of the legal business form) for which the financial statements are being prepared. The accounting entity principle states that there is a "business entity" separate from its owners ... a fictional "person" called a company for which the books are written.

2. Going Concern Unless there is evidence to the contrary, accountants assume that the life of the business entity is infinitely long. Obviously this assumption cannot be verified and is hardly ever true. But this assumption does greatly simplify the presentation of the financial position of the firm and aids in the preparation of financial statements.

If during the review of a corporation's books, the accountant has reason to believe that the company may go bankrupt, he must issue a "qualified opinion" stating the potential of the company's demise. More on this concept later.

3. Measurement Accounting deals with things that can be quantified — resources and obligations upon which there is an agreed-upon value. Accounting only deals with things that can be measured.

This measurement assumption leaves out many very valuable company "assets." For example, loyal customers, while necessary for company success, still cannot be quantified and assigned a value and thus are not stated in the books.

Financial statements contain only the quantifiable estimates of assets (what the business owns) and liabilities (what the business owes). The difference between the two equals owner's equity.

4. Units of Measure U.S. dollars are the units of value reported in the financial statements of U.S. companies. Results of any foreign subsidiaries are translated into dollars for consolidated reporting of results. As exchange rates vary, so do the values of any assets and liabilities denominated in foreign currency

5. Historical Cost What a company owns and what it owes are recorded at their original (historical) cost with no adjustment for inflation.

A company can own a building valued at $50 million yet carry it on the books at its $5 million original purchase price (less accumulated depreciation), a gross understatement of value.

This assumption can greatly understate the value of some assets purchased in the past and depreciated to a very low amount on the books. Why, you ask, do accountants demand that we obviously understate assets? Basically, it is the easiest thing to do. You do not have to appraise and re-appraise all the time.

6. Materiality Materiality refers to the relative importance of different financial information. Accountants don't sweat the small stuff. But all transactions must be reported if they would materially affect the financial condition of the company.

Remember, what is material for a corner drug store is not material for IBM (lost in the rounding errors). Materiality is a straightforward judgment call.

7. Estimates and Judgments Complexity and uncertainty make any measurement less than exact. Estimates and judgments must often be made for financial reporting. It is okay to guess if: (a) that is the best you can do, and (b) the expected error would not matter much anyway. But accountants should use the same guessing method for each period. Be consistent in your guesses and do the best you can. See "consistency" below.

8. Consistency Sometimes identical transactions can be accounted for differently. You could do it this way or that way, depending upon some preference. The principle of consistency states that each individual enterprise must choose a single method of reporting and use it consistently over time. You cannot switch back and forth. Measurement techniques must be consistent from any one fiscal period to another.

9. Conservatism Accountants have a downward measurement bias, preferring understatement to overvaluation.

For example, losses are recorded when you feel that they have a great probability of occurring, not later, when they actually do occur. Conversely, the recording of a gain is postponed until it actually happens, not when it is only anticipated.

10. Periodicity Accountants assume that the life of a corporation can be divided into periods of time for which profits and losses can be reported, usually a month, quarter or year.

What is so special about a month, quarter or year? They are just convenient periods; short enough so that management can remember what has happened, long enough to have meaning and not just be random fluctuations. These periods are called "fiscal" periods. For example, a "fiscal year" could extend from October 1 in one year till September 30 in the next year. Or a company's fiscal year could be the same as the calendar year starting on January 1 and ending on December 31.

11. Substance over Form Accountants report the economic "substance" of a transaction rather than just its form. For example, an equipment lease that is really a purchase dressed-up in a costume, should be booked as a purchase and not as a lease on financial statements. This substance over form rule states that if it's a duck … then you must report it as a duck.

12. Accrual Basis of Presentation This concept is very important to understand. Accountants translate into dollars of profit or loss all the money-making (or losing) activities that take place during a fiscal period. In accrual accounting, if a business action in a period makes money, then all its product costs and its business expenses should be reported in that period. Otherwise, profits and losses could flop around depending on which period the entries were made. In accrual accounting, this documentation is accom-

FASB[1] makes the rules and they are called GAAP.[2]

[1] Financial Accounting Standards Board
[2] Generally Accepted Accounting Principles

plished by matching for presentation: (a) the revenue received in selling product and (b) the costs to make that specific product sold. Fiscal period expenses such as selling, legal, administrative and so forth are then subtracted.

Key to accrual accounting is determining: (a) when you may report a sale on the financial statements, (b) matching and then reporting the appropriate costs of products sold, and (c) using a systematic and rational method allocating all the other costs of being in business for the period. We will deal with each point separately.

Revenue Recognition In accrual accounting, a sale is recorded when all the necessary activities to provide the good or service have been completed regardless of when cash changes hands. A customer just ordering a product has not yet generated any revenue. Revenue is recorded when the product is shipped.

Matching Principle In accrual accounting, the costs associated with making products (Cost of Goods Sold, COGS) are recorded at the same time the matching revenue is recorded.

Allocation Many costs cannot be specifically associated with a product. These costs must be allocated to fiscal periods in a reasonable fashion. For example, each month can be charged with one-twelfth of the general business insurance policy even though the policy was paid in full at the beginning of the year. Other expenses are recorded when they arise (period expenses).

Note that all businesses with inventory must use the accrual basis of accounting. Other businesses may use a "cash basis" if they desire. Cash basis financial statements are just like the *Cash Flow Statement* or a simple checkbook. We'll describe features of accrual accounting in the chapters that follow.

~

Who makes all these rules? The simple answer is that "FASB" makes the rules and they are called "GAAP." Note also that FASB is made up of "CPAs." Got that?

Financial statements in the United States must be prepared according to the accounting profession's set of rules and guiding principles called the Generally Accepted Accounting Principles, GAAP for short. Other countries use different rules.

GAAP is a series of conventions, rules and procedures for preparing and reporting financial statements. The Financial Accounting Standards Board, FASB for short, lays out the GAAP conventions, rules and procedures.

The FASB's mission is "to establish and improve standards of financial accounting and reporting for guidance and education of the public, including issuers, auditors, and users of financial information." The Securities and Exchange Commission (SEC) designates FASB as the organization responsible for setting accounting standards for all U.S. public companies.

CPAs CPAs are, of course, Certified Public Accountants. These very exalted individuals are specially trained in college and have practiced auditing companies for a number of years. In addition, they have passed a series of exams testing their clear understanding of both accounting principles and auditing procedures. Note that FASB is made up mostly of CPAs and that CPAs both develop, interpret and apply GAAP when they audit a company. All this is fairly incestuous.

Single and Double Lines

"Lines" are perhaps not as important as principles, but they can be confusing if you don't know how accountants use them in financial statements. Financial statements often have two types of lines to indicate types of numeric computations above and below the lines.

Single lines on a financial statement indicate that a calculation (addition or subtraction) has been made on the numbers just preceding in the column.

The double underline is saved for the last. That is, use of a double underline signifies the very last amount in the statement.

Note that while all the numbers in the statement represent currency, only the top line and the bottom line of the statement normally show a dollar sign. This use is just a convention.

Income Statement *(for the period)*

NET SALES	$a
COST OF GOODS SOLD	b
GROSS MARGIN	a – b = c
SALES & MARKETING	d
RESEARCH & DEVELOPMENT	e
GENERAL & ADMINISTRATIVE	f
OPERATING EXPENSES	d + e + f = g
INCOME FROM OPERATIONS	c – g = h
INTEREST INCOME	i
INCOME TAX	j
NET INCOME	$h + i – j = k

Single line shows an arithmetic operation with the above lines.

Double line shows the end of the statement.

Chapter 2. Balance Sheet

One of the two main financial statements
of a business ... the other is the *Income Statement*.

The Basic Equation of Accounting

- The basic equation of accounting states: "What you have minus what you owe is what you're worth."

$$Assets \; - \; Liabilities \; = \; Worth$$

    "have"   "owe"   "value to owners"

- Worth, net worth, equity, owners' equity and shareholders' equity all mean the same thing—the value of the enterprise belonging to its owners.

The Balance Sheet

- The *Balance Sheet* presents the basic equation of accounting in a slightly rearranged form:

$$Assets \; = \; Liabilities \; + \; Worth$$

    "have"   "owe"   "value to owners"

- By definition, this equation must always be "in balance," with assets equaling the sum of liabilities and worth.

- So, if you add an asset to the left side of the equation, you must also increase the right side by adding a liability or increasing worth. Two entries are required to keep the equation in balance.

Balance Sheet *(as of a specific date)*

Assets	Liabilities & Equity
CASH	ACCOUNTS PAYABLE
ACCOUNTS RECEIVABLE	ACCRUED EXPENSES
INVENTORY	CURRENT PORTION OF DEBT
PREPAID EXPENSES	INCOME TAXES PAYABLE
CURRENT ASSETS	CURRENT LIABILITIES
OTHER ASSETS	LONG-TERM DEBT
FIXED ASSETS @ COST	CAPITAL STOCK
ACCUMULATED DEPRECIATION	RETAINED EARNINGS
NET FIXED ASSETS	SHAREHOLDERS' EQUITY
TOTAL ASSETS	TOTAL LIABILITIES & EQUITY

The Balance Sheet — a snapshot in time.

- The *Balance Sheet* presents the financial picture of the enterprise on one particular day, an instant in time, the date it was written.

- The *Balance Sheet* presents:

  what the enterprise has today: **assets**
  how much the enterprise owes today: **liabilities**
  what the enterprise is worth today: **equity**

- The *Balance Sheet* reports:

  Has today = Owes today + Worth today

  "assets"   "liabilities"   "shareholders' equity"

Balance Sheet *(as of a specific date)*

Assets

CASH	a
ACCOUNTS RECEIVABLE	b
INVENTORY	c
PREPAID EXPENSES	d
CURRENT ASSETS	a + b + c + d = e
OTHER ASSETS	f
FIXED ASSETS @ COST	g
ACCUMULATED DEPRECIATION	h
NET FIXED ASSETS	g – h = i
TOTAL ASSETS	e + f + i = j

What are Assets?

- **ASSETS** are everything you've got — cash in the bank, inventory, machines, buildings — all of it.

- **ASSETS** are also certain "rights" you own that have a monetary value ... like the right to collect cash from customers who owe you money.

- **ASSETS** are *valuable* and this value must be *quantifiable* for an asset to be listed on the Balance Sheet. Everything in a company's financial statements must be translated into dollars and cents.

Balance Sheet *(as of a specific date)*

Assets

CASH	a	*most liquid*
ACCOUNTS RECEIVABLE	b	
INVENTORY	c	
PREPAID EXPENSES	d	
CURRENT ASSETS	a + b + c + d = e	
OTHER ASSETS	f	
FIXED ASSETS @ COST	g	*least liquid*
ACCUMULATED DEPRECIATION	h	
NET FIXED ASSETS	g – h = i	
TOTAL ASSETS	e + f + i = j	

Grouping Assets for Presentation

- Assets are grouped for presentation on the *Balance Sheet* according to their characteristics:

    very liquid assets ..... cash and securities
    productive assets ..... plant and machinery
    assets for sale .... inventory

- **ACCOUNTS RECEIVABLE** are a special type of asset group — the obligations of customers of a company to pay the company for goods shipped to them on credit. See page 22.

- **ASSETS** are displayed in the asset section of the *Balance Sheet* in the *descending order of liquidity (the ease of convertibility into cash)*. **CASH** itself is the most liquid of all assets; **FIXED ASSETS** are normally the least liquid.

Balance Sheet *(as of a specific date)*

Current Assets

Assets

CASH .... a
ACCOUNTS RECEIVABLE .... b
INVENTORY c
PREPAID EXPENSES .... d
CURRENT ASSETS .... a + b + c + d = e

OTHER ASSETS .... f

FIXED ASSETS @ COST .... g
ACCUMULATED DEPRECIATION .... h
NET FIXED ASSETS .... g – h = i

TOTAL ASSETS .... e + f + i = j

Current Assets

- By definition, **CURRENT ASSETS** are those assets that are expected to be converted into cash in less than 12 months.

- **CURRENT ASSET** groupings are listed in order of liquidity with the most easy to convert into cash listed first: (a) **CASH**, (b) **ACCOUNTS RECEIVABLE**, (c) **INVENTORY**, and (d) **PREPAID EXPENSES**.

- **PREPAID EXPENSES** are a special type of **CURRENT ASSETS** — expenditures for services to be rendered to the company within the next 12 months. See page 24.

- The money the company will use to pay its bills in the near term (within the year) will come when its **CURRENT ASSETS** are converted into cash (that is when inventory is sold, and **ACCOUNTS RECEIVABLE** are then paid to the company by customers).

Balance Sheet *(as of a specific date)*

Assets

CASH	a
ACCOUNTS RECEIVABLE	b
INVENTORY	c
PREPAID EXPENSES	d
CURRENT ASSETS	a + b + c + d = e
OTHER ASSETS	f
FIXED ASSETS @ COST	g
ACCUMULATED DEPRECIATION	h
NET FIXED ASSETS	g – h = i
TOTAL ASSETS	e + f + i = j

Current Assets: Cash

- **CASH** is the ultimate liquid asset: on-demand deposits in a bank as well as the dollars and cents in the petty cash drawer.

- When you write a check to pay a bill, you are taking money out of **CASH** assets.

- Like all of the rest of the *Balance Sheet*, **CASH** is denominated in U.S. dollars for corporations in the United States. A U.S. company with foreign subsidiaries would convert the value of any foreign currency it holds (and also other foreign assets) into dollars for financial reporting.

Balance Sheet *(as of a specific date)*

Assets

CASH	a
ACCOUNTS RECEIVABLE	b
INVENTORY	c
PREPAID EXPENSES	d
CURRENT ASSETS	a + b + c + d = e
OTHER ASSETS	f
FIXED ASSETS @ COST	g
ACCUMULATED DEPRECIATION	h
NET FIXED ASSETS	g – h = i
TOTAL ASSETS	e + f + i = j

Current Assets: Accounts Receivable

- When the enterprise ships a product to a customer on credit, the enterprise acquires a *right* to collect money from that customer at a specified time in the future.

- These collection rights are totaled and reported on the *Balance Sheet* as **ACCOUNTS RECEIVABLE.**

- **ACCOUNTS RECEIVABLE** are owed to the enterprise from customers (called "accounts") who were shipped goods but have not yet paid for them. Credit customers — most business between companies is done on credit — are commonly given payment terms that allow 30 or 60 days to pay.

Balance Sheet *(as of a specific date)*

Assets

CASH	a
ACCOUNTS RECEIVABLE	b
INVENTORY	c
PREPAID EXPENSES	d
CURRENT ASSETS	a + b + c + d = e
OTHER ASSETS	f
FIXED ASSETS @ COST	g
ACCUMULATED DEPRECIATION	h
NET FIXED ASSETS	g − h = i
TOTAL ASSETS	e + f + i = j

Current Assets: Inventory

- **INVENTORY** is both finished products for ready sale to customers and also materials to be made into products. A manufacturer's **INVENTORY** includes three groupings:

  1. **Raw material inventory** is unprocessed materials that will be used in manufacturing products.
  2. **Work-in-process inventory** is partially finished products in the process of being manufactured.
  3. **Finished goods inventory** is completed products ready for shipment to customers when they place orders.

- As *finished goods inventory* is sold it becomes an **ACCOUNTS RECEIVABLE** and then **CASH** when the customer pays.

Balance Sheet *(as of a specific date)*

Assets

CASH .... a

ACCOUNTS RECEIVABLE .... b

INVENTORY c

PREPAID EXPENSES .... d

CURRENT ASSETS .... a + b + c + d = e

OTHER ASSETS .... f

FIXED ASSETS @ COST .... g

ACCUMULATED DEPRECIATION .... h

NET FIXED ASSETS .... g – h = i

TOTAL ASSETS .... e + f + i = j

Current Assets: Prepaid Expenses

- **PREPAID EXPENSES** are bills the company has already paid ... but for services not yet received.

- **PREPAID EXPENSES** are things like prepaid insurance premiums, prepayment of rent, deposits paid to the telephone company, salary advances, etc.

- **PREPAID EXPENSES** are current assets not because they can be turned into cash, but because the enterprise will not have to use cash to pay them in the near future. They have been paid already.

Current Asset Cycle

Current assets are said to be "working assets" because they are in a constant cycle of being converted into cash. The repeating current asset cycle of a business is shown below:

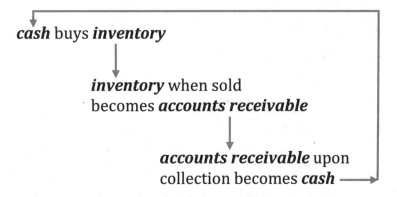

More Asset Types

- In addition to a company's current assets, there are two other major asset groups listed on the *Balance Sheet*: OTHER ASSETS and FIXED ASSETS. These so-called *"non-current assets"* are not converted into cash during the normal course of business.

- OTHER ASSETS is a catchall category that includes intangible assets such as the value of patents, trade names and so forth.

- The company's FIXED ASSETS (so-called *property, plant and equipment, or PP&E*) is generally the largest and most important non-current asset grouping.

Balance Sheet *(as of a specific date)*

Assets

CASH	a
ACCOUNTS RECEIVABLE	b
INVENTORY	c
PREPAID EXPENSES	d
CURRENT ASSETS	a + b + c + d = e
OTHER ASSETS	f
FIXED ASSETS @ COST	g
ACCUMULATED DEPRECIATION	h
NET FIXED ASSETS	g – h = i
TOTAL ASSETS	e + f + i = j

Fixed Assets at Cost

- Fixed assets are productive assets not intended for sale. They will be used over and over again to manufacture the product, display it, warehouse it, transport it and so forth.

- Fixed assets commonly include land, buildings, machinery, equipment, furniture, automobiles, trucks, etc.

- **FIXED ASSETS AT COST** are reported on the *Balance Sheet* at original purchased price. Fixed assets are also shown as *net fixed assets* — valued at original cost minus an allowance for depreciation. See the *depreciation* discussion on the facing page.

Balance Sheet *(as of a specific date)*

Assets

CASH	a
ACCOUNTS RECEIVABLE	b
INVENTORY	c
PREPAID EXPENSES	d
CURRENT ASSETS	a + b + c + d = e
OTHER ASSETS	f
FIXED ASSETS @ COST	g
ACCUMULATED DEPRECIATION	h
NET FIXED ASSETS	g − h = i
TOTAL ASSETS	e + f + i = j

Accumulated Depreciation

- Depreciation is an *accounting convention* reporting (on the Income Statement) the decline in useful value of a fixed asset due to wear and tear from use and the passage of time.

- "Depreciating" an asset means spreading the cost to acquire the asset over the asset's whole useful life. **ACCUMULATED DEPRECIATION** (on the *Balance Sheet*) is the sum of all the depreciation charges taken since the asset was first acquired.

- Depreciation charges taken in a period do lower *profits* for the period, but do not lower *cash*. Cash was required to purchase the fixed asset originally.

Balance Sheet *(as of a specific date)*

Assets

CASH	a
ACCOUNTS RECEIVABLE	b
INVENTORY	c
PREPAID EXPENSES	d
CURRENT ASSETS	a + b + c + d = e
OTHER ASSETS	f
FIXED ASSETS @ COST	g
ACCUMULATED DEPRECIATION	h
NET FIXED ASSETS	g – h = i
TOTAL ASSETS	e + f + i = j

Net Fixed Assets

- The **NET fIXED ASSETS** of a company are the sum of its fixed assets' purchase prices *(***FIXED ASSETS @ COST***)* minus the depreciation charges taken on the *Income Statement* over the years *(***ACCUMULATED DEPRECIATION***)*.

- The so-called *book value* of an asset — its value as reported on the books of the company — is the asset's purchase price minus its **ACCUMULATED DEPRECIATION.**

- Note that depreciation does not necessarily relate to an actual decrease in value. In fact, some assets appreciate in value over time. However, such appreciated assets are by convention still reported on the *Balance Sheet* at their lower book value.

Balance Sheet *(as of a specific date)*

Assets

CASH	a
ACCOUNTS RECEIVABLE	b
INVENTORY	c
PREPAID EXPENSES	d
CURRENT ASSETS	$a + b + c + d = e$
OTHER ASSETS	f
FIXED ASSETS @ COST	g
ACCUMULATED DEPRECIATION	h
NET FIXED ASSETS	$g - h = i$
TOTAL ASSETS	$e + f + i = j$

Other Assets

- The **OTHER ASSETS** category on the *Balance Sheet* includes assets of the enterprise that cannot be properly classified into the current assets or fixed assets categories.

- Intangible assets (a major type of other assets) are things owned by the company that have value but are not tangible (that is, not physical property) in nature.

- For example, a patent, a copyright, or a brand name can have considerable value to the enterprise, yet these are not tangible as a machine or inventory is.

- Intangible assets are valued by management according to various accounting conventions too complex, arbitrary and confusing to be of interest here.

Balance Sheet *(as of a specific date)*

Liabilities & *Shareholders' Equity*

a	ACCOUNTS PAYABLE
b	ACCRUED EXPENSES
c	CURRENT PORTION OF DEBT
d	INCOME TAXES PAYABLE
a + b + c + d = e	CURRENT LIABILITIES
f	LONG-TERM DEBT
g	CAPITAL STOCK
h	RETAINED EARNINGS
g + h = i	SHAREHOLDERS' EQUITY
e + f + i = j	TOTAL LIABILITIES & EQUITY

What are Liabilities?

- **LIABILITIES** are economic obligations of the enterprise, such as money that the corporation owes to lenders, suppliers, employees, etc.

- **LIABILITIES** are categorized and grouped for presentation on the *Balance Sheet* by: (1) to whom the debt is owed and (2) whether the debt is payable within the year (*current liabilities*) or is a long-term obligation.

- **SHAREHOLDERS' EQUITY** is a special kind of liability. It represents the value of the corporation that belongs to its owners. However, this "debt" will never be repaid in the normal course of business.

Current Liabilities

Balance Sheet *(as of a specific date)*
Liabilities & Shareholders' Equity

a .... ACCOUNTS PAYABLE
b .... ACCRUED EXPENSES
c .... CURRENT PORTION OF DEBT
d .... INCOME TAXES PAYABLE
a + b + c + d = e .... CURRENT LIABILITIES

 f .... LONG-TERM DEBT

g .... CAPITAL STOCK
h .... RETAINED EARNINGS
g + h = i .... SHAREHOLDERS' EQUITY

e + f + i = j .... TOTAL LIABILITIES & EQUITY

Current Liabilities

- **CURRENT LIABILITIES** are bills that must be paid within one year of the date of the Balance Sheet. **CURRENT LIABILITIES** are the reverse of current assets:

  CURRENT ASSETS provide cash within 12 months.
  CURRENT LIABILITIES take cash within 12 months.

- The cash generated from current assets is used to pay **CURRENT LIABILITIES** as they become due.

- **CURRENT LIABILITIES** are grouped depending on to whom the debt is owed: (a) **ACCOUNTS PAYABLE** owed to suppliers, (b) **ACCRUED EXPENSES** owed to employees and others for services, (c) **CURRENT DEBT** owed to lenders and (d) **INCOME TAXES PAYABLE** owed to the government.

Balance Sheet *(as of a specific date)*

Liabilities & Shareholders' Equity

a	ACCOUNTS PAYABLE
b	ACCRUED EXPENSES
c	CURRENT PORTION OF DEBT
d	INCOME TAXES PAYABLE
a + b + c + d = e	CURRENT LIABILITIES
f	LONG-TERM DEBT
g	CAPITAL STOCK
h	RETAINED EARNINGS
g + h = i	SHAREHOLDERS' EQUITY
e + f + i = j	TOTAL LIABILITIES & EQUITY

Current Liabilities: Accounts Payable

- **ACCOUNTS PAYABLE** are bills, generally to other companies for materials and equipment bought on credit, that the corporation must pay soon.

- When it receives materials, the corporation can either pay for them immediately with cash or wait and let what is owed become an **ACCOUNT PAYABLE.**

- Business-to-business transactions are most often done on credit. Common trade payment terms are usually 30 or 60 days with a discount for early payment, such as 2% off if paid within 10 days, or the total due in 30 days *("2% 10; net 30").*

Balance Sheet *(as of a specific date)*

Liabilities & Shareholders' Equity

a	**ACCOUNTS PAYABLE**
b	ACCRUED EXPENSES
c	**CURRENT PORTION OF DEBT**
d	**INCOME TAXES PAYABLE**
a + b + c + d = e	**CURRENT LIABILITIES**
f	**LONG-TERM DEBT**
g	**CAPITAL STOCK**
h	**RETAINED EARNINGS**
g + h = i	**SHAREHOLDERS' EQUITY**
e + f + i = j	**TOTAL LIABILITIES & EQUITY**

Current Liabilities: Accrued Expenses

- **ACCRUED EXPENSES** are monetary obligations similar to accounts payable. The business uses one or the other classification depending on to whom the debt is owed.

- **ACCOUNTS PAYABLE** is used for debts to regular suppliers of merchandise or services bought on credit. See facing page.

- Examples of **ACCRUED EXPENSES** are salaries earned by employees but not yet paid to them, lawyers' bills not yet paid, interest due but not yet paid on bank debt and so forth.

Balance Sheet *(as of a specific date)*

Liabilities & Shareholders' Equity

a	ACCOUNTS PAYABLE
b	ACCRUED EXPENSES
c	CURRENT PORTION OF DEBT
d	INCOME TAXES PAYABLE
a + b + c + d = e	CURRENT LIABILITIES
f	LONG-TERM DEBT
g	CAPITAL STOCK
h	RETAINED EARNINGS
g + h = i	SHAREHOLDERS' EQUITY
e + f + i = j	TOTAL LIABILITIES & EQUITY

Current Debt and Long-Term Debt

- Any *notes payable* and the *current portion of long-term debt* are both components of current liabilities and are listed on the Balance Sheet under **CURRENT PORTION OF DEBT.**

- If the enterprise owes money to a bank and the terms of the loan say it must be repaid in less than 12 months, then the debt is called a *note payable* and is a current liability.

- A loan with an overall term of more than 12 months from the date of the Balance Sheet is called **LONG-TERM DEBT.** A mortgage on a building is a common example.

- The so-called *current portion of long-term debt* is that amount due for payment within 12 months and is a current liability listed under **CURRENT PORTION OF DEBT.**

Balance Sheet *(as of a specific date)*

Liabilities & Shareholders' Equity

a	ACCOUNTS PAYABLE
b	ACCRUED EXPENSES
c	CURRENT PORTION OF DEBT
d	INCOME TAXES PAYABLE
a + b + c + d = e	CURRENT LIABILITIES
f	LONG-TERM DEBT
g	CAPITAL STOCK
h	RETAINED EARNINGS
g + h = i	SHAREHOLDERS' EQUITY
e + f + i = j	TOTAL LIABILITIES & EQUITY

Current Liabilities: Taxes Payable

- Every time the company sells something and makes a profit on the sale, a percentage of the profit will be owed the government as *income taxes.*

- **INCOME TAXES PAYABLE** are income taxes that the company owes the government but that the company has not yet paid.

- Every three months or so the company will send the government a check for the income taxes owed. For the time between when the profit was made and the time when the taxes are actually paid, the company will show the amount to be paid as **INCOME TAXES PAYABLE** on the *Balance Sheet.*

Working Capital

- The company's **working capital** is the amount of money left over after you subtract current liabilities from current assets.

"the good stuff"	*"the less good stuff"*	*"the great stuff"*
Current Assets	– Current Liabilities	= Working Capital
CASH	ACCOUNTS PAYABLE	
ACCOUNTS RECEIVABLE	ACCRUED EXPENSES	
INVENTORY	CURRENT PORTION OF DEBT	
PREPAID EXPENSES	INCOME TAXES PAYABLE	

- **Working capital** is the amount of money the enterprise has to "work with" in the short term. **Working capital** feeds the operations of the enterprise with dollar bills. **Working capital** is also called *"net current assets"* or simply *"funds."*

Sources and Uses of Working Capital

- **Sources** of working capital are ways working capital *increases* in the normal course of business. This increase in working capital happens when:

    1. **CURRENT LIABILITIES** decrease and/or
    2. **CURRENT ASSETS** increase

- **Uses** of working capital (also called *applications*) are ways working capital *decreases* during the normal course of business. For example, when:

    1. **CURRENT ASSETS** decrease and/or
    2. **CURRENT LIABILITIES** increase

- With lots of working capital it will be easy to pay your "current" financial obligations ... bills that come due in the next 12 months.

Liabilities

Balance Sheet *(as of a specific date)*
Liabilities & Shareholders' Equity

a	ACCOUNTS PAYABLE
b	ACCRUED EXPENSES
c	CURRENT PORTION OF DEBT
d	INCOME TAXES PAYABLE
a + b + c + d = e	CURRENT LIABILITIES
f	LONG-TERM DEBT
g	CAPITAL STOCK
h	RETAINED EARNINGS
g + h = i	SHAREHOLDERS' EQUITY
e + f + i = j	TOTAL LIABILITIES & EQUITY

Total Liabilities

- **Note:** In most *Balance Sheet* formats there is not a separate line for **TOTAL LIABILITIES.**

- A company's **TOTAL LIABILITIES.** are just the sum of its **CURRENT LIABILITIES** and its **LONG-TERM DEBT.**

- **LONG-TERM DEBT** is any loan to the company to be repaid more than 12 months after the date of the *Balance Sheet.*

- Common types of **LONG-TERM DEBT** include mortgages for land and buildings and the so-called *chattel mortgages* for machinery and equipment.

Balance Sheet *(as of a specific date)*

Liabilities & Shareholders' Equity

a	ACCOUNTS PAYABLE
b	ACCRUED EXPENSES
c	CURRENT PORTION OF DEBT
d	INCOME TAXES PAYABLE
a + b + c + d = e	CURRENT LIABILITIES
f	LONG-TERM DEBT
g	CAPITAL STOCK
h	RETAINED EARNINGS
g + h = i	SHAREHOLDERS' EQUITY
e + f + i = j	TOTAL LIABILITIES & EQUITY

Shareholders' Equity

- If you subtract what the company owes *(total liabilities)* from what it has *(total assets)*, you are left with the company's value to its owners ... its SHAREHOLDERS' EQUITY.

- SHAREHOLDERS' EQUITY has two components:

  1. CAPITAL STOCK: The original amount of money the owners contributed as their investment in the stock of the company.

  2, RETAINED EARNINGS: All the earnings of the company that have been retained, that is, not paid out as dividends to owners.

- Note: Both *"net worth"* and *"book value"* mean the same thing as SHAREHOLDERS' EQUITY.

Balance Sheet *(as of a specific date)*

Liabilities & Shareholders' Equity

a	ACCOUNTS PAYABLE
b	ACCRUED EXPENSES
c	CURRENT PORTION OF DEBT
d	INCOME TAXES PAYABLE
a + b + c + d = e	CURRENT LIABILITIES
f	LONG-TERM DEBT
g	CAPITAL STOCK
h	RETAINED EARNINGS
g + h = i	SHAREHOLDERS' EQUITY
e + f + i = j	TOTAL LIABILITIES & EQUITY

Capital Stock

- The original money to start and any add-on money invested in the business is represented by shares of **CAPITAL STOCK** held by owners of the enterprise.

- **Common stock** is the regular *"denomination of ownership"* for all corporations. All companies issue common stock, but they may issue other kinds of stock, too.

- Companies often issue **preferred stock** that have certain contractual rights or *"preferences"* over the common stock. These rights may include a specified dividend and/or a preference over common stock to receive company assets if the company is liquidated.

Balance Sheet *(as of a specific date)*

Liabilities & Shareholders' Equity

a	ACCOUNTS PAYABLE
b	ACCRUED EXPENSES
c	CURRENT PORTION OF DEBT
d	INCOME TAXES PAYABLE
a + b + c + d = e	CURRENT LIABILITIES
f	LONG-TERM DEBT
g	CAPITAL STOCK
h	RETAINED EARNINGS
g + h = i	SHAREHOLDERS' EQUITY
e + f + i = j	TOTAL LIABILITIES & EQUITY

Retained Earnings

- All the company's profits that have not been returned to the shareholders as dividends are called **RETAINED EARNINGS.**

retained earnings = sum of all profits – sum of all dividends

- **RETAINED EARNINGS** can be viewed as a "pool" of money from which future dividends could be paid. In fact, dividends cannot be paid to shareholders unless sufficient retained earnings are on the *Balance Sheet* to cover the total amount of the dividend checks.

- If the company has not made a profit but rather has sustained losses, it has *"negative retained earnings"* that are called its accumulated deficit.

Balance Sheet *(as of a specific date)*

Liabilities & Shareholders' Equity

a	**ACCOUNTS PAYABLE**
b	**ACCRUED EXPENSES**
c	**CURRENT PORTION OF DEBT**
d	**INCOME TAXES PAYABLE**
a + b + c + d = e	**CURRENT LIABILITIES**
f	**LONG-TERM DEBT**
g	CAPITAL STOCK
h	RETAINED EARNINGS
g + h = i	SHAREHOLDERS' EQUITY
e + f + i = j	**TOTAL LIABILITIES & EQUITY**

Changes in Shareholders' Equity

- **SHAREHOLDERS' EQUITY** is just the sum of the investment made in the stock of the company plus any profits (less any losses) minus any dividends that have been paid to shareholders.

- The value of **SHAREHOLDERS' EQUITY** increases when the company:
    1. *Makes a profit,* thereby increasing **RETAINED EARNINGS**, or
    2. *Sells new stock* to investors, thereby increasing **CAPITAL STOCK**.

- The value of **shareholders' equity** decreases when the company:
    1. *Has a loss,* thereby lowering **RETAINED EARNINGS**, or
    2. *Pays dividends* to shareholders, thereby lowering **RETAINED EARNINGS**.

Balance Sheet *(as of a specific date)*

Assets	Liabilities **& Equity**
CASH	ACCOUNTS PAYABLE
ACCOUNTS RECEIVABLE	ACCRUED EXPENSES
INVENTORY	CURRENT PORTION OF DEBT
PREPAID EXPENSES	INCOME TAXES PAYABLE
CURRENT ASSETS	CURRENT LIABILITIES
OTHER ASSETS	LONG-TERM DEBT
FIXED ASSETS @ COST	**CAPITAL STOCK**
ACCUMULATED DEPRECIATION	**RETAINED EARNINGS**
NET FIXED ASSETS	**SHAREHOLDERS' EQUITY**
TOTAL ASSETS	TOTAL LIABILITIES & EQUITY

Balance Sheet Summary

- The *Balance Sheet* presents the financial picture of the enterprise on one day, an instant in time, the date it was written.

- The *Balance Sheet* presents:

  what the enterprise has today: assets
  how much the enterprise owes today: liabilities
  what the enterprise is worth today: equity

- The *Balance Sheet* reports:

  Has today = *Owes today* + *Worth today*

  "assets"   "liabilities"   "shareholders' equity"

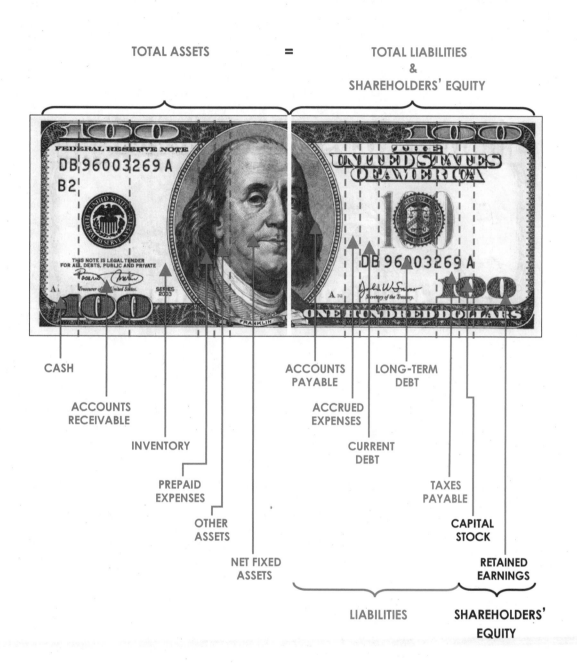

TOTAL ASSETS = TOTAL LIABILITIES & SHAREHOLDERS' EQUITY

CASH

ACCOUNTS RECEIVABLE

INVENTORY

PREPAID EXPENSES

OTHER ASSETS

NET FIXED ASSETS

ACCOUNTS PAYABLE

ACCRUED EXPENSES

CURRENT DEBT

LONG-TERM DEBT

TAXES PAYABLE

CAPITAL STOCK

RETAINED EARNINGS

LIABILITIES

SHAREHOLDERS' EQUITY

Chapter 3. Income Statement

One of the two main financial statements
of a business ... the other is the *Balance Sheet*.

Income Statement *(for the period)*

NET SALES	a
COST OF GOODS SOLD	b
GROSS MARGIN	a – b = c
SALES & MARKETING	d
RESEARCH & DEVELOPMENT	e
GENERAL & ADMINISTRATIVE	f
OPERATING EXPENSES	d + e + f = g
INCOME FROM OPERATIONS	c – g = h
INTEREST INCOME	i
INCOME TAX	j
NET INCOME	h + i – j = k

The Income Statement

- The *Income Statement* gives one important perspective on the health of a business—its *profitability*.

  Note: The *Income Statement* does not tell the whole picture about a company's financial health.

- The Balance Sheet reports on assets, liabilities and equity.

- The Cash Flow Statement reports on cash movements.

  Also note: The *Income Statement* says nothing about when the company receives cash or how much cash it has on hand.

The Income Statement (continued)

- The Income Statement reports on making and selling activities of a business over a period of time:

what's **sold** in the period

minus

what it **cost** *(COGS)* to make

minus

operating expenses for the period

equals

income for the period.

- The **Income Statement** documents for a specific period (a month, quarter or year) the *second basic equation of accounting:*

Sales — *Costs & Expenses* = *Income*

NET SALES

COST OF GOODS SOLD   OPERATING EXPENSES   INCOME

Income Statement *(for the period)*

NET SALES	a
COST OF GOODS SOLD	b
GROSS MARGIN	a − b = c
SALES & MARKETING	d
RESEARCH & DEVELOPMENT	e
GENERAL & ADMINISTRATIVE	f
OPERATING EXPENSES	d + e + f = g
INCOME FROM OPERATIONS	c − g = h
INTEREST INCOME	i
INCOME TAX	j
NET INCOME	h + i − j = k

Net Sales

- **SALES** are recorded on the *Income Statement* when the company actually ships products to customers. Customers now have an obligation to pay for the product and the company has the right to collect.

- When the company ships a product to a customer, it also sends an invoice (a bill). The company's right to collect is called an **ACCOUNT RECEIVABLE** and is entered on the company's *Balance Sheet*.

- **Note: NET SALES** means the total amount the company will ultimately collect from the sale — that is, list price less any discounts offered to the customer to induce purchase.

Sales vs. Orders

- A **sale** is made when the company actually ships a product to a customer. **Orders,** however, are something different.

- **Orders** become **sales** only when the products ordered have left the company's loading dock and are en route to the customer.

- When a **sale** is made, income is generated on the *Income Statement.* **Orders** only increase the "backlog" of products to be shipped and do not have an impact on the *Income Statement* in any way. Simply receiving an order does not result in income.

Costs

- **Costs** are expenditures for raw materials, workers' wages, manufacturing overhead and so forth. **Costs** are what you spend when you buy (or make) products for inventory.

- When this inventory is sold, that is, shipped to customers, its total **cost** is taken out of inventory and entered in the *Income Statement* as a special type of expense called ***cost of goods sold***.

- **Costs** lower cash and increase inventory values on the *Balance Sheet.* Only when inventory is sold does its value move from the *Balance Sheet* to the *Income Statement* as ***cost of goods sold.***

Income Statement *(for the period)*

NET SALES	a
COST OF GOODS SOLD	b
GROSS MARGIN	a – b = c
SALES & MARKETING	d
RESEARCH & DEVELOPMENT	e
GENERAL & ADMINISTRATIVE	f
OPERATING EXPENSES	d + e + f = g
INCOME FROM OPERATIONS	c – g = h
INTEREST INCOME	i
INCOME TAX	j
NET INCOME	h + i – j = k

Cost of Goods Sold

- When a product is shipped and a sale is booked, the company records the total cost of manufacturing the product as **COST OF GOODS SOLD** on the *Income Statement*.

- Remember: When the company made the product, it took all the product's costs and added them to the value of inventory.

- The costs to manufacture products are accumulated in inventory until the products are sold. Then these costs are *"expensed"* through the *Income Statement* as **COST OF GOODS SOLD.**

Income Statement *(for the period)*

NET SALES	a
COST OF GOODS SOLD	b
GROSS MARGIN	a – b = c
SALES & MARKETING	d
RESEARCH & DEVELOPMENT	e
GENERAL & ADMINISTRATIVE	f
OPERATING EXPENSES	d + e + f = g
INCOME FROM OPERATIONS	c – g = h
INTEREST INCOME	i
INCOME TAX	j
NET INCOME	h + i – j = k

Gross Margin

- **GROSS MARGIN** is the amount left over from sales after product manufacturing costs (cost of goods sold) are subtracted. **GROSS MARGIN** is sometimes called *gross profit* or the company's *manufacturing margin.*

NET SALES

COST OF GOODS SOLD   GROSS MARGIN

Cost vs. Expense

- Two different terms, **cost** and **expense,** are used to describe how the company spends its money:

- *Manufacturing expenditures* to build inventories are called **costs.**

- All of the other business expenditures are called **expenses.**

  Note: Using the terms **cost** and **expense** correctly will make it easier to understand how the *Income Statement* and *Balance Sheet* work together.

  Also note: An *expenditure* can be either a cost or an expense. The word "expenditure" simply means the use of cash to pay for an item purchased.

Expenses

- **Expenses** pay for developing and selling products and for running the "general and administrative" aspects of the business.

- Examples of **expenses** are paying legal fees and a salesperson's salary, buying chemicals for the R&D laboratory and so forth.

- **Expenses** directly lower INCOME on the *Income Statement.*

  Note: The words *profit* and *income* mean the same thing; that is, what's left over from sales after you have subtracted all the costs and expenses.

Income Statement *(for the period)*

NET SALES	a
COST OF GOODS SOLD	b
GROSS MARGIN	a – b = c
SALES & MARKETING	d
RESEARCH & DEVELOPMENT	e
GENERAL & ADMINISTRATIVE	f
OPERATING EXPENSES	d + e + f = g
INCOME FROM OPERATIONS	c – g = h
INTEREST INCOME	i
INCOME TAX	j
NET INCOME	h + i – j = k

Operating Expenses

- **OPERATING EXPENSES** are those expenditures (that is, cash out) that a company makes to generate income.

- Common groupings of **OPERATING EXPENSES** are:
  1. **SALES & MARKETING** expenses.
  2. **RESEARCH & DEVELOPMENT** ("R&D") expenses.
  3. **GENERAL & ADMINISTRATIVE** ("G&A") expenses.

- **OPERATING EXPENSES** are sometimes called SG&A expenses, meaning *"sales, general & administrative expenses."*

Income or Loss

- If sales exceed costs plus expenses (as reported on the *Income Statement)*, the business has earned **income.** If costs plus expenses exceed sales, then a **loss** has occurred.

- The terms *income* and *profit* and *earnings* all have the same meaning — what's left over when you subtract expenses and costs from sales.

- Note: The *Income Statement* is often referred to as the *Profit & Loss Statement,* the *Earnings Statement,* or simply the *P&L.*

    Remember: **Income** is the difference between two very large numbers: *sales* less *costs* and *expenses.* Slightly lower *sales* and/or slightly higher *costs* and *expenses* can eliminate any expected profit and result in a **loss.**

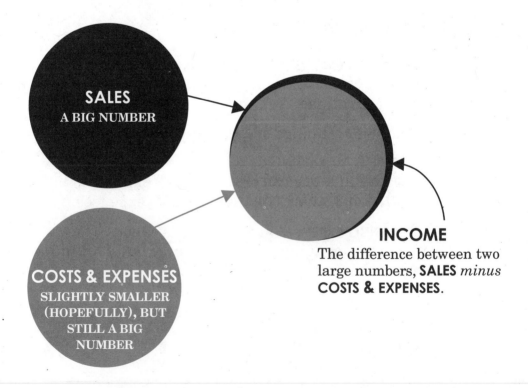

SALES
A BIG NUMBER

COSTS & EXPENSES
SLIGHTLY SMALLER
(HOPEFULLY), BUT
STILL A BIG
NUMBER

INCOME
The difference between two
large numbers, **SALES** *minus*
COSTS & EXPENSES.

Income Statement *(for the period)*

NET SALES	a
COST OF GOODS SOLD	b
GROSS MARGIN	a – b = c
SALES & MARKETING	d
RESEARCH & DEVELOPMENT	e
GENERAL & ADMINISTRATIVE	f
OPERATING EXPENSES	d + e + f = g
INCOME FROM OPERATIONS	c – g = h
INTEREST INCOME	i
INCOME TAX	j
NET INCOME	h + i – j = k

Income from Operations

- A manufacturing company's *operations* are all its actions taken in making and selling products, resulting in both expenses and costs. The term **INCOME FROM OPERATIONS** refers to what is left over after expenses and costs are subtracted from sales.

  Note: Companies can also generate income and have expenses from financial (non-operating) activities. For example, a manufacturing company makes a non-operating profit when it sells a piece of real estate for more than its book value.

Income Statement *(for the period)*

NET SALES	a
COST OF GOODS SOLD	b
GROSS MARGIN	a − b = c
SALES & MARKETING	d
RESEARCH & DEVELOPMENT	e
GENERAL & ADMINISTRATIVE	f
OPERATING EXPENSES	d + e + f = g
INCOME FROM OPERATIONS	c − g = h
INTEREST INCOME	i
INCOME TAX	j
NET INCOME	h + i − j = k

Non-operating Income & Expense

- Paying interest on a loan is a **non-operating expense.** Likewise, receiving interest on cash balances in the company's bank account is **non-operating income.**

- Because it is from non-operating sources, INTEREST INCOME (or expense) is reported on the *Income Statement* just below the INCOME FROM OPERATIONS line. Likewise INCOME TAXES.

- Note: A company's operations can be producing income, but the company as a whole can still show an overall loss. This sad state of affairs comes about when **non-operating expenses** (such as very high interest expenses) exceed the total INCOME FROM OPERATIONS.

Income Statement *(for the period)*

NET SALES .... a

COST OF GOODS SOLD .... b

GROSS MARGIN .... a − b = c

SALES & MARKETING .... d

RESEARCH & DEVELOPMENT .... e

GENERAL & ADMINISTRATIVE .... f

OPERATING EXPENSES .... d + e + f = g

INCOME FROM OPERATIONS .... c − g = h

INTEREST INCOME i

INCOME TAX .... j

NET INCOME .... h + i − j = k

Net Income

- **Income** is the difference between two large numbers: (1) *sales* and (2) *costs* plus *expenses*. More *costs* plus *expenses* than sales and the company will show a loss. Less *costs* plus *expenses* than *sales* and the company will show a profit. See page 54.

- Remember: **Income is not cash.** In fact, a very profitable company with lots of net income can also be insolvent; that is, with no cash left to pay its bills.

- Often rapidly growing companies are short of cash — even though they are highly profitable. They simply cannot supply out of earnings the capital required for such rapid growth.

> Top Line

Income Statement *(for the period)*

NET SALES	a
COST OF GOODS SOLD	b
GROSS MARGIN	a – b = c
SALES & MARKETING	d
RESEARCH & DEVELOPMENT	e
GENERAL & ADMINISTRATIVE	f
OPERATING EXPENSES	d + e + f = g
INCOME FROM OPERATIONS	c – g = h
INTEREST INCOME	i
INCOME TAX	j
NET INCOME	h + i – j = k

> Bottom Line

Income *(Profits)* vs. Sales *(Revenue)*

- The words **income** and **revenue** are often confused. They mean very different things:

    Profit and *income* do mean the same thing.

    Sales and *revenue* do mean the same thing.

- NET INCOME (also called **profits**) is at the bottom of the *Income Statement*. NET SALES (also called **revenue**) is at the top of the *Income Statement*.

- NET INCOME is often referred to as *the bottom line* because it is the last line of the *Income Statement*.

- NET SALES are often referred to as *the top line* because it is at the top of the *Income Statement*.

Income Statement *(for the period)*

NET SALES	a
COST OF GOODS SOLD	b
GROSS MARGIN	a − b = c
SALES & MARKETING	d
RESEARCH & DEVELOPMENT	e
GENERAL & ADMINISTRATIVE	f
OPERATING EXPENSES	d + e + f = g
INCOME FROM OPERATIONS	c − g = h
INTEREST INCOME	i
INCOME TAX	j
NET INCOME	h + i − j = k

Income Statement Summary

- The *Income Statement* summarizes and displays the financial impact of:

  movement of goods to customers (**SALES**)
  minus
  efforts to make and sell goods (**COSTS & EXPENSES**)
  equals
  any value created in the process (**INCOME**)

- All business activities that generate income or result in a loss for a company — *that is, all transactions that change* the value of **SHAREHOLDERS' EQUITY** on the *Balance Sheet* — are recorded here on the *Income Statement*.

Accrual Basis vs. Cash Basis

- The two major ways of running a company's books — *cash basis* or *accrual basis* —differ on when the company records expenses and income.

- If income is measured when cash is received and expenses are measured when cash is spent, the business is said to be operating on a **cash basis** —just like your checkbook.

- If income and expenses are measured when the transactions occur — regardless of the physical flow of cash — the business is said to be operating on an **accrual basis**.

Cash Basis

- **Cash basis** books are the simplest...functioning just like the proverbial cookie jar. When the books are on a **cash basis,** accounting transactions are triggered only by the movement of cash.

- With the books on a **cash basis,** the *Income Statement* and the *Cash Flow Statement* are the same.

- In general, people run their lives on a **cash basis**, but most businesses run their books on an accrual basis.

  Note: All businesses that maintain inventories of product for sale must use accrual accounting to report income — so says the IRS. In businesses with inventory, using accrual accounting helps compute income (profit) properly.

Accrual Basis

- In **accrual basis** accounting, the *Income Statement* does not reflect the movement of cash, but rather, the generation of obligations (**PAYABLES**) to pay cash in the future.

- With **accrual basis** accounting, expenses occur when the company incurs the obligation to pay, not when it actually parts with the cash. In **accrual basis** accounting, sales and costs are recorded when the goods are shipped and customers incur the obligation to pay, not when they actually pay.

- For example, under **accrual basis** accounting you would lower your net worth when you use your charge card rather than when you ultimately paid the bill.

Income Statement & Balance Sheet

- The enterprise's *Income Statement* and *Balance Sheet* are inexorably linked.

- If the enterprise's *Income Statement* shows income, then retained earnings are *increased* on the *Balance Sheet*.

- Then, also, either the enterprise's *assets* must increase or its *liabilities* decrease for the *Balance Sheet* to remain in balance.

- Thus, the *Income Statement* shows for a period all the actions taken by the enterprise to either *increase assets* or *decrease liabilities* on the *Balance Sheet*.

Chapter 4. Cash Flow Statement

Where the company gets cash,

and where that cash goes.

Cash Flow Statement *(for the period)*

BEGINNING CASH BALANCE .... a

CASH RECEIPTS .... b
CASH DISBURSEMENTS c

CASH FROM OPERATIONS .... b – c + d

FIXED ASSET PURCHASES .... e
NET BORROWINGS .... f
INCOME TAXES PAID .... g
SALE OF STOCK .... h

ENDING CASH BALANCE .... a + b – e + f – g + h = i

Cash Flow Statement

- The *Cash Flow Statement* tracks the *movement of cash* through the business *over a period of time.*

- A company's *Cash Flow Statement* is just like a check register ... recording all the company's transactions that use cash *(checks)* or supply cash *(deposits).*

- The *Cash Flow Statement* shows:

  cash on-hand at the start of the period
  plus
  cash received in the period
  minus
  cash spent in the period
  equals
  cash on-hand at the end of the period.

Cash Transactions

- So-called **cash transactions** affect cash flow. For example:

  Paying salaries lowers **cash**.
  Paying for equipment lowers **cash**.
  Paying off a loan lowers **cash**.

  Receiving money borrowed from a bank raises **cash**.
  Receiving money from investors for stock raises **cash**.
  Receiving money from customers raises **cash**.

- Notice using the words "paying" and "receiving" money for those transactions where cash actually changes hands.

Non-cash Transactions

- **Non-cash transactions** are company activities where no cash moves into or out of the company's accounts. Non-cash transactions have no effect on the *Cash Flow Statement*, but they can affect the *Income Statement* and *Balance Sheet*.

- Examples of non-cash transactions include shipping product to a customer, receiving supplies from a vendor and receiving raw materials required to make the product. For these material transfer transactions, no cash actually changes hands during the transaction proper, only later.

- Cash comes into the company when the customer pays for the product, not when the company ships it. Cash moves out of the company when it pays for materials, not when the company orders or receives them.

Cash Flow

- A **positive cash flow** for a period means the company has more cash at the end of the period than at the beginning.

- A negative cash flow for a period means that the company has less cash at the end of the period than at the beginning.

- If a company has a continuing negative cash flow, it runs the risk of running out of cash and not being able to pay its bills when due — just another way of saying *broke...tapped-out...insolvent.*

- Most rapidly growing companies experience a negative cash flow. Their need for more cash outstrips the cash the business is generating. Everything is fine, so long as the company can borrow or sell more equity. Otherwise, growth must slow.

Sources and Uses of Cash

- **Cash** comes into the business (*sources*) in two major ways:

  1. Operating activities such as receiving payment from customers.
  2. Financing activities such as selling stock or borrowing money.

- **Cash** goes out of the business (*uses*) in four major ways:

  1. Operating activities such as paying suppliers and employees.
  2. Financial activities such as paying interest and principal on debt or paying dividends to shareholders.
  3. Making major capital investments in long-lived productive assets like machines.
  4. Paying income taxes to the government.

Cash Flow Statement *(for the period)*

BEGINNING CASH BALANCE .... a

CASH RECEIPTS .... b
CASH DISBURSEMENTS c

CASH FROM OPERATIONS .... b – c + d

FIXED ASSET PURCHASES .... e
NET BORROWINGS .... f
INCOME TAXES PAID .... g
SALE OF STOCK .... h

ENDING CASH BALANCE .... a + b – e + f – g + h = i

Cash from Operations

- The normal day-to-day business activities (making and selling product) of a business are called its "operations."

- The *Cash Flow Statement* shows CASH FROM OPERATIONS separately from other cash flows.

- *Cash receipts* are inflows of money coming from operating the business.

- *Cash disbursements* are outflows of money used in operating the business.

- *Cash receipts* (money in) minus *cash disbursements* (money out) equals CASH FROM OPERATIONS.

Cash Flow Statement *(for the period)*

BEGINNING CASH BALANCE .... a

CASH RECEIPTS .... b

CASH DISBURSEMENTS c

CASH FROM OPERATIONS .... b – c + d

FIXED ASSET PURCHASES .... e

NET BORROWINGS .... f

INCOME TAXES PAID .... g

SALE OF STOCK .... h

ENDING CASH BALANCE .... a + b – e + f – g + h = i

Cash Receipts

- **CASH RECEIPTS** (also called *collections* or simply *receipts*) come from collecting money from customers.

- **CASH RECEIPTS** increase the amount of cash the company has on hand.

- **Note:** Receiving cash from customers decreases the amount that is due the company as accounts receivable shown on the *Balance Sheet*.

- **CASH RECEIPTS** are not profits. Profits are something else altogether. Don't confuse the two. Profits are reported on the *Income Statement*.

Cash Flow Statement *(for the period)*

BEGINNING CASH BALANCE .... a

CASH RECEIPTS .... b

CASH DISBURSEMENTS c

CASH FROM OPERATIONS .... b – c + d

FIXED ASSET PURCHASES .... e

NET BORROWINGS .... f

INCOME TAXES PAID .... g

SALE OF STOCK .... h

ENDING CASH BALANCE .... a + b – e + f – g + h = i

Cash Disbursements

- A **CASH DISBURSEMENT** is writing a check to pay for the rent, for inventory and supplies or for a worker's salary. **CASH DISBURSEMENT** *lower* the amount of cash the company has on hand.

- **CASH DISBURSEMENTS** (payments) to suppliers *lower* the amount the company owes as reported in **ACCOUNTS PAYABLE** on the *Balance Sheet*.

- **CASH DISBURSEMENTS** are also called *payments* or simply *disbursements*.

Other elements of cash flow...

- **CASH FROM OPERATIONS** reports the flow of money into and out of the business from the making and selling of products.

- **CASH FROM OPERATIONS** is a good measure of how well the enterprise is doing in its day-to-day business activities, its so-called *operations.*

- But remember, **CASH FROM OPERATIONS** is just one of the important elements of cash flow. Other major cash flows are:

  1. *Investment in fixed assets* such as buying a manufacturing facility and machinery to make product.
  2. *Financial activities* such as selling stock to investors, borrowing money from banks, paying dividends, or paying taxes to the government.

Cash Flow Statement *(for the period)*

BEGINNING CASH BALANCE .... a

CASH RECEIPTS .... b
CASH DISBURSEMENTS c

CASH FROM OPERATIONS .... b − c + d
FIXED ASSET PURCHASES .... e
NET BORROWINGS .... f
INCOME TAXES PAID .... g
SALE OF STOCK .... h

ENDING CASH BALANCE .... a + b − e + f − g + h = i

Fixed Asset Purchases

- Money spent to buy *property, plant* and *equipment* (PP&E) is an investment in the long-term capability of the company to manufacture and sell product.

- Paying for PP&E is not considered part of operations and thus is not reported in *cash disbursements from operations*. Cash payments for PP&E are reported on a separate line on the *Cash Flow Statement*. PP&E purchases are investments in productive assets.

- Needless to say, after paying for PP&E the business has less cash. Cash is used when the PP&E is purchased originally. Note, however, when the enterprise *depreciates* a fixed asset, it does not use any cash at that time. No check is written to anyone.

Cash Flow Statement *(for the period)*

BEGINNING CASH BALANCE .... a

CASH RECEIPTS .... b

CASH DISBURSEMENTS c

CASH FROM OPERATIONS .... b – c + d

FIXED ASSET PURCHASES .... e

NET BORROWINGS .... f

INCOME TAXES PAID .... g

SALE OF STOCK .... h

ENDING CASH BALANCE .... a + b – e + f – g + h = i

Net Borrowings

- Borrowing money *increases* the amount of cash the company has on hand.

- Conversely, paying back a loan *decreases* the company's supply of cash on hand.

- The difference between any new borrowings in a period and the amount paid back in the period is called NET BORROWINGS and is reported for the period on a separate line in the *Cash Flow Statement*.

Cash Flow Statement *(for the period)*

BEGINNING CASH BALANCE .... a

CASH RECEIPTS .... b
CASH DISBURSEMENTS c

CASH FROM OPERATIONS .... b – c + d

FIXED ASSET PURCHASES .... e
NET BORROWINGS .... f
INCOME TAXES PAID .... g
SALE OF STOCK .... h

ENDING CASH BALANCE .... a + b – e + f – g + h = i

Income Taxes Paid

- Owing *income taxes* is different from paying them. The business owes some more *income tax* every time it sells something for a profit.

- But just owing taxes does not reduce cash. *Only writing a check to the government and thus paying the taxes due actually reduces the company's cash on-hand.*

- Paying *income taxes* to the government decreases the company's supply of cash. **INCOME TAXES PAID** are reported on the *Cash Flow Statement.*

Cash Flow Statement *(for the period)*

BEGINNING CASH BALANCE .... a

CASH RECEIPTS .... b

CASH DISBURSEMENTS c

CASH FROM OPERATIONS .... b − c + d

FIXED ASSET PURCHASES .... e

NET BORROWINGS .... f

INCOME TAXES PAID .... g

SALE OF STOCK .... h

ENDING CASH BALANCE .... a + b − e + f − g + h = i

Sale of Stock: New Equity

- When people invest in a company's *stock*, they exchange one piece of paper for another: real U.S. currency for a fancy stock certificate.

- When a company sells *stock* to investors, it receives money and increases the amount of cash it has on hand.

- Selling *stock* is the closest thing to *printing money* that a company can do...and it's perfectly legal — unless you mislead widows and orphans as to the real value of the *stock,* in which case the S.E.C. (U.S. Securities and Exchange Commission) will send you to jail. Really.

Cash Flow Statement *(for the period)*

BEGINNING CASH BALANCE .... a

CASH RECEIPTS ....…....... b

CASH DISBURSEMENTS c

CASH FROM OPERATIONS .... b − c + d

FIXED ASSET PURCHASES .... e

NET BORROWINGS .... f

INCOME TAXES PAID .... g

SALE OF STOCK .... h

ENDING CASH BALANCE .... a + b − e + f − g + h = i

Ending Cash Balance

The **BEGINNING CASH BALANCE** (at the start of the period) plus or minus all cash transactions that took place during the period equals the **ENDING CASH BALANCE**. In summary,

> beginning **cash** on-hand *(at start of period)*
> *plus*
> **cash** received *(during the period)*
> *minus*
> **cash** spent *(during the period)*
> *equals*
> ending **cash** on hand (at the end period)

Cash Flow Statement *(for the period)*

BEGINNING CASH BALANCE .... a

CASH RECEIPTS .... b
CASH DISBURSEMENTS c

CASH FROM OPERATIONS .... b − c + d

FIXED ASSET PURCHASES .... e
NET BORROWINGS .... f
INCOME TAXES PAID .... g
SALE OF STOCK .... h

ENDING CASH BALANCE .... a + b − e + f − g + h = i

Cash Flow Statement Summary

- Think of the company's *Cash Flow Statement* as a check register reporting all the company's payments *(cash outflows — checks)* and deposits *(cash inflows)* for a period of time.

- If no actual cash changes hands in a particular transaction, then the *Cash Flow Statement* is not changed.

- **Note however**, that the *Balance Sheet* and the *Income Statement* may be changed by a *non-cash transaction.*

- **Note also**, that *cash transactions* — those reported on the *Cash Flow Statement* — usually do have some effect on the *Income Statement* and *Balance Sheet* as well.

Chapter 5.
Connections

These pages will begin our formal study of how the three major financial statements interact — how they work in concert to give a true picture of the enterprise's financial health.

In the prior chapters, we studied separately the vocabulary/structure of the three main financial statements. What follows here is an opportunity to put the statements together as a financial reporting tool. We will see how the *Income Statement* relates to the *Balance Sheet* and vice versa and how changes to each can affect the *Cash Flow Statement*.

Remember the fundamental reporting function of each of the three main financial statements:

1. The ***Income Statement*** shows the manufacturing and selling actions of the enterprise that results in a profit or loss.

2. The ***Cash Flow Statement*** details the movements of cash into and out of the coffers of the enterprise.

3. The ***Balance Sheet*** records what the company owns and what it owes, including the owner's stake.

Each statement views the enterprise's financial health from a different — and very necessary — perspective. Each statement relates to the other two in specific ways. Review these following examples of the natural "connections" between the three main financial statements.

Balance Sheet Connections — See the basic structural connections between the *Balance Sheet* and the other two major financial statements.

Sales Cycle — Next shown is the sale cycle describing those repeating financial statement entries that the company must make in order to report a sale and receive payment.

Expense Cycle — Then follow the documenting entries for SG&A and research expenses and their subsequent payment.

Investment Cycle — Next shown are the connection entries relating to the investment of capital and the acquisition of debt (borrowing).

Asset Purchase/Depreciation — Last shown are entries for asset purchases and depreciation.

～

Here is a hint as you study the reporting of dollars and goods entering or leaving the business (and the statements):

1. **Watch the flow of cash money,**
2. **Watch the flow of goods and services.**

Fundamentally, financial statements document the movement of cash and goods and services into and out of the enterprise. That is all the financial statements are about. It's no more complicated than that. Everything else is details.

Financial statements document the movement of cash, and goods & services into and out of the enterprise. That is all financial statements do. It is no more complicated. Everything else is details. Don't sweat the details.

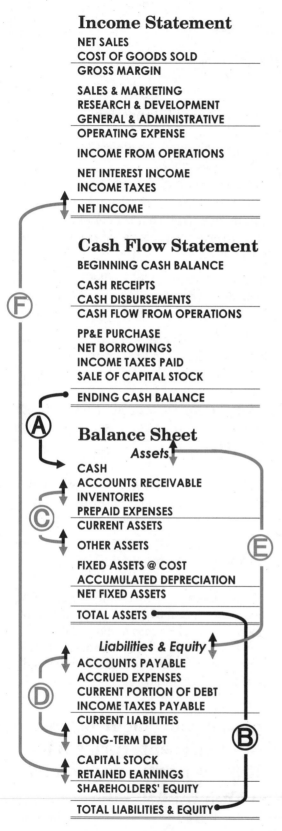

Income Statement

NET SALES
COST OF GOODS SOLD
GROSS MARGIN

SALES & MARKETING
RESEARCH & DEVELOPMENT
GENERAL & ADMINISTRATIVE
OPERATING EXPENSE

INCOME FROM OPERATIONS

NET INTEREST INCOME
INCOME TAXES

NET INCOME

Cash Flow Statement

BEGINNING CASH BALANCE

CASH RECEIPTS
CASH DISBURSEMENTS
CASH FLOW FROM OPERATIONS

PP&E PURCHASE
NET BORROWINGS
INCOME TAXES PAID
SALE OF CAPITAL STOCK

ENDING CASH BALANCE

Balance Sheet
Assets

CASH
ACCOUNTS RECEIVABLE
INVENTORIES
PREPAID EXPENSES
CURRENT ASSETS

OTHER ASSETS

FIXED ASSETS @ COST
ACCUMULATED DEPRECIATION
NET FIXED ASSETS

TOTAL ASSETS

Liabilities & Equity
ACCOUNTS PAYABLE
ACCRUED EXPENSES
CURRENT PORTION OF DEBT
INCOME TAXES PAYABLE
CURRENT LIABILITIES

LONG-TERM DEBT

CAPITAL STOCK
RETAINED EARNINGS
SHAREHOLDERS' EQUITY

TOTAL LIABILITIES & EQUITY

Balance Sheet Connections
Structural Connections

(A) **ENDING CASH BALANCE** on the *Cash Flow Statement* for the period always equals **CASH** at period end on the *Balance Sheet*.

(B) As the basic equation of accounting says (see page 16), **TOTAL ASSETS** will always equal **TOTAL LIABILITIES & SHAREHOLDERS' EQUITY** on the *Balance Sheet*.

"Balancing" Connections

(C) To keep the *Balance Sheet* in balance, when a transaction amount is **added** (or subtracted) to an asset account, an equal amount must be **subtracted** (or added) from another asset account.

(D) Likewise, for liability accounts. In both cases, **TOTAL ASSETS** or **TOTAL LIABILITIES & SHAREHOLDERS' EQUITY** do not change and maintain the balance in the *Balance Sheet*. Got that?

(E) Also, the *Balance Sheet* remains in balance if an equal amount is added (or subtracted) from an asset account and a liability account. Thus, **TOTAL ASSETS** and **TOTAL LIABILITIES & SHAREHOLDERS' EQUITY** increase (or decrease) by the same amount to maintain the balance in the *Balance Sheet*.

(F) An increase in **NET INCOME** on the *Income Statement* is added to **RETAINED EARNINGS** on the *Balance Sheet*. A loss would be subtracted. A change in another *Balance Sheet* account will always balance that entry and thus maintain *Balance Sheet* balance.

See the following "cycle" descriptions to better understand how this all works.

Sales Cycle
Recording Sales

(A) When a sale is made on credit, **NET SALES** increases at the top of the *Income Statement* and **ACCOUNTS RECEIVABLE** increases on the *Balance Sheet* by the same amount.

(B) When a sale is made and the product purchased is shipped, the product value is moved from **INVENTORY** on the *Balance Sheet* to **COST OF GOODS SOLD** (**COGS**) on the *Income Statement*.

(C) When a sale is entered on the *Income Statement*, **NET INCOME** is generated and is added to **RETAINED EARNINGS** on the *Balance Sheet*.

~

Recording Payments

(D) When the customer pays for the products shipped, the **ACCOUNTS RECEIVABLE** on the *Balance Sheet* becomes a **CASH RECEIPT** on the *Cash Flow Statement*.

(E) **ENDING CASH BALANCE** is increased by the amount added as a **CASH RECEIPT** in **(C)** and equals **CASH** on the *Balance Sheet*.

~

Balance Sheet Summary

TOTAL ASSETS on the *Balance Sheet* increase by the **CASH** added in **(E)** and decrease by the **INVENTORY** shipped in **(B)**. **ACCOUNTS RECEIVABLE** does not change because the same amount was added in **(A)** and then subtracted in **(C)**.

TOTAL LIABILITIES & SHAREHOLDERS' EQUITY increases by the **NET INCOME** added to **RETAINED EARNINGS** in **(D)**. This amount is the same as the increase in **TOTAL ASSETS** as computed in the prior paragraph.

Thus, the *Balance Sheet* remains in balance. ***Hallelujah!***

Income Statement

NET SALES
COST OF GOODS SOLD
GROSS MARGIN

SALES & MARKETING
RESEARCH & DEVELOPMENT
GENERAL & ADMINISTRATIVE
OPERATING EXPENSE

INCOME FROM OPERATIONS

NET INTEREST INCOME
INCOME TAXES

NET INCOME

Cash Flow Statement
BEGINNING CASH BALANCE

CASH RECEIPTS
CASH DISBURSEMENTS
CASH FLOW FROM OPERATIONS

PP&E PURCHASE
NET BORROWINGS
INCOME TAXES PAID
SALE OF CAPITAL STOCK

ENDING CASH BALANCE

Balance Sheet
Assets

CASH
ACCOUNTS RECEIVABLE
INVENTORIES
PREPAID EXPENSES
CURRENT ASSETS

OTHER ASSETS

FIXED ASSETS @ COST
ACCUMULATED DEPRECIATION
NET FIXED ASSETS

TOTAL ASSETS

Liabilities & Equity
ACCOUNTS PAYABLE
ACCRUED EXPENSES
CURRENT PORTION OF DEBT
INCOME TAXES PAYABLE
CURRENT LIABILITIES

LONG-TERM DEBT

CAPITAL STOCK
RETAINED EARNINGS
SHAREHOLDERS' EQUITY

TOTAL LIABILITIES & EQUITY

Income Statement

NET SALES
COST OF GOODS SOLD

GROSS MARGIN

SALES & MARKETING
RESEARCH & DEVELOPMENT
GENERAL & ADMINISTRATIVE
OPERATING EXPENSE

INCOME FROM OPERATIONS

NET INTEREST INCOME
INCOME TAXES

NET INCOME

Cash Flow Statement

BEGINNING CASH BALANCE

CASH RECEIPTS
CASH DISBURSEMENTS

CASH FLOW FROM OPERATIONS

PP&E PURCHASE
NET BORROWINGS
INCOME TAXES PAID
SALE OF CAPITAL STOCK

ENDING CASH BALANCE

Balance Sheet
Assets

CASH
ACCOUNTS RECEIVABLE
INVENTORIES
PREPAID EXPENSES

CURRENT ASSETS

OTHER ASSETS

FIXED ASSETS @ COST
ACCUMULATED DEPRECIATION

NET FIXED ASSETS

TOTAL ASSETS

Liabilities & Equity

ACCOUNTS PAYABLE
ACCRUED EXPENSES
CURRENT PORTION OF DEBT
INCOME TAXES PAYABLE

CURRENT LIABILITIES

LONG-TERM DEBT

CAPITAL STOCK
RETAINED EARNINGS

SHAREHOLDERS' EQUITY

TOTAL LIABILITIES & EQUITY

Expense Cycle
Recording Expenses

Ⓐ **EXPENSES,** when incurred and entered on the *Income Statement,* become **ACCOUNTS PAYABLE** on the *Balance Sheet* by the same amount.

Ⓑ **EXPENSES** when entered on the *Income Statement* also reduce the **NET INCOME.**

Ⓒ This **NET INCOME** reduction on the *Income Statement* reduces **RETAINED EARNINGS** on the *Balance Sheet* by the same amount.

~

Recording Expenditures (Cash Out)

Ⓓ When paid, the **ACCOUNTS PAYABLE** on the *Balance Sheet* becomes an actual **CASH DISBURSEMENT** on the *Cash Flow Statement*. Voila, the expense has become an expenditure (actual cash out)!

Ⓔ **ENDING CASH BALANCE** is lowered by the amount of the **CASH DISBURSEMENT** in Ⓓ and equals **CASH** on the *Balance Sheet*.

~

Balance Sheet Summary

RETAINED EARNINGS on the liabilities & equity section of the *Balance Sheet* is reduced by the amount of the **EXPENSE. ACCOUNTS PAYABLE** is increased by the same amount, thus keeping the *Balance Sheet* in balance so far.

When the **ACCOUNTS PAYABLE** is paid with cash, **CASH** in the assets section of the *Balance Sheet* is lowered and **ACCOUNTS PAYABLE** is lowered too, by the same amount.

Thus, in summary, **TOTAL ASSETS** and **TOTAL LIABILITIES & EQUITY** are lowered equally and the *Balance Sheet* remains in balance. *Hallelujah* again!

Investment Cycle
Recording Debt

NET BORROWINGS when entered on the *Cash Flow Statement* increase both **CASH** and **DEBT** by the same amount. This new debt is entered into either of the two different accounts depending on when it is due for repayment.

 SHORT-TERM DEBT is the portion to be repaid within 12 months.

 LONG-TERM DEBT is for repayment required in more than 12 months.

 Borrowing increases **CASH** on the *Balance Sheet*. Note, Ⓐ + Ⓑ = Ⓒ.

~

Selling Stock

Ⓓ Selling stock increases both **CASH** and **CAPITAL STOCK** by the same amount on the *Balance Sheet*.

Balance Sheet Summary

NET BORROWINGS on the *Cash Flow Statement* increase **CASH** in the asset section and **DEBT** in the liabilities & equity section of the *Balance Sheet* by the same amount.

SALE OF CAPITAL STOCK on the *Cash Flow Statement* increases **CASH** in the asset section and **CAPITAL STOCK** in the liabilities & equity section of the *Balance Sheet* by the same amount.

Since these are balancing entries, there is no change in **TOTAL ASSETS** or in **TOTAL LIABILITIES & EQUITY.** The *Balance Sheet* remains in balance. **Hallelujah** again, again!

Income Statement

NET SALES
COST OF GOODS SOLD
GROSS MARGIN

SALES & MARKETING
RESEARCH & DEVELOPMENT
GENERAL & ADMINISTRATIVE
OPERATING EXPENSE

INCOME FROM OPERATIONS

NET INTEREST INCOME
INCOME TAXES

NET INCOME

Cash Flow Statement

BEGINNING CASH BALANCE

CASH RECEIPTS
CASH DISBURSEMENTS
CASH FLOW FROM OPERATIONS

PP&E PURCHASE
NET BORROWINGS
INCOME TAXES PAID
SALE OF CAPITAL STOCK

ENDING CASH BALANCES

Balance Sheet
Assets

CASH
ACCOUNTS RECEIVABLE
INVENTORIES
PREPAID EXPENSES
CURRENT ASSETS

OTHER ASSETS

FIXED ASSETS @ COST
ACCUMULATED DEPRECIATION
NET FIXED ASSETS

TOTAL ASSETS

Liabilities & Equity

ACCOUNTS PAYABLE
ACCRUED EXPENSES
CURRENT PORTION OF DEBT
INCOME TAXES PAYABLE
CURRENT LIABILITIES

LONG-TERM DEBT

CAPITAL STOCK
RETAINED EARNINGS
SHAREHOLDERS' EQUITY

TOTAL LIABILITIES & EQUITY

Income Statement

NET SALES
COST OF GOODS SOLD
GROSS MARGIN

SALES & MARKETING
RESEARCH & DEVELOPMENT
GENERAL & ADMINISTRATIVE
OPERATING EXPENSE

INCOME FROM OPERATIONS

NET INTEREST INCOME
INCOME TAXES

NET INCOME

Cash Flow Statement

BEGINNING CASH BALANCE

CASH RECEIPTS
CASH DISBURSEMENTS
CASH FLOW FROM OPERATIONS

PP&E PURCHASE
NET BORROWINGS
INCOME TAXES PAID
SALE OF CAPITAL STOCK

ENDING CASH BALANCE

Balance Sheet
Assets

CASH
ACCOUNTS RECEIVABLE
INVENTORIES
PREPAID EXPENSES
CURRENT ASSETS

OTHER ASSETS

FIXED ASSETS @ COST
ACCUMULATED DEPRECIATION
NET FIXED ASSETS

TOTAL ASSETS

Liabilities & Equity

ACCOUNTS PAYABLE
ACCRUED EXPENSES
CURRENT PORTION OF DEBT
INCOME TAXES PAYABLE
CURRENT LIABILITIES

LONG-TERM DEBT

CAPITAL STOCK
RETAINED EARNINGS
SHAREHOLDERS' EQUITY

TOTAL LIABILITIES & EQUITY

Fixed Asset Cycle
PP&E Purchase

(A) When equipment is originally purchased, the account **PP&E PURCHASE** is increased on the *Cash Flow Statement* and **FIXED ASSETS @ COST** is increased on the *Balance Sheet* by the same amount.

(B) **ENDING CASH BALANCE** is lowered on the *Cash Flow Statement* and so is **CASH** on the *Balance Sheet.*

~

Depreciation Charges

(C) Regularly over time, according to a calculated depreciation schedule, a **depreciation charge** is entered on the *Income Statement* as an **OPERATING EXPENSE** and thus lowers **NET INCOME** on the *Income Statement*, and …

(D) Since **NET INCOME** has been lowered, **RETAINED EARNINGS** on the *Balance Sheet* goes down by the same amount.

(E) Also, **ACCUMULATED DEPRECIATION** is increased as an expense, thus lowering **NET INCOME** and **NET FIXED ASSETS**.

~

Depreciation expenses are so-called *non-cash expenses.* Note, when a depreciation expense is entered on the *Income Statement*, no actual **CASH DISBURSEMENT** is made and entered on the *Cash Flow Statement.* **ENDING CASH BALANCE** on the *Cash Flow Statement* and **CASH** on the *Balance Sheet* are not lowered.

CASH was originally lowered (see **(A)** above) by the full purchase price when the equipment was acquired and paid for.

~

Balance Sheet Summary

TOTAL ASSETS and **TOTAL LIABILITIES & EQUITY** remain in balance. **(A)** and **(B)** above result in offsetting entries. **(C)**, **(D)**, and **(E)** result in offsetting entries, too.

Section B.
Transactions: Exploits
of AppleSeed Enterprises, Inc.

About This Section

We are now at the heart of learning how financial statements work. In the previous section, we reviewed financial statement structure and vocabulary, and saw examples of how the three main financial statements interact.

The following pages chronicle thirty-three specific business transactions in Appleseed's financial life. We'll show how Appleseed constructs and maintains its books to report accurately the company's financial position.

Each new business transaction means new "postings" to AppleSeed's financial statements as our company goes about its business of making and selling delicious applesauce. As we discuss each transaction, you'll get a hands-on feel for how a company's books are constructed. Each transaction is described in a two-page spread. See the "annotated" transaction spread on the next two pages.

Right-Hand Page The right-hand page of each two-page transaction spread describes an AppleSeed business transaction, discussing both business rationale and financial effect. Note that numbered circles are placed beside descriptions of specific financial postings for the transaction. The large number circles correspond to the entries beside the smaller numbered circles on the left-hand page that shows the company's three main financial statements.

As you begin to study each new transaction, first read and understand the right-hand page description. Then go to the left-hand page to see actual postings to AppleSeed's three financial statements.

Left-Hand Page The left-hand page of each transaction spread shows required entries into Apple-Seed's *Income Statement, Balance Sheet* and *Cash Flow Statement*. Depending on the type of transaction, all three financial statements may be changed, or just two, or one or none may change.

Note, entries are only made in the account lines with boxes at the right. The other lines are just additions or subtractions to show running and grand totals.

The account deck pages 18, 30, 46, and 64 show how the various account lines are summed.

~

That is all there is to accounting and financial reporting. It is really not rocket science at all, just a little addition and subtraction. With some effort and this book, you will find enlightenment.

However, remember, our analysis is just an overview. If you need details (and there are many), just ask an accountant a good question based upon the knowledge you have acquired from this book. They will be so happy to get an intelligent question from a non-financial type, they will bend over backwards to answer.

Welcome to AppleSeed Enterprises!

Transaction Spread
— Left-Hand Page

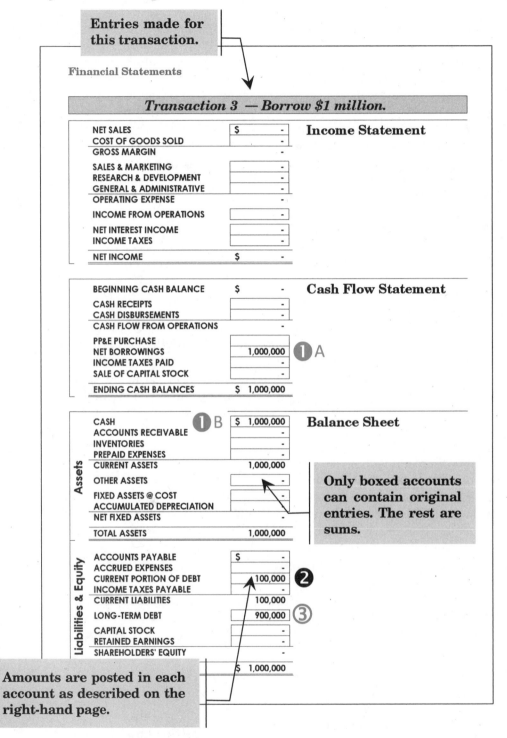

Entries made for this transaction.

Financial Statements

Transaction 3 — Borrow $1 million.

Income Statement

NET SALES	$	-
COST OF GOODS SOLD		-
GROSS MARGIN		-
SALES & MARKETING		-
RESEARCH & DEVELOPMENT		-
GENERAL & ADMINISTRATIVE		-
OPERATING EXPENSE		-
INCOME FROM OPERATIONS		-
NET INTEREST INCOME		-
INCOME TAXES		-
NET INCOME	$	-

Cash Flow Statement

BEGINNING CASH BALANCE	$	-
CASH RECEIPTS		-
CASH DISBURSEMENTS		-
CASH FLOW FROM OPERATIONS		-
PP&E PURCHASE		
NET BORROWINGS	1,000,000	❶A
INCOME TAXES PAID		-
SALE OF CAPITAL STOCK		-
ENDING CASH BALANCES	$ 1,000,000	

Balance Sheet

Assets			
CASH	❶B	$ 1,000,000	
ACCOUNTS RECEIVABLE		-	
INVENTORIES		-	
PREPAID EXPENSES		-	
CURRENT ASSETS		1,000,000	
OTHER ASSETS		-	
FIXED ASSETS @ COST		-	
ACCUMULATED DEPRECIATION		-	
NET FIXED ASSETS		-	
TOTAL ASSETS		1,000,000	

Only boxed accounts can contain original entries. The rest are sums.

Liabilities & Equity			
ACCOUNTS PAYABLE	$	-	
ACCRUED EXPENSES		-	
CURRENT PORTION OF DEBT	100,000	❷
INCOME TAXES PAYABLE		-	
CURRENT LIABILITIES	100,000	
LONG-TERM DEBT	900,000	③
CAPITAL STOCK		-	
RETAINED EARNINGS		-	
SHAREHOLDERS' EQUITY		-	
	$ 1,000,000	

Amounts are posted in each account as described on the right-hand page.

Transaction Spread — Right-Hand Page

Transactions are described in detail at the top of the right-hand page.

Startup Financing and Staffing

T3. Borrow $1 million to buy a building. Terms of this 10-year mortgage are 10% interest per annum.

Go to the bank and apply for a loan to buy a building to (1) manufacture and warehouse applesauce, and (2) house the administrative and sales activities of the company.

The friendly loan officer agrees that AppleSeed has a strong equity capital base and good prospects. She agrees to lend you a cool million to buy the building but demands that you pledge all the assets of the company to collateralize the loan. That's okay.

She also asks for your personal guarantee to repay the loan if the company cannot. What do you say? The correct answer is **no**. *If the business fails, you don't want to lose your home too.*

You and your friendly banker agree on a 10-year loan amortization (that is, "payback") schedule shown on the right.

Loan Amortization Schedule

YEAR	INTEREST PAYMENTS	PRINCIPAL PAYMENTS	OUTSTANDING PRINCIPAL
1	$100,000	$100,000	$900,000
3	$80,000	$100,000	$700,000
4	$70,000	$100,000	$600,000
5	$60,000	$100,000	$500,000
6	$50,000	$100,000	$400,000
7	$40,000	$100,000	$300,000
8	$30,000	$100,000	$200,000
9	$20,000	$100,000	$100,000
10	$10,000	$100,000	$0
TOTAL	$550,000	$1,000,000	

Transaction: Borrow $1 million to purchase an all-purpose building. This term note will run for 10 years, calling for yearly principal payments of $100,000 plus interest at a rate of 10% per annum.

1 (1A) At the loan closing the friendly banker deposits $1 million in your checking account, thus increasing NET BORROWINGS in the *Cash Flow Statement.* (1B) Remember also, CASH increases by $1 million in the assets section of the *Balance Sheet.*

2 The CURRENT PORTION OF DEBT (that is, the amount that will be repaid this year) is $100,000 and is listed in the current liabilities section of the *Balance Sheet.*

3 The remaining debt of $900,000 will be repaid more than one year in the future and thus is listed as LONG-TERM DEBT in the *Balance Sheet.*

Note: This transaction just books the loan. We will pay down the principal and interest in a later transaction.

Read the account posting descriptions on the right-hand page. Then look at the corresponding numbered circles in the financial statements on the left-hand page. See how the changes to the statements are recorded.

Chapter 6.
Startup Financing and Staffing

Welcome to our little business — AppleSeed Enterprises, Inc. Imagine that you are AppleSeed's entrepreneurial CEO. You also double as treasurer and chief financial officer.

You have just incorporated (in Delaware) and invested $50,000 of your own money into the company — well, actually it's your Great Aunt Lillian's money. You're going to need much more capital to get into production, but these initial transactions will start up the business. Follow along ... we have a lot to do.

~

Transaction 1.   Sell 150,000 shares of AppleSeed's common stock ($1 par value) for $10 per share.

Transaction 2.   Pay yourself your first month's salary. Book all payroll-associated fringe benefits and taxes.

Transaction 3.   Borrow $1 million to buy a building. Terms of this 10-year mortgage are 10% per annum.

Transaction 4.   Pay $1.5 million for a building to be used for office, manufacturing and warehouse space. Set up a depreciation schedule.

Transaction 5.   Hire administrative and sales staff. Pay first month's salaries and book fringe benefits and taxes.

Transaction 6.   Pay employee health, life and disability insurance premiums plus FICA, unemployment and also withholding taxes.

Transaction 1. — Sell Stock

Income Statement

NET SALES	$	-
COST OF GOODS SOLD		-
GROSS MARGIN		-
SALES & MARKETING		-
RESEARCH & DEVELOPMENT		-
GENERAL & ADMINISTRATIVE		-
OPERATING EXPENSE		-
INCOME FROM OPERATIONS		-
NET INTEREST INCOME		-
INCOME TAXES		-
NET INCOME	$	-

Cash Flow Statement

BEGINNING CASH BALANCE	$	-
CASH RECEIPTS		-
CASH DISBURSEMENTS		-
CASH FLOW FROM OPERATIONS		-
PP&E PURCHASE		-
NET BORROWINGS		-
INCOME TAXES PAID		-
SALE OF CAPITAL STOCK	1,500,000	❶
ENDING CASH BALANCES	$ 1,500,000	

Balance Sheet

Assets

CASH ❷	$ 1,500,000	
ACCOUNTS RECEIVABLE		-
INVENTORIES		-
PREPAID EXPENSES		-
CURRENT ASSETS	1,500,000	
OTHER ASSETS		-
FIXED ASSETS @ COST		-
ACCUMULATED DEPRECIATION		-
NET FIXED ASSETS		-
TOTAL ASSETS	1,500,000	

Liabilities & Equity

ACCOUNTS PAYABLE	$	-
ACCRUED EXPENSES		-
CURRENT PORTION OF DEBT		-
INCOME TAXES PAYABLE		-
CURRENT LIABILITIES		-
LONG-TERM DEBT		-
CAPITAL STOCK	1,500,000	③
RETAINED EARNINGS		-
SHAREHOLDERS' EQUITY	1,500,000	
TOTAL LIABILITIES & EQUITY	$ 1,500,000	

Note: Review account line sumations for **ASSETS** (page 18), **LIABILITIES** (page 37), the *Income Statement* (page 48), and the *Cash Flow Statement* (page 67).

T1. Sell 150,000 shares of AppleSeed's common stock ($1 par value) for $10 per share.

Shares of stock represent ownership in a corporation. A corporation can issue a single class or multiple classes of stock, each with different rights and privileges.

Common stock has the lowest preference to receive assets if the corporation is liquidated. Common stockholders vote for the board of directors.

Preferred stock has a preference over common stock when the corporation pays a dividend or distributes assets in liquidation. Usually, preferred stockholders do not have the right to vote for directors.

Note that claims of both the common and preferred stockholders are junior to claims of bondholders or other creditors of the company.

Par value is the dollar amount that is assigned to shares by the company's charter. Par value has little significance other than to keep track of stock splits.

There is no connection between the stated par value and any *underlying worth* of the stock or the enterprise.

Transaction: A group of investors is willing to exchange their $1.5 million in cash for stock certificates representing 150,000 common shares of AppleSeed Enterprises, Inc.

Note: When the company formed, you bought 50,000 shares of "founder's stock" at $1.00 per share for a total investment of $50,000 in cash. Thus after this sale to the investor group there will be 200,000 shares outstanding. They will own 75% of AppleSeed and you will own the rest.

① Take the money, issue the investors common stock certificates, and run to the bank to deposit the check in AppleSeed's checking account. The company has received cash, so on the *Cash Flow Statement* record the $1.5 million as **SALE OF CAPITAL STOCK**.

② This $1.5 million in cash is a new asset for the corporation, so increase **CASH** in the *Balance Sheet* by the amount received from the investors.

③ Each new asset must create a corresponding liability (or offsetting asset) or the *Balance Sheet* will be out of balance. Issuing stock creates a liability for the company. In effect, AppleSeed "owes" the new stockholders a portion of its assets. So, increase the liability **CAPITAL STOCK** on the *Balance Sheet* by $1.5 million.

~

Transaction 2. — Pay Salary & Book Fringes

Income Statement

NET SALES	$	-
COST OF GOODS SOLD		
GROSS MARGIN		-
SALES & MARKETING		-
RESEARCH & DEVELOPMENT		-
GENERAL & ADMINISTRATIVE		6,230
OPERATING EXPENSE		6,230
INCOME FROM OPERATIONS		-
NET INTEREST INCOME		-
INCOME TAXES		-
NET INCOME	$	(6,230)

❶ A

Cash Flow Statement

BEGINNING CASH BALANCE	$	-
CASH RECEIPTS		-
CASH DISBURSEMENTS		3,370
CASH FLOW FROM OPERATIONS		(3,370)
PP&E PURCHASE		-
NET BORROWINGS		-
INCOME TAXES PAID		-
SALE OF CAPITAL STOCK		-
ENDING CASH BALANCE	$	(3,370)

❷ A

Balance Sheet

Assets

CASH	$	(3,370)
ACCOUNTS RECEIVABLE		-
INVENTORIES		-
PREPAID EXPENSES		-
CURRENT ASSETS		(3,370)
OTHER ASSETS		-
FIXED ASSETS @ COST		-
ACCUMULATED DEPRECIATION		-
NET FIXED ASSETS		-
TOTAL ASSETS		(3,370)

❷ B

Liabilities & Equity

ACCOUNTS PAYABLE	$	-
ACCRUED EXPENSES		2,860
CURRENT PORTION OF DEBT		-
INCOME TAXES PAYABLE		-
CURRENT LIABILITIES		2,860
LONG-TERM DEBT		-
CAPITAL STOCK		-
RETAINED EARNINGS		(6,230)
SHAREHOLDERS' EQUITY		(6,230)
TOTAL LIABILITIES & EQUITY	$	(3,370)

③

❶ B

T2. Pay yourself a month's salary. Book all payroll-associated fringe benefits and taxes.

Congratulations! The board of directors of AppleSeed Enterprises, Inc., has hired you to manage the company at the grand salary of $5,000 per month.

Before you spend all your newfound wealth, let's calculate: (1) your actual take-home pay; (2) the cut for taxes; and (3) the total expense to the company for fringe benefits and payroll taxes.

See the table at right. It costs Apple-Seed a total of $6,230 to pay your $5,000 in salary, even though you only receive $3,370 in your paycheck.

Salary & Employment Expenses

	PAY TO EMPLOYEES	PAY TO OTHERS
MONTHLY SALARY	$5,000	-
EMPLOYEE'S FICA	$(380)	$380
FEDERAL/STATE WITHHOLDING	$(1,250)	$1,250
EMPLOYER'S FICA	-	$380
WORKMEN'S COMPENSATION	-	$100
UNEMPLOYMENT INSURANCE	-	$250
HEALTH & LIFE INSURANCE	-	$500
TOTALS PER MONTH	$3,370	$2,860
TOTAL PAID TO EMPLOYEES & OTHERS		$6,230

Transaction: Book all payroll-associated company expenses totaling $6,230 including salary, employer's contribution to FICA (Social Security) and various insurance expenses. Issue yourself a payroll check for $3,370 (your $5,000 monthly salary minus $1,250 in federal and state withholding tax and $380 for your own contribution to FICA).

1 (1A) Salary and fringes are expenses that decrease income. Add the total monthly payroll expense of $6,230 to GENERAL & ADMINISTRATIVE expenses in the *Income Statement*. (1B) Also decrease RETAINED EARNINGS in the *Balance Sheet* by the same amount.

2 (2A) So far your payroll check is the only cash that has left the company. List the $3,370 check under CASH DISBURSEMENTS in the *Cash Flow Statement*. (2B) Also decrease CASH in the *Balance Sheet* by the same amount.

3 The remaining $2,860 in expenses — due to the government and to various insurance companies — is an obligation of the company not yet discharged (that is, owed but not yet paid). Enter this amount under ACCRUED EXPENSES in the liability section of the *Balance Sheet*.

~

Transaction 3. — Borrow $1 million

Income Statement

NET SALES	$	-
COST OF GOODS SOLD		-
GROSS MARGIN		-
SALES & MARKETING		-
RESEARCH & DEVELOPMENT		-
GENERAL & ADMINISTRATIVE		-
OPERATING EXPENSE		-
INCOME FROM OPERATIONS		-
NET INTEREST INCOME		-
INCOME TAXES		-
NET INCOME	$	-

Cash Flow Statement

BEGINNING CASH BALANCE	$	-
CASH RECEIPTS		-
CASH DISBURSEMENTS		-
CASH FLOW FROM OPERATIONS		-
PP&E PURCHASE		
NET BORROWINGS		1,000,000	❶ A
INCOME TAXES PAID		-
SALE OF CAPITAL STOCK		-
ENDING CASH BALANCE	$	1,000,000

Balance Sheet

Assets

CASH ❶ B	$	1,000,000
ACCOUNTS RECEIVABLE		-
INVENTORIES		-
PREPAID EXPENSES		-
CURRENT ASSETS		1,000,000
OTHER ASSETS		-
FIXED ASSETS @ COST		-
ACCUMULATED DEPRECIATION		-
NET FIXED ASSETS		-
TOTAL ASSETS		1,000,000

Liabilities & Equity

ACCOUNTS PAYABLE	$	-
ACCRUED EXPENSES		-
CURRENT PORTION OF DEBT		100,000	❷
INCOME TAXES PAYABLE		-
CURRENT LIABILITIES		100,000
LONG-TERM DEBT		900,000	③
CAPITAL STOCK		-
RETAINED EARNINGS		-
SHAREHOLDERS' EQUITY		-
TOTAL LIABILITIES & EQUITY	$	1,000,000

T3. Borrow $1 million to buy a building. Terms of this 10-year mortgage are 10% interest per annum.

Go to the bank and apply for a loan to buy a building to (1) manufacture and warehouse applesauce, and (2) house the administrative and sales activities of the company.

The friendly loan officer agrees that AppleSeed has a strong equity capital base and good prospects. She agrees to lend you a cool million to buy the building but demands that you pledge all the assets of the company to collateralize the loan. That's okay.

She also asks for your personal guarantee to repay the loan if the company cannot. What do you say? The correct answer is **no**. *If the business fails, you don't want to lose your home too.*

You and your friendly banker agree on a 10-year loan amortization (that is, "payback") schedule shown on the right.

Loan Amortization Schedule

YEAR	INTEREST PAYMENTS	PRINCIPAL PAYMENTS	OUTSTANDING PRINCIPAL
1	$100,000	$100,000	$900,000
3	$80,000	$100,000	$700,000
4	$70,000	$100,000	$600,000
5	$60,000	$100,000	$500,000
6	$50,000	$100,000	$400,000
7	$40,000	$100,000	$300,000
8	$30,000	$100,000	$200,000
9	$20,000	$100,000	$100,000
10	$10,000	$100,000	$0
TOTAL	$550,000	$1,000,000	

Transaction: Borrow $1 million to purchase an all-purpose building. This term note will run for 10 years, calling for yearly principal payments of $100,000 plus interest at a rate of 10% per annum.

1 (1A) At the loan closing the friendly banker deposits $1 million in your checking account, thus increasing NET BORROWINGS in the *Cash Flow Statement*. (1B) Remember also, CASH increases by $1 million in the assets section of the *Balance Sheet*.

2 The CURRENT PORTION OF DEBT (that is, the amount that will be repaid this year) is $100,000 and is listed in the current liabilities section of the *Balance Sheet*.

3 The remaining debt of $900,000 will be repaid more than one year in the future and thus is listed as LONG-TERM DEBT in the *Balance Sheet*.

Note: This transaction just books the loan. We will pay down the principal and interest in a later transaction.

∼

Transaction 4. — Buy a Building

Income Statement

NET SALES	$	-
COST OF GOODS SOLD		-
GROSS MARGIN		-
SALES & MARKETING		-
RESEARCH & DEVELOPMENT		-
GENERAL & ADMINISTRATIVE		-
OPERATING EXPENSE		-
INCOME FROM OPERATIONS		-
NET INTEREST INCOME		-
INCOME TAXES		-
NET INCOME	$	-

Cash Flow Statement

BEGINNING CASH BALANCE	$	-
CASH RECEIPTS		-
CASH DISBURSEMENTS		-
CASH FLOW FROM OPERATIONS		-
PP&E PURCHASE	1,500,000	❶
NET BORROWINGS		-
INCOME TAXES PAID		-
SALE OF CAPITAL STOCK		-
ENDING CASH BALANCE	$ (1,500,000)	

Balance Sheet

Assets	CASH	❷ $ (1,500,000)	
	ACCOUNTS RECEIVABLE	-	
	INVENTORIES	-	
	PREPAID EXPENSES	-	
	CURRENT ASSETS	(1,500,000)	
	OTHER ASSETS	-	
	FIXED ASSETS @ COST	1,500,000	③
	ACCUMULATED DEPRECIATION	-	
	NET FIXED ASSETS	1,500,000	
	TOTAL ASSETS	$0	
Liabilities & Equity	ACCOUNTS PAYABLE	$ -	
	ACCRUED EXPENSES	-	
	CURRENT PORTION OF DEBT	-	
	INCOME TAXES PAYABLE	-	
	CURRENT LIABILITIES	-	
	LONG-TERM DEBT	-	
	CAPITAL STOCK	-	
	RETAINED EARNINGS	-	
	SHAREHOLDERS' EQUITY	-	
	TOTAL LIABILITIES & EQUITY	$0	

T4. Pay $1.5 million for a building to be used for office, manufacturing and warehouse space.

You have found the perfect building for AppleSeed Enterprises, Inc. This 100,000 square-foot building is appraised at $1.1 million and the land at $550,000. The building is nicely laid out with 90,000 square feet of manufacturing and warehouse space and 10,000 square feet for of offices.

You negotiate well and drive a hard bargain. You and the seller agree on a sale price for building and land of $1.5 million, a good deal for AppleSeed.

In this transaction we will buy the building, AppleSeed Enterprises' first fixed asset. Fixed assets (also called *PP&E for Property, Plant & Equipment*) are long-lived productive assets such as

buildings, machinery and fixtures, that are used to make, store, ship and sell product. Fixed assets are also sometimes called capital equipment. When you acquire a fixed asset, you add its value to the *Balance Sheet* as an asset.

Accounting convention and IRS regulations do not allow you to immediately "expense" the cost of acquiring a fixed asset. Because fixed assets have a long productive life, you can expense only a portion of their purchase price each year as you use them. ***This yearly expense is called depreciation.***

We will set up a depreciation schedule on page 113 and book a depreciation charge in Transaction 13.

Transaction: Purchase 100,000 square foot building and land for $1.5 million in cash. This facility will serve as AppleSeed Enterprises' headquarters, manufacturing facility and warehouse.

① Write a check for $1.5 million to the seller of the building. Record this cash transaction under **PP&E PURCHASE** in the *Cash Flow Statement*.

② Then, lower **CASH** in the *Balance Sheet* by the $1.5 million check that you wrote to buy the building.

③ Now you must make another entry to bring the *Balance Sheet* back into balance. Increase **FIXED ASSETS @ COST** on the *Balance Sheet* by the $1.5 million purchase price of the building. Note that this asset is recorded at actual cost, not at an appraised or any other valuation.

~

Transaction 5. — Pay SG&A Salaries & Book Fringes

Income Statement

NET SALES	$	-
COST OF GOODS SOLD		-
GROSS MARGIN		-
SALES & MARKETING		7,680
RESEARCH & DEVELOPMENT		-
GENERAL & ADMINISTRATIVE		7,110
OPERATING EXPENSE		14,790
INCOME FROM OPERATIONS		(14,790)
NET INTEREST INCOME		-
INCOME TAXES		-
NET INCOME	$	(14,790)

① A
① B

Cash Flow Statement

BEGINNING CASH BALANCE	$	-
CASH RECEIPTS		-
CASH DISBURSEMENTS		7,960
CASH FLOW FROM OPERATIONS		(7,960)
PP&E PURCHASE		-
NET BORROWINGS		-
INCOME TAXES PAID		-
SALE OF CAPITAL STOCK		-
ENDING CASH BALANCE	$	(7,960)

③ A

Balance Sheet

Assets	CASH	$	(7,960)
	ACCOUNTS RECEIVABLE		-
	INVENTORIES		-
	PREPAID EXPENSES		-
	CURRENT ASSETS		(7,960)
	OTHER ASSETS		-
	FIXED ASSETS @ COST		-
	ACCUMULATED DEPRECIATION		-
	NET FIXED ASSETS		-
	TOTAL ASSETS		(7,960)

③ B

Liabilities & Equity	ACCOUNTS PAYABLE	$	-
	ACCRUED EXPENSES		6,830
	CURRENT PORTION OF DEBT		-
	INCOME TAXES PAYABLE		-
	CURRENT LIABILITIES		6,830
	LONG-TERM DEBT		-
	CAPITAL STOCK		-
	RETAINED EARNINGS		(14,790)
	SHAREHOLDERS' EQUITY		(14,790)
	TOTAL LIABILITIES & EQUITY	$	(7,960)

④
②

T5. Hire administrative and sales staff. Pay first month's salaries, book fringe benefits and taxes.

AppleSeed will soon be in production, so you had better figure out how to sell applesauce! You will also need help with administrative tasks.

Hire some SG&A employees. SG&A stands for *"sales, general and administrative."* SG&A is a catchall for all expenses not involved in manufacturing; that is, not added to inventory. More on this topic later.

Add to AppleSeed's SG&A payroll a secretary at the wage of $13 per hour ($2,250 per month), a bookkeeper at a salary of $3,000 per month, salesperson at $4,000 per month and a salesclerk at $10 per hour ($1,750 per month).

The table below computes SG&A take-home pay and fringe benefit costs.

SG&A Payroll-Related Expenses

	PAY TO EMPLOYEES	PAY TO OTHERS
MONTHLY SALARY	$11,000	-
EMPLOYEE'S FICA	$(840)	$840
FEDERAL/STATE WITHHOLDING	$(2,200)	$2,200
EMPLOYER'S FICA	-	$840
WORKMEN'S COMPENSATION	-	$400
UNEMPLOYMENT INSURANCE	-	$550
HEALTH & LIFE INSURANCE	-	$2,000
TOTALS PER MONTH	$7,960	$6,830
TOTAL PAID TO EMPLOYEES & OTHERS		$14,790

Transaction: Book this month's payroll-associated expenses of $14,790 ($7,680 for **SALES MARKETING** expense and $7,110 for **GENERAL & ADMINISTRATIVE** expense). These expenses include salaries, wages, insurance, and other fringe benefits. Issue payroll checks totaling $7,960 to SG&A employees.

1 (1A) On the *Income Statement* add total monthly payroll expense of $7,680 for the salesperson and clerk to **SALES & MARKETING** expenses. (1B) Also add the payroll expense of $7,110 for the secretary and the bookkeeper to **GENERAL & ADMINISTRATIVE** expenses.

2 Decrease **RETAINED EARNINGS** in the *Balance Sheet* by the total SG&A payroll of $14,790.

3 (3A) Issue payroll checks totaling $7,960 and list as a **CASH DISBURSEMENTS** in the *Cash Flow Statement*. (3B) Decrease **CASH** in the *Balance Sheet* by the same amount.

4 The $6,830 due to others is owed, but not yet paid. Place this amount as **ACCRUED EXPENSES** in the liability section of the *Balance Sheet*.

~

Transaction 6. — Pay Fringes, FICA, & Withholding Taxes

Income Statement

NET SALES	$	-
COST OF GOODS SOLD		-
GROSS MARGIN		-
SALES & MARKETING		-
RESEARCH & DEVELOPMENT		-
GENERAL & ADMINISTRATIVE		-
OPERATING EXPENSE		-
INCOME FROM OPERATIONS		-
NET INTEREST INCOME		-
INCOME TAXES		-
NET INCOME	$	-

Cash Flow Statement

BEGINNING CASH BALANCE	$	-	
CASH RECEIPTS		-	
CASH DISBURSEMENTS		9,690	❶
CASH FLOW FROM OPERATIONS		(9,690)	
PP&E PURCHASE		-	
NET BORROWINGS		-	
INCOME TAXES PAID		-	
SALE OF CAPITAL STOCK		-	
ENDING CASH BALANCE	$	(9,690)	

Balance Sheet

Assets	CASH	❷ $	(9,690)	
	ACCOUNTS RECEIVABLE		-	
	INVENTORIES		-	
	PREPAID EXPENSES		-	
	CURRENT ASSETS		(9,690)	
	OTHER ASSETS		-	
	FIXED ASSETS @ COST		-	
	ACCUMULATED DEPRECIATION		-	
	NET FIXED ASSETS		-	
	TOTAL ASSETS		(9,690)	
Liabilities & Equity	ACCOUNTS PAYABLE	$	-	
	ACCRUED EXPENSES		(9,690)	③
	CURRENT PORTION OF DEBT		-	
	INCOME TAXES PAYABLE		-	
	CURRENT LIABILITIES		(9,690)	
	LONG-TERM DEBT		-	
	CAPITAL STOCK		-	
	RETAINED EARNINGS		-	
	SHAREHOLDERS' EQUITY		-	
	TOTAL LIABILITIES & EQUITY	$	(9,690)	

T6. Pay employee health, life, and disability insurance premiums plus FICA, unemployment and withholding taxes.

When you put yourself on AppleSeed's payroll in Transaction 2 and then hired an SG&A staff in Transaction 5, you issued payroll checks to all new AppleSeed employees.

However, you did not at that time pay all the payroll-associated expenses for fringe benefits such as health and life insurance or the withholding taxes and the FICA that you deducted from the employees' paychecks.

These expenses were booked in the *Income Statement* at the time they were incurred, but since they were not at that time actually paid, they became accrued expenses. Such is the accrual basis of accounting

If an expense is booked in the *Income Statement* but you have not yet "satisfied the obligation" by paying it immediately, you must record the expense as "accrued" on the *Balance Sheet*.

Transaction: Pay all the payroll-associated expenses that were accrued in Transaction 2 and Transaction 5, including FICA, withholding tax and unemployment insurance to be paid to the government. Also pay to private insurance companies the workmen's compensation and health and life insurance premiums.

1 Write checks totaling $9,690 — $2,860 from Transaction 2 plus $6,830 from Transaction 5 for these accrued expenses. Show payments in **CASH DISBURSEMENTS** in the *Cash Flow Statement*.

2 Lower **CASH** in the asset section of the *Balance Sheet* by the same amount paid above.

3 Lower **ACCRUED EXPENSES** in the liabilities section of the *Balance Sheet* by the $9,690 paid above. Payment of these expenses had been deferred (accrued). Now that you have paid them you can, in effect, reverse the original deferring entry.

Note: Actually paying these accrued expenses does not affect the *Income Statement* now. The *Income Statement* was already charged when the expenses were incurred as described in Transaction 2 and Transaction 5.

∼

Appleseed Summary Financial Statements: T1 thru T6.

Income Statement

	T1 +	T2 +	T3 +	T4 +	T5 +	T6 =	T1 thru T6
NET SALES	$ -	$ -	$ -	$ -	$ -	$ -	$ -
COST OF GOODS SOLD	-	-	-			-	-
GROSS MARGIN							$0
SALES & MARKETING	-	-	-	-	7,680	-	7,680
RESEARCH & DEVELOPMENT	-	-	-	-			-
GENERAL & ADMINISTRATIVE	-	6,230	-	-	7,110		13,340
OPERATING EXPENSE							$ 21,020
INCOME FROM OPERATIONS							$0
NET INTEREST INCOME		-	-	-	-	-	-
INCOME TAXES		-	-	-	-	-	-
NET INCOME							$ (21,020)

Cash Flow Statement

	T1 +	T2 +	T3 +	T4 +	T5 +	T6 =	T1 thru T6
BEGINNING CASH BALANCE							$ 0
CASH RECEIPTS	-	-	-	-	-	-	-
CASH DISBURSEMENTS	-	3,370	-	-	7,960	9,690	21,020
CASH FLOW FROM OPERATIONS							$ (21,020)
PP&E PURCHASE	-	-	-	1,500,000	-	-	1,500,000
NET BORROWINGS	-	-	1,000,000	-	-	-	1,000,000
INCOME TAXES PAID	-	-	-	-	-	-	-
SALE OF CAPITAL STOCK	1,550,000	-	-	-	-	-	1,550,000
ENDING CASH BALANCES							$1,028,980

Balance Sheet

		T1 +	T2 +	T3 +	T4 +	T5 +	T6 =	T1 thru T6
Assets	CASH							$1,028,980
	ACCOUNTS RECEIVABLE	-	-	-	-	-	-	-
	INVENTORIES	-	-	-	-	-	-	-
	PREPAID EXPENSES	-	-	-	-	-	-	-
	CURRENT ASSETS							1,028,980
	OTHER ASSETS	-	-	-	-	-	-	-
	FIXED ASSETS @ COST	-	-	-	1,500,000	-	-	1,500,000
	ACCUMULATED DEPRECIATION	-	-	-	-	-	-	-
	NET FIXED ASSETS							1,500,000
	TOTAL ASSETS							$2,528,980
Liabilities & Equity	ACCOUNTS PAYABLE	$ -	$ -	$ -	$ -	$ -	$ -	$ -
	ACCRUED EXPENSES	-	2,860	-	6,830	-	(9,690)	0
	CURRENT PORTION OF DEBT	-	-	100,000	-	-	-	100,000
	INCOME TAXES PAYABLE	-	-	-	-	-	-	-
	CURRENT LIABILITIES							100,000
	LONG-TERM DEBT	-	-	900,000	-	-	-	900,000
	CAPITAL STOCK + Founding $50K	1,500,000	-	-	-	-	-	1,550,000
	RETAINED EARNINGS	-	(6,230)	-	(14,790)	-	-	(21,020)
	SHAREHOLDERS' EQUITY							1,528,980
	TOTAL LIABILITIES & EQUITY							$2,528,980

Chapter 7.
Staffing and Equipping Facility; Planning for Manufacturing

Now begins the fun stuff. In a few short weeks, we will be producing thousands of cases of the best applesauce you have ever tasted.

In anticipation of beginning applesauce production, we will design our production techniques, determine raw material requirements, labor needs, figure our costs and establish methods to keep track of our inventories.

Finally, we will order our first raw materials and get everything ready to begin trial production in our new manufacturing plant.

~

Transaction 7. Order $250,000 worth of manufacturing Pay 1/2 down now.

Transaction 8. Receive and install applesauce-making machinery. Pay the $125,000 balance due.

Transaction 9. Hire supervisor. Expense first month's salary and wages.

- Prepare bill of materials and establish labor requirements.

- Set up plant and machinery depreciation schedules.

- Plan monthly production schedule and set standard costs.

Transaction 10. Place standing orders for raw materials with suppliers. Receive one million jar labels.

Appleseed Enterprises Inc. Summary Financial Statements: Transaction 1 thru Transaction 6.

At the end of a period, all the financial transaction entries that have taken place in the period are added and then presented as the summary consolidated financial statement for the period. See the example of how this is accomplished on the facing page. Note, only the actual account transaction figures are listed in the consolidation. Final sums are computed as always.

Transaction 7. — Order Machinery

Income Statement

NET SALES	$	-
COST OF GOODS SOLD		-
GROSS MARGIN		-
SALES & MARKETING		-
RESEARCH & DEVELOPMENT		-
GENERAL & ADMINISTRATIVE		-
OPERATING EXPENSE		-
INCOME FROM OPERATIONS		-
NET INTEREST INCOME		-
INCOME TAXES		-
NET INCOME	$	-

Cash Flow Statement

BEGINNING CASH BALANCE	$	-
CASH RECEIPTS		-
CASH DISBURSEMENTS		-
CASH FLOW FROM OPERATIONS		-
PP&E PURCHASE	125,000	❶
NET BORROWINGS		-
INCOME TAXES PAID		-
SALE OF CAPITAL STOCK		-
ENDING CASH BALANCE	$	(125,000)

Balance Sheet

	CASH	❷ $	(125,000)
	ACCOUNTS RECEIVABLE		-
	INVENTORIES		-
	PREPAID EXPENSES		-
Assets	CURRENT ASSETS		(125,000)
	OTHER ASSETS		125,000 ③
	FIXED ASSETS @ COST		-
	ACCUMULATED DEPRECIATION		-
	NET FIXED ASSETS		-
	TOTAL ASSETS		-
	ACCOUNTS PAYABLE	$	-
	ACCRUED EXPENSES		-
	CURRENT PORTION OF DEBT		-
	INCOME TAXES PAYABLE		-
Liabilities & Equity	CURRENT LIABILITIES		-
	LONG-TERM DEBT		-
	CAPITAL STOCK		-
	RETAINED EARNINGS		-
	SHAREHOLDERS' EQUITY		-
	TOTAL LIABILITIES & EQUITY	$	-

T7. Order $250,000 worth of manufacturing machinery. Pay 1/2 down now.

We will need a lot of specialized machinery to make our special applesauce: presses, large stainless-steel holding tanks, bottling machines, a labeling machine and so forth.

We contract with ABC AppleCrushing Machinery Inc. (ABCACM, Inc., for short) to construct and install our equipment at a total cost to AppleSeed of $250,000 including delivery charges.

Before beginning all its important work, ABCACM demands a prepayment of $125,000 in cash. The remaining payment of $125,000 will be due upon the completion of installation and qualification of the equipment.

Transaction: Place an order for $250,000 worth of applesauce-making machinery. Make a prepayment of $125,000 with the remaining balance due upon successful installation.

1 Enclose a check for $125,000 with the purchase order to the machinery contractor. Show this prepayment as a **PROPERTY PLANT & EQUIPMENT PURCHASE** on the *Cash Flow Statement*.

2 Lower **CASH** in the assets section of the *Balance Sheet* by the $125,000 contractor prepayment.

3 This prepayment is an asset that AppleSeed "owns." It can be viewed as a "right" to receive in the future $250,000 of equipment and only have to issue another $125,000 check to the equipment builder. Since this asset does not fit into any of the other asset categories in our abbreviated sample statements, increase **OTHER ASSETS** on the *Balance Sheet* by the $125,000 machinery prepayment.

~

Transaction 8. — Receive Machinery & Pay Balance Due

Income Statement

NET SALES	$	-
COST OF GOODS SOLD		-
GROSS MARGIN		-
SALES & MARKETING		-
RESEARCH & DEVELOPMENT		-
GENERAL & ADMINISTRATIVE		-
OPERATING EXPENSE		-
INCOME FROM OPERATIONS		-
NET INTEREST INCOME		-
INCOME TAXES		-
NET INCOME	$	-

Cash Flow Statement

BEGINNING CASH BALANCE	$	-
CASH RECEIPTS		-
CASH DISBURSEMENTS		-
CASH FLOW FROM OPERATIONS		-
PP&E PURCHASE		125,000 ❶
NET BORROWINGS		-
INCOME TAXES PAID		-
SALE OF CAPITAL STOCK		-
ENDING CASH BALANCE	$	(125,000)

Balance Sheet

Assets

CASH ❷	$	(125,000)
ACCOUNTS RECEIVABLE		-
INVENTORIES		-
PREPAID EXPENSES		-
CURRENT ASSETS		(125,000)
OTHER ASSETS		(125,000) ③
FIXED ASSETS @ COST ④		250,000
ACCUMULATED DEPRECIATION		-
NET FIXED ASSETS		250,000
TOTAL ASSETS		-

Liabilities & Equity

ACCOUNTS PAYABLE	$	-
ACCRUED EXPENSES		-
CURRENT PORTION OF DEBT		-
INCOME TAXES PAYABLE		-
CURRENT LIABILITIES		-
LONG-TERM DEBT		-
CAPITAL STOCK		-
RETAINED EARNINGS		-
SHAREHOLDERS' EQUITY		-
TOTAL LIABILITIES & EQUITY	$	-

T8. Receive and install applesauce-making machinery. Pay the $125,000 balance due.

ABCACM does a super job — on time and on budget. They submit an invoice for their work, and you are happy to pay. Our applesauce machinery is installed and ready for operation.

These new machines are a productive asset ... so-called because they will be used to produce our product and make a profit for AppleSeed.

Note that when you paid for these machines you just shifted money from one asset category on the *Balance Sheet* into another, from cash to fixed assets. The *Income Statement* was not affected. When we use and then depreciate these assets, the *Income Statement* will take a hit.

More later in Transaction 13.

Transaction: Make final payment of $125,000, the balance due on our new applesauce-making machinery.

(1) Everything is working well. Accept delivery on the machinery and write a check for the $125,000 balance due. Show this payment as a **PROPERTY PLANT & EQUIPMENT PURCHASE** in the *Cash Flow Statement*.

(2) Lower **CASH** in the assets section of the *Balance Sheet* by the $125,000 paid to the contractor.

(3) Lower **OTHER ASSETS** by the $125,000 prepayment that now will be converted (below) to a fixed asset.

(4) Increase **FIXED ASSETS @ COST** by the total $250,000 cost of the machinery. Half of this amount comes from this transaction (payment of the $125,000 balance due) and half from reversing the **OTHER ASSETS** account (prepayment of $125,000 that was done in Transaction 7) now that we have received the machinery.

~

Transaction 9. — Expense Pre-Production Salaries

Income Statement

NET SALES	$	-
COST OF GOODS SOLD		
GROSS MARGIN		-
SALES & MARKETING		
RESEARCH & DEVELOPMENT		
GENERAL & ADMINISTRATIVE	4,880	❶ A
OPERATING EXPENSE	4,880	
INCOME FROM OPERATIONS	(4,880)	
NET INTEREST INCOME		
INCOME TAXES		
NET INCOME	$	(4,880)

Cash Flow Statement

BEGINNING CASH BALANCE	$	-
CASH RECEIPTS		
CASH DISBURSEMENTS	2,720	❷ A
CASH FLOW FROM OPERATIONS	(2,720)	
PP&E PURCHASE		
NET BORROWINGS		
INCOME TAXES PAID		
SALE OF CAPITAL STOCK		
ENDING CASH BALANCES	$	(2,720)

Balance Sheet

Assets

CASH ❷ B	$	(2,720)
ACCOUNTS RECEIVABLE		
INVENTORIES		
PREPAID EXPENSES		
CURRENT ASSETS		(2,720)
OTHER ASSETS		
FIXED ASSETS @ COST		
ACCUMULATED DEPRECIATION		
NET FIXED ASSETS		-
TOTAL ASSETS		(2,720)

Liabilities & Equity

ACCOUNTS PAYABLE	$	-
ACCRUED EXPENSES	2,160	③
CURRENT PORTION OF DEBT		
INCOME TAXES PAYABLE		
CURRENT LIABILITIES		2,160
LONG-TERM DEBT		
CAPITAL STOCK		
RETAINED EARNINGS	(4,880)	❶ B
SHAREHOLDERS' EQUITY		(4,880)
TOTAL LIABILITIES & EQUITY	$	(2,720)

T9. Hire supervisor. Expense first month's salary and wages.

Hire the supervisor at a salary of $3,750 per month and have her start immediately. Using similar calculations to those in the table for Transaction 5, the supervisor will receive $2,720 per month in take-home pay. The company will also pay $2,160 in fringes and various taxes to the government. Salary and fringes for the supervisor total $4,880 per month.

Production Labor Costs

	TAKE-HOME PAY TO EMPLOYEES	FRINGE BENEFITS AND TAXES	TOTALS
SUPERVISOR	$2,720	$2,160	$4,880
HOURLY WORKERS	$6,300	$6,000	$12,300
MANUFACTURING PAYROLL	$9,020	$8,160	$17,180

We will begin paying the supervisor right away. However, since we have not yet started production, we will charge this month's salary to G&A as a start-up expense. Normally the manufacturing salary and wage expense is charged to inventory. More later.

The supervisor starts interviewing hourly production workers. Wages will be $12.50 per hour plus fringes with an expected 40-hour week. Hire five workers and tell them to report next month when we expect to start production.

AppleSeed's manufacturing payroll now totals $17,180 per month: $4,880 for the supervisor and also $12,300 for the five hourly workers.

Transaction: Book supervisor's salary and associated payroll expenses as a **GENERAL & ADMINISTRATIVE EXPENSE** since we have not yet started production. Issue first month's salary check. Make no entries for hourly workers since they have not yet reported for work.

1 (1A) On the *Income Statement* add $4,880 (the total salary and payroll costs for the supervisor) to **GENERAL & ADMINISTRATIVE EXPENSE**. (1B) Decrease **RETAINED EARNINGS** in the liabilities section of the *Balance Sheet* by the same amount.

2 (2A) Issue a payroll check totaling $2,720 and list under **CASH DISBURSEMENTS** in the *Cash Flow Statement*. (2B) Decrease **CASH** in the *Balance Sheet* by the same amount.

3 The remaining $2,160 in benefits and taxes is owed but not yet paid. Place this amount in **ACCRUED EXPENSES** on the *Balance Sheet*.

$\sim$

Manufacturing Costing

How much will it cost to make our fine applesauce? How should we account for manufacturing costs? How will we correctly value our inventory? These are essential questions for managing the books (and profitability) of our business.

～

Manufacturing businesses such as AppleSeed Enterprises compute product cost by determining and then adding three separate cost elements. The three common cost elements are: (a) raw material costs, (b) direct labor costs, and (c) overhead costs.

We will discuss so-called *direct costs* first and then overhead costs. Direct costs (basically materials and labor) are simple and easy to understand. After discussing each element of manufacturing cost separately, we will then summarize them into a product "standard" cost for use in: (a) inventory valuation on the *Balance Sheet,* and (b) computing the cost of goods sold for entry on the *Income Statement*.

Overhead costs is a catchall category for costs that cannot be assigned to a specific product, but rather are ongoing costs required just to keep the plant open. Examples of overhead costs include costs for plant space, heat, light, power, supervisory labor, depreciation, and so forth.

Cost of Raw Materials See AppleSeed's applesauce "Bill of Materials" below. This table lists all of the materials that go into our product and the unit cost of these materials in normal commercial purchase quantities. Also shown are the amount and cost of materials that go into a single shipping "unit" of our product, in this instance a case containing 12 jars of applesauce.

From the Bill of Materials we see that we buy apples in ton quantities at a price of $120 per ton delivered to our plant. Also, each 12-jar case of our applesauce takes 33 lbs. of apples to produce. Because 2,000 lbs. of apples costs us $120, we will pay $1.98 for the 33 lbs. of apples that will go into a case of applesauce.

Using a similar calculation for all the other raw materials in our product, yields a total materials cost of $8.55 per 12-jar case.

Cost of Direct Labor We have designed our plant to manufacture up to 20,000 cases of applesauce each month. Because the plant is highly automated, we will need only five hourly workers to achieve this production level.

AppleSeed Enterprises's Applesauce Bill of Materials

	PRICE PER UNIT OF RAW MATERIAL	UNIT OF MEASURE FOR RAW MATERIAL	QUANTITY REQUIRED PER CASE OF 12 JARS	EXTENDED COST PER CASE OF 12 JARS
APPLES	$120	TON	33.00 LBS.	$1.98
SUGAR	$140	1000 LBS.	2.30 LBS.	$0.32
CINNAMON	$280	100 LBS.	0.35 OZ.	$0.06
GLASS JAR	$55	GROSS	12	$4.60
JAR CAP	$10	GROSS	12	$0.83
JAR LABEL	$200	10,000	12	$0.24
LARGE BOX	$75	GROSS	1	$0.52
			COST PER CASE	$8.55

Our total hourly labor payroll for a single month is $12,300 (as computed in Transaction 9). Divide this labor cost by the 20,000 cases we plan to produce each month. We compute a direct labor cost of $0.62 for each case of applesauce made.

Manufacturing Labor Cost per Case:

Hourly payroll per month	$12,000.00
÷ Cases produced	20,000
= hourly payroll per case	$0.62

We have just estimated the first two elements of product cost — materials and direct labor. They were easy compared to what follows: overhead and depreciation.

Overhead

It is not difficult to see how material cost should be added as a part of product costs. Same for the direct labor. However, "overhead" is not so simple.

It takes more than just materials and labor to make a product. It takes a manufacturing building; it takes machinery; it takes heat, light and power; and it takes supervisors to make things run smoothly. These costs don't go "directly" into the product as do materials and labor, but they are costs to make the product nonetheless.

We'll next study depreciation charges for AppleSeed and then come back to compute total overhead costs and total manufacturing costs for our applesauce.

Depreciation

A major cost for AppleSeed is the depreciation of machinery and buildings used to make our product. Basically, depreciation is a way of charging to current activities a prorated portion of the original purchase price of long-lived assets.

For example, suppose we purchase a $100,000 machine. Over its useful life, it will make 500,000 jars of applesauce. Therefore, each jar should be charged a $0.20 cost for its prorated use of that machine. Thus, we would add $0.20 to the cost of each jar as a depreciation charge.

To simplify, both accounting practice and tax laws say that fixed assets such as buildings and machinery can be "written off" or "depreciated" each year by a certain specified portion of their value. Some assets are written off over a longer useful life (buildings over 20 to 30 years) or a shorter useful life (automobiles over 5 years).

Depreciation Schedule Look at the AppleSeed Enterprises' fixed asset depreciation schedule on the facing page. Listed in the left-most column are AppleSeed's fixed assets. Note that the total amount under "original purchase price" is the same amount shown on AppleSeed's *Balance Sheet* for Fixed Assets @ Cost.

The next column lists the useful life that AppleSeed will use to compute depreciation for each asset class. In the next

Depreciation is just a method of dribbling over time a portion of the purchase price of a fixed assets through the *Income Statement* as a period expense, thus lowering profit for that period.

When you originally purchased the fixed asset, you pay for the asset all at once with cash, but you only book a calculated portion (the depreciation charge) of the cost each month based on the expected useful life of the asset.

AppleSeed Enterprises' Fixed Asset Depreciation Schedule

	ORIGINAL PURCHASE PRICE	YEARS OF USEFUL LIFE	DEPRECIATION CHARGE EACH YEAR	BOOK VALUE AT END OF YEAR 1	BOOK VALUE AT END OF YEAR 2	BOOK VALUE AT END OF YEAR 3
BUILDING	$1,000,000	20	$50,000	$950,000	$900,000	$850,000
LAND	$500,000	forever	$0	$500,000	$500,000	$500,000
MACHINERY	$250,000	7	$35,714	$214,286	$178,572	$142,858
TOTALS	$1,750,000		$85,714	$1,664,286	$1,578,572	$1,492,858

column, we list the actual yearly depreciation amount when using the "straight-line" method to compute depreciation. Straight-line yearly depreciation equals original cost divided by years of useful life.

Note that with straight-line depreciation, the same amount of depreciation is taken for each year. Sometimes used, "accelerated" depreciation methods can allow you to depreciate more in early years.

Book Value The remaining three columns show the "book value" of Apple-Seed's fixed assets at the end of each of the next three years. Book value is just the original purchase price of a fixed asset less all the depreciation charges taken over the years — the so-called "accumulated depreciation." The book value of the fixed assets is shown on the *Balance Sheet* as *Net Fixed Assets*.

Note that book value is an accounting definition of "value." It does not necessarily correspond to any actual resale value or replacement value.

Effect on Income Each year Apple-Seed will add $85,714 (or $7,143 per month) to its costs to account for its use of fixed assets throughout the year. This charge will hit the *Income Statement* as an element of product cost shown in cost of goods sold (COGS). More later.

Effect on Cash Unlike most other expenses, you do not pay a depreciation charge with cash. That is to say, cash balance and cash flow are not affected as you depreciate a fixed asset. Why is this so? Sounds like a free lunch?

Depreciation is not free. When you originally purchased the fixed asset, you paid its total cost with cash. The *Cash Flow Statement* showed the payment at full purchase price. However, this purchase price was not posted on the *Income Statement* as an expense at that time. However, we will depreciate the full cost of that long-lived asset, but over time.

Depreciation is just a method of dribbling the costs of fixed assets through the Income Statement over time, as you use the assets.

~

AppleSeed Enterprises' manufacturing overhead is made up of the supervisor's salary, depreciation charges and other odds and ends such as heat, light and power, and general supplies. Most of these costs must be paid regardless of the production volume. That is, these costs are generally the same whether we produce a lot or a little applesauce.

Let's compute AppleSeed's manufacturing overhead. From Transaction 9, we see that the supervisor's total payroll cost is $4,880 per month. From computations shown above, we see that depreciation is $7,143 per month. Let's assume that all other elements of overhead (heat, power,

Product Cost @ Three Different Production Levels

	COSTS PER CASE	COSTS PER MONTH	TOTAL COSTS FOR 10,000 CASES PER MONTH PRODUCTION	TOTAL COSTS FOR 20,000 CASES PER MONTH PRODUCTION	TOTAL COSTS FOR 30,000 CASES PER MONTH PRODUCTION
RAW MATERIALS	$8.55		$85,500	$171,000	$256,500
DIRECT LABOR	$0.62		$6,150	$12,300	$18,450
OVERHEAD— SUPERVISOR		$4,880	$4,880	$4,880	$4,880
DEPRECIATION		$7,143	$7,143	$7,143	$7,143
ALL OTHER		$8,677	$8,677	$8,677	$8,677
TOTAL MANUFACTURING $ COST IN MONTH			$112,350	$204,000	$295,650
CASES MANUFACTURED IN MONTH			10,000	20,000	30,000
$ MANUFACTURING COST PER CASE			$11.24	$10.20	$9.86

etc.) will cost $8,677 per month. Thus, AppleSeed's total manufacturing overhead is $20,700 each and every month as shown below:

Supervisory payroll	$4,880
Depreciation	$7,143
all other costs	$8,677
Total monthly overhead	$20,700

But note that it all does not go out as cash each month. Remember, depreciation is a non-cash expense — just a book-keeping entry. The actual cash outlay for overhead is only the supervisor's salary and the "all other" expense that totals $13,577 each month.

Variable Costs

Some of AppleSeed's manufacturing costs get larger (in total) with each additional case the company makes. For example, with more cases produced, more raw material is consumed. Ten cases require $85.50 worth of raw materials; 100 cases require $855 worth of raw materials. This type of cost, one that varies directly and proportionally with production volume, is called a *variable cost.* Direct labor is another example of a variable cost.

Fixed Costs

A cost that does not normally change with the volume level of production is called a *fixed cost.* Examples of AppleSeed fixed costs are supervisory labor costs and depreciation. Generally, the elements of overhead are fixed costs.

What is important about the concept of fixed and variable costs? Costs to produce a manufactured product can vary greatly depending on the:

1. production volume and
2. proportion of fixed versus variable costs elements in product cost.

Thus, when we talk about the cost of an individual case of applesauce to manufacture, we must also state a production volume. Then the total fixed manufacturing costs can be "allocated" proportionally to each individual unit of production. Thus, we can establish a cost for inventory valuation and the cost of goods sold.

See the table above. It shows different product costs at different production volumes. Actual costs to produce a case of applesauce vary between $11.24 and $9.86, depending on whether we produce 10,000 or up to 30,000 cases. The lower case cost is at the higher volume.

When we talk about what an individual case of applesauce costs us to make, we must also state a production volume.

Now we are ready to compute Apple-Seed's product costs and determine how to value our inventory.

Standard Cost System

Okay, let's pull all the manufacturing costs together and compute what a case of applesauce costs to make. But remember, we cannot compute the unit cost of a case of applesauce until we set a monthly level of production.

In the production costing chart shown on the previous page, we have computed the total monthly costs to produce applesauce at three different production volumes: 10,000, 20,000 or 30,000 cases per month. We have also computed for these production volumes AppleSeed's cost per case. Depending on our monthly production volume, a single case of applesauce can cost between $11.24 (at 10,000 cases per month) and $9.86 (at 30,000 cases per month). Quite a significant difference!

The so-called *standard cost* is an estimate of product unit cost assuming a certain production volume. Accountants use standard cost as a good estimate of the real costs, to simplify posting of day-to-day accounting transactions.

Establishing a standard cost will be useful for maintaining AppleSeed Enterprises' books. We will use this standard cost to value inventory and to establish cost of goods sold (COGS) when we sell our product.

AppleSeed's planned production is 20,000 cases per month. From the table on the previous page, we expect our actual costs will be $10.20 per case of applesauce we manufacture. The table shows this standard cost broken down by element of cost. We will be using this breakdown in later transactions.

Variances

What happens if at the end of a period we find that we manufactured either more (or less) than 20,000 cases per month? Won't the "costs" then change? Yes, costs will change. We will account for this overestimate or underestimate of costs by making manufacturing variance adjustments to the books.

More on how manufacturing variances affect product cost will be discussed in detail on pages 132-133.

**AppleSeed Enterprises' Standard Cost Calculations by
Cost Element @ 20,000 Cases per Month Production Level**

	TOTAL COST PER MONTH AT 20,000 CASE PRODUCTION	COST PER CASE	TO EMPLOYEES	FRINGES AND TAXES	TO SUPPLIERS	DEPRECIATION CHARGE
RAW MATERIALS	$171,000	$8.55			$8.55	
DIRECT LABOR	$12,300	$0.62	$0.32	$0.30		
OVERHEAD—SUPERVISOR	$4,880	$0.24	$0.14	$0.10		
DEPRECIATION	$7,143	$0.36				$0.36
ALL OTHER	$8,677	$0.43			$0.43	
	$204,000	$10.20	$.46	$0.40	$8.98	$0.36
TOTALS PER MONTH			$9,020	$8,160	$179,677	$7,143

Transaction 10. — Receive raw materials

Income Statement

NET SALES	$	-
COST OF GOODS SOLD		-
GROSS MARGIN		-
SALES & MARKETING		-
RESEARCH & DEVELOPMENT		-
GENERAL & ADMINISTRATIVE		-
OPERATING EXPENSE		-
INCOME FROM OPERATIONS		-
NET INTEREST INCOME		-
INCOME TAXES		-
NET INCOME	$	-

Cash Flow Statement

BEGINNING CASH BALANCE	$	-
CASH RECEIPTS		-
CASH DISBURSEMENTS		-
CASH FLOW FROM OPERATIONS		-
PP&E PURCHASE		-
NET BORROWINGS		-
INCOME TAXES PAID		-
SALE OF CAPITAL STOCK		-
ENDING CASH BALANCE	$	-

Balance Sheet

Assets

CASH	$	-
ACCOUNTS RECEIVABLE		-
INVENTORIES		20,000
PREPAID EXPENSES		-
CURRENT ASSETS		20,000
OTHER ASSETS		-
FIXED ASSETS @ COST		-
ACCUMULATED DEPRECIATION		-
NET FIXED ASSETS		-
TOTAL ASSETS		20,000

Liabilities & Equity

ACCOUNTS PAYABLE	$	20,000 ❷
ACCRUED EXPENSES		-
CURRENT PORTION OF DEBT		-
INCOME TAXES PAYABLE		-
CURRENT LIABILITIES		20,000
LONG-TERM DEBT		-
CAPITAL STOCK		-
RETAINED EARNINGS		-
SHAREHOLDERS' EQUITY		-
TOTAL LIABILITIES & EQUITY	$	20,000

T10. Place an order for raw materials (apples, spices, and packaging materials). Receive one million specialty printed jar labels at 2¢ each.

We must order and receive raw materials before AppleSeed can start production. The table below shows the quantities of the various materials required for our monthly planned production level of 20,000 cases. Place a standing order with your suppliers for delivery of these quantities of raw materials each month. To get a good price and rapid delivery on very special four-color labels, the printer demands a press run of one million labels at $0.02 each.

Place the label order and receive the labels from the printer.

Raw Material Costs and Monthly Production Requirements

	QUANTITY PER CARTON	COST PER CARTON	QUANTITY NEEDED FOR 20,000 CARTONS	EXTENDED COST FOR 20,000 CARTONS
APPLES	33.00 LBS.	$1.98	330 TONS	$39,600
SUGAR	2.30 LBS.	$0.32	52 TONS	$6,400
CINNAMON	0.35 OZ.	$0.06	438 LBS.	$1,200
GLASS JAR	12	$4.60	1,667 GROSS	$92,000
JAR CAP	12	$0.83	1,667 GROSS	$16,600
JAR LABEL	12	$0.24	1,667 GROSS	$4,800
LARGE BOX	1	$0.52	139 GROSS	$10,400
TOTALS		$8.55		$171,000

Transaction: Order and receive one million applesauce jar labels at a cost of 2¢ each for a total of $20,000 to be paid 30 days after delivery.

1 Place the labels in raw material inventory for use when we start production. Increase **INVENTORIES** by $20,000 in the assets section of the *Balance Sheet*.

2 We owe our printer for the labels, but we will pay the bill later. Increase **ACCOUNTS PAYABLE** by $20,000 in the liabilities section of the *Balance Sheet*.

Note: Simply placing an order for raw materials has no effect on any of the three financial statements. However, when you do receive the materials ordered, the *Balance Sheet* is modified to account for these new assets and the balancing new liabilities you owe for the materials is listed as an **ACCOUNTS PAYABLE.**

∼

Chapter 8.
Startup of Manufacturing Operations

We are ready to start producing applesauce. The machinery is up and running, the workers are hired, and we are about to receive a supply of raw materials.

While manufacturing goes fairly smoothly, we do botch a half-day's production and have to scrap it. We will learn how to value our inventory "at standard" and book our first manufacturing variance. Raw materials keep rolling in. Now begins the fun stuff. In a few short weeks, we will be producing thousands of cases of the best applesauce you have ever tasted.

~

Transaction 11. Receive two months' supply of raw materials.

Transaction 12. Start up production. Pay supervisor and workers for the month.

Transaction 13. Book depreciation and other manufacturing overhead costs for the month.

Transaction 14. Pay for the labels received in Transaction 10.

Transaction 15. Finish manufacturing 19,500 cases of applesauce and move them into finished goods inventory.

Transaction 16. Scrap 500 cases worth of work-in-process inventory.

- Manufacturing variances: what can go wrong and what can go right.

Transaction 17. Pay for the two months' supply of raw materials received in Transaction 11 above.

Transaction 18. Manufacture another month's supply of applesauce.

Transaction 11. — Receive Raw Materials

Income Statement

NET SALES	$	-
COST OF GOODS SOLD		-
GROSS MARGIN		-
SALES & MARKETING		-
RESEARCH & DEVELOPMENT		-
GENERAL & ADMINISTRATIVE		-
OPERATING EXPENSE		-
INCOME FROM OPERATIONS		-
NET INTEREST INCOME		-
INCOME TAXES		-
NET INCOME	$	-

Cash Flow Statement

BEGINNING CASH BALANCE	$	-
CASH RECEIPTS		-
CASH DISBURSEMENTS		-
CASH FLOW FROM OPERATIONS		-
PP&E PURCHASE		-
NET BORROWINGS		-
INCOME TAXES PAID		-
SALE OF CAPITAL STOCK		-
ENDING CASH BALANCE	$	-

Balance Sheet

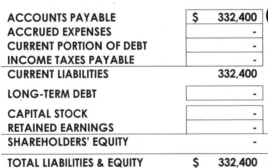

Assets

CASH	$	-
ACCOUNTS RECEIVABLE		-
INVENTORIES		332,400 ❶
PREPAID EXPENSES		-
CURRENT ASSETS		332,400
OTHER ASSETS		-
FIXED ASSETS @ COST		-
ACCUMULATED DEPRECIATION		-
NET FIXED ASSETS		-
TOTAL ASSETS		332,400

Liabilities & Equity

ACCOUNTS PAYABLE	$	332,400 ❷
ACCRUED EXPENSES		-
CURRENT PORTION OF DEBT		-
INCOME TAXES PAYABLE		-
CURRENT LIABILITIES		332,400
LONG-TERM DEBT		-
CAPITAL STOCK		-
RETAINED EARNINGS		-
SHAREHOLDERS' EQUITY		-
TOTAL LIABILITIES & EQUITY	$	332,400

T11. Receive two months' supply of raw materials.

Receive two months' supply of the rest of the raw materials necessary to manufacture our splendid applesauce. We will buy these materials on credit. Our suppliers will ship the materials to us now and not expect payment for a little while.

> Now is the time for AppleSeed to set up an *Inventory Valuation Worksheet.* (See table below.) This worksheet will help us compute the value of our inventory as we make and sell applesauce.
>
> The worksheet will list the effects of all transactions that change inventory values. The "Total Inventory" value at the bottom of the worksheet will always equal the **INVENTORY** value as shown on the company's *Balance Sheet.*

Our inventory will be divided into three groups depending on where it is in the manufacturing process. These categories will not show up on the *Balance Sheet.* The *Balance Sheet* lists only the total inventory figure. But you'll see in future transactions how useful it is to account for inventory valuation using these three classifications:

Raw Material Inventory is just what it says, "raw" purchased goods unmodified by us and waiting to be processed.

Work-In-Process ("WIP") refers to materials that are being processed by our machines and by our labor force. Work-in-process has added value because of our processing. More on this concept later.

Finished Goods Inventory is product finished, in our warehouse, and ready to ship. For inventory valuation purposes we will use the "standard cost" we computed earlier to value our finished goods.

Transaction: Receive two months' supply of all raw materials (apples, sugar, cinnamon, jars, caps, boxes) worth $332,400 in total. (That is, $8.55 total materials per case less $0.24 for the already received labels times 40,000 cases.)

 Increase **INVENTORIES** account on the Balance Sheet by the $332,400 cost of these materials.

 Increase **ACCOUNTS PAYABLE** on the *Balance Sheet* by the value of the materials received.

Inventory Valuation Worksheet	RAW MATERIAL	WORK IN PROCESS	FINISHED GOODS
INVENTORY VALUES AT STARTUP	$0	$0	$0
A. Receive labels **(T10)**	$20,000	$0	$0
B. Receive 2 months' supply of other raw materials **(T11)**	$332,400	$0	$0
INVENTORY SUBTOTALS AFTER THIS TRANSACTION	$352,400	$0	$0

TOTAL INVENTORY	$352,400

Transaction 12. — Start Production

Income Statement

NET SALES	$	-
COST OF GOODS SOLD		-
GROSS MARGIN		-
SALES & MARKETING		-
RESEARCH & DEVELOPMENT		-
GENERAL & ADMINISTRATIVE		-
OPERATING EXPENSE		-
INCOME FROM OPERATIONS		-
NET INTEREST INCOME		-
INCOME TAXES		-
NET INCOME	$	-

Cash Flow Statement

BEGINNING CASH BALANCE	$	-
CASH RECEIPTS		-
CASH DISBURSEMENTS		9,020	❶ A
CASH FLOW FROM OPERATIONS		(9,020)
PP&E PURCHASE		-
NET BORROWINGS		-
INCOME TAXES PAID		-
SALE OF CAPITAL STOCK		-
ENDING CASH BALANCES	$	(9,020)

Balance Sheet

Assets

CASH ❶ B	$	(9,020)
ACCOUNTS RECEIVABLE		-
INVENTORIES		17,180 ③
PREPAID EXPENSES		-
CURRENT ASSETS		8,160
OTHER ASSETS		-
FIXED ASSETS @ COST		-
ACCUMULATED DEPRECIATION		-
NET FIXED ASSETS		-
TOTAL ASSETS		8,160

Liabilities & Equity

ACCOUNTS PAYABLE	$	-
ACCRUED EXPENSES		8,160 ❷
CURRENT PORTION OF DEBT		-
INCOME TAXES PAYABLE		-
CURRENT LIABILITIES		8,160
LONG-TERM DEBT		-
CAPITAL STOCK		-
RETAINED EARNINGS		-
SHAREHOLDERS' EQUITY		-
TOTAL LIABILITIES & EQUITY	$	8,160

T12. Start production. Pay supervisor and workers for the month. Book payroll-associated fringes and taxes.

We are finally ready to produce apple-sauce. The plant is all set up and the workers have all shown up for work. Yeah!

A month's supply of raw material ($8.55 per case times 20,000 cases equals a total of $171,000) is on its way from storage onto the plant floor to await processing. On the inventory worksheet we will "move" this raw material into work-in-process.

Also, with this transaction we will pay our workers and the supervisor a month's salary and wages. Because these salary and wages go toward producing product, they are called costs. These manufactur

ing costs will be accounted for by adding them to our work-in-process inventory. Thus, our inventory will increase in value by the amount of labor that we add while we process our product.

Transaction 9. showed the amounts for our manufacturing payroll. Because we were not yet in production then, we charged the *Income Statement* with the expense covering the supervisor's salary. Now that we are manufacturing product, these salary and wages are costs that increase the value of our product and are shown as an increase in the value of inventory.

Transaction: Pay production workers' wages and supervisor's salary for the month. Book associated fringe benefits and payroll taxes. Cut checks for $9,020 for take-home salary and workers' wages:

① **(1A)** Increase **CASH DISBURSEMENTS** by $9,020 in the *Cash Flow Statement*. **(1B)** Lower **CASH** by that amount in the *Balance Sheet*.

② Book payroll-associated fringes and taxes of $8,160 as **ACCRUED EXPENSES** on the *Balance Sheet*.

③ Increase **INVENTORIES** on the *Balance Sheet* by $17,180; that is, $9,020 in salary and wages plus $8,160 in benefits and taxes.

~

Inventory Valuation Worksheet	RAW MATERIAL	WORK IN PROCESS	FINISHED GOODS
PRIOR INVENTORY VALUES	$0	$0	$0
C. Move materials from raw materials to WIP.	($171,000)	$171,000	$0
D. Pay supervisor and workers for the month. See **T9**.	$0	$17,180	$0
INVENTORY SUBTOTALS AFTER THIS TRANSACTION	$181,400	$188,180	$0

	TOTAL INVENTORY	$369,580

Transaction 13. — Record Depreciation & Overhead

Income Statement

NET SALES	$	-
COST OF GOODS SOLD		-
GROSS MARGIN		-
SALES & MARKETING		-
RESEARCH & DEVELOPMENT		-
GENERAL & ADMINISTRATIVE		-
OPERATING EXPENSE		-
INCOME FROM OPERATIONS		-
NET INTEREST INCOME		-
INCOME TAXES		-
NET INCOME	$	-

Cash Flow Statement

BEGINNING CASH BALANCE	$	-
CASH RECEIPTS		-
CASH DISBURSEMENTS		-
CASH FLOW FROM OPERATIONS		-
PP&E PURCHASE		-
NET BORROWINGS		-
INCOME TAXES PAID		-
SALE OF CAPITAL STOCK		-
ENDING CASH BALANCE	$	-

Balance Sheet

Assets

CASH	$	-
ACCOUNTS RECEIVABLE		-
INVENTORIES		15,820 ③
PREPAID EXPENSES		-
CURRENT ASSETS		15,820
OTHER ASSETS		-
FIXED ASSETS @ COST		-
ACCUMULATED DEPRECIATION		7,143 ❷
NET FIXED ASSETS		(7,143)
TOTAL ASSETS		8,677

Liabilities & Equity

ACCOUNTS PAYABLE	$	8,677 ❶
ACCRUED EXPENSES		-
CURRENT PORTION OF DEBT		-
INCOME TAXES PAYABLE		-
CURRENT LIABILITIES		8,677
LONG-TERM DEBT		-
CAPITAL STOCK		-
RETAINED EARNINGS		-
SHAREHOLDERS' EQUITY		-
TOTAL LIABILITIES & EQUITY	$	8,677

T13. Book a month's depreciation and other manufacturing overhead costs.

As we are busily working on applesauce-making, there are a few bean-counting details that must be performed.

We are using our new machines in our very beautifully refurbished building. Something has to pay for all this splendor. With this transaction we will depreciate our machinery and building.

This depreciation charge is a manufacturing cost ... a legitimate cost of making our applesauce. Thus, when we book this depreciation, we will add it in as a cost of manufacturing by increasing the value of our work-in-process inventory. Remember, all the manufacturing costs go into inventory value.

Depreciation is a "non-cash" transaction, so we will not alter cash or accounts payable when we book Apple-Seed's depreciation charges. No such luck with the other elements of overhead. We will eventually have to pay for them. Thus, accounts payable will be increased by what we owe.

Transaction: Book this month's manufacturing depreciation of $7,143 and $8,677 covering other overhead costs. Note that depreciation is not a cash expense and will not lower our cash balance. But, for all the other overhead, we will eventually have to pay with cash.

1 Increase **ACCOUNTS PAYABLE** on the *Balance Sheet* by $8,677 covering the "all other" manufacturing overhead.

2 Increase **ACCUMULATED DEPRECIATION** on the *Balance Sheet* by this month's $7,143 depreciation charge.

3 Increase **INVENTORIES** on the *Balance Sheet* by $15,820 covering this month's depreciation of $7,143 plus the $8,677 "all other" manufacturing overhead.

~

Inventory Valuation Worksheet	RAW MATERIAL	WORK IN PROCESS	FINISHED GOODS
PRIOR INVENTORY VALUES	$181,400	$188,180	$0
E. Book manufacturing depreciation for the month.	$0	$7,143	$0
F. Book all other manufacturing overhead costs.	$0	$8,677	$0
INVENTORY SUBTOTALS AFTER THIS TRANSACTION	$181,400	$204,000	$0
	TOTAL INVENTORY		$385,400

Transaction 14. — Pay for Materials

Income Statement

NET SALES	$	-
COST OF GOODS SOLD		-
GROSS MARGIN		-
SALES & MARKETING		-
RESEARCH & DEVELOPMENT		-
GENERAL & ADMINISTRATIVE		-
OPERATING EXPENSE		-
INCOME FROM OPERATIONS		-
NET INTEREST INCOME		-
INCOME TAXES		-
NET INCOME	$	-

Cash Flow Statement

BEGINNING CASH BALANCE	$	-
CASH RECEIPTS		-
CASH DISBURSEMENTS		20,000	❶
CASH FLOW FROM OPERATIONS		(20,000)
PP&E PURCHASE		-
NET BORROWINGS		-
INCOME TAXES PAID		-
SALE OF CAPITAL STOCK		-
ENDING CASH BALANCE	$	(20,000)

Balance Sheet

Assets

CASH ❷	$	(20,000)
ACCOUNTS RECEIVABLE		-
INVENTORIES		-
PREPAID EXPENSES		-
CURRENT ASSETS		(20,000)
OTHER ASSETS		-
FIXED ASSETS @ COST		-
ACCUMULATED DEPRECIATION		-
NET FIXED ASSETS		-
TOTAL ASSETS		(20,000)

Liabilities & Equity

ACCOUNTS PAYABLE	$	(20,000)	③
ACCRUED EXPENSES		-
CURRENT PORTION OF DEBT		-
INCOME TAXES PAYABLE		-
CURRENT LIABILITIES		(20,000)
LONG-TERM DEBT		-
CAPITAL STOCK		-
RETAINED EARNINGS		-
SHAREHOLDERS' EQUITY		-
TOTAL LIABILITIES & EQUITY	$	(20,000)

T14. Pay for labels received in Transaction 10.

We received our applesauce jar labels a month ago and the printer is very anxious to get paid. When we received the jar labels, we created an **ACCOUNTS PAYABLE**. When we pay this vendor with cash, we will "reverse" the payable at the same time we lower cash.

Note, paying for this raw material does not affect the values in our Inventory Valuation Worksheet. The inventory was increased by the cost of the labels when we received them and also created an **ACCOUNTS PAYABLE**.

Transaction: Pay for 1 million labels received in Transaction 10. Issue a check to our vendor for $20,000 as payment in full.

1 Cut a check for $20,000 to pay the label printer. Increase **CASH DISBURSEMENTS** by that amount in the *Cash Flow Statement*.

2 Lower **CASH** by $20,000 in the assets section of the *Balance Sheet* since we wrote the check.

3 Lower **ACCOUNTS PAYABLE** in the liabilities section of the *Balance Sheet* by the $20,000 that we no longer owe (since we just paid as described above).

~

Inventory Valuation Worksheet	RAW MATERIAL	WORK IN PROCESS	FINISHED GOODS
PRIOR INVENTORY VALUES	$181,400	$204,000	$0
G. Pay for labels received on **T10**.	$0	$0	$0
INVENTORY VALUES AFTER THIS TRANSACTION	$181,400	$204,000	$0
	TOTAL INVENTORY		$385,400

Transaction 15. — Move Inventory WIP to FG

Income Statement

NET SALES	$	-
COST OF GOODS SOLD		-
GROSS MARGIN		-
SALES & MARKETING		-
RESEARCH & DEVELOPMENT		-
GENERAL & ADMINISTRATIVE		-
OPERATING EXPENSE		-
INCOME FROM OPERATIONS		-
NET INTEREST INCOME		-
INCOME TAXES		-
NET INCOME	$	-

Cash Flow Statement

BEGINNING CASH BALANCE	$	-
CASH RECEIPTS		-
CASH DISBURSEMENTS		-
CASH FLOW FROM OPERATIONS		-
PP&E PURCHASE		-
NET BORROWINGS		-
INCOME TAXES PAID		-
SALE OF CAPITAL STOCK		-
ENDING CASH BALANCE	$	-

Balance Sheet

Assets			
CASH	$	-
ACCOUNTS RECEIVABLE		-
INVENTORIES		-
PREPAID EXPENSES		-
CURRENT ASSETS		-
OTHER ASSETS		-
FIXED ASSETS @ COST		-
ACCUMULATED DEPRECIATION		-
NET FIXED ASSETS		-
TOTAL ASSETS		-

Liabilities & Equity		
ACCOUNTS PAYABLE	$	-
ACCRUED EXPENSES		-
CURRENT PORTION OF DEBT		-
INCOME TAXES PAYABLE		-
CURRENT LIABILITIES		-
LONG-TERM DEBT		-
CAPITAL STOCK		-
RETAINED EARNINGS		-
SHAREHOLDERS' EQUITY		-
TOTAL LIABILITIES & EQUITY	$	-

T15. Finish Manufacturing 19,500 cases of applesauce and move from work-in-process (WIP) into finished goods inventory.

When we have finally boxed our finished jars of applesauce and they are ready for shipping, we place them in our finished goods warehouse. We will value this inventory at "standard cost," ready to become a COST OF GOODS SOLD amount when we ship.

On our Inventory Valuation Worksheet, we will decrease work-in-process inventory and also increase finished goods inventory by the same amount, the value of goods we moved from work-in-process to finished goods.

Remember, we started out to make 20,000 cases. But somewhere in the process we lost some product and only ended up with 19,500 cases. We will "move"

these 19,500 cases into finished goods inventory. In the next transaction we will deal with what happened and how to account for the remaining 500 cases.

The inventory value of the 19,500 cases to be transferred is $198,900 — a $10.20 standard cost times 19,500 cases. Note that while accounting entries (see below) are made in our Inventory Valuation Worksheet as we move work-in-process inventory into finished goods, no change is made in the company's *Income Statement, Balance Sheet* or *Cash Flow Statement.*

Inventory values will become COST OF GOODS SOLD only when we ship product to customers.

Transaction: This movement of inventory into a different class is just an internal management control transaction as far as the financial statements are concerned. There is no effect on the three major financial statements of AppleSeed. INVENTORIES on the *Balance Sheet* remains the same regardless of the transfer. However, our Inventory Valuation Worksheet, as shown below, reflects the change in inventory status.

~

INVENTORY VALUATION WORKSHEET	RAW MATERIAL	WORK IN PROCESS	FINISHED GOODS
PRIOR INVENTORY VALUES	$181,400	$204,000	$0
H. Move 19,500 cases from WIP into FG @ standard cost.	$0	$(198,900)	$198,900
INVENTORY SUBTOTALS AFTER THIS TRANSACTION	$181,400	$204,000	$0
TOTAL INVENTORY			$385,400

Transaction 16. — Write Off Damaged Inventory

Income Statement

NET SALES	$	-
COST OF GOODS SOLD ❷		5,100
GROSS MARGIN		(5,100)
SALES & MARKETING		-
RESEARCH & DEVELOPMENT		-
GENERAL & ADMINISTRATIVE		-
OPERATING EXPENSE		-
INCOME FROM OPERATIONS		(5,100)
NET INTEREST INCOME		-
INCOME TAXES		-
NET INCOME	$	(5,100)

Cash Flow Statement

BEGINNING CASH BALANCE	$	-
CASH RECEIPTS		-
CASH DISBURSEMENTS		-
CASH FLOW FROM OPERATIONS		-
PP&E PURCHASE		-
NET BORROWINGS		-
INCOME TAXES PAID		-
SALE OF CAPITAL STOCK		-
ENDING CASH BALANCE	$	-

Balance Sheet

Assets			
	CASH	$	-
	ACCOUNTS RECEIVABLE		-
	INVENTORIES		(5,100) ❶
	PREPAID EXPENSES		-
	CURRENT ASSETS		(5,100)
	OTHER ASSETS		-
	FIXED ASSETS @ COST		-
	ACCUMULATED DEPRECIATION		-
	NET FIXED ASSETS		-
	TOTAL ASSETS		(5,100)

Liabilities & Equity			
	ACCOUNTS PAYABLE	$	-
	ACCRUED EXPENSES		-
	CURRENT PORTION OF DEBT		-
	INCOME TAXES PAYABLE		-
	CURRENT LIABILITIES		-
	LONG-TERM DEBT		-
	CAPITAL STOCK		-
	RETAINED EARNINGS		(5,100) ③
	SHAREHOLDERS' EQUITY		(5,100)
	TOTAL LIABILITIES & EQUITY	$	(5,100)

T16. Scrap 500 cases' worth of work-in-process inventory.

After we moved all the product that we could find (19,500 cases) into finished goods, we looked around for the remaining 500 cases we had expected to make.

We started out with enough material to make 20,000 cases but seem to have produced only 19,500 cases. The material and labor expenditures for these remaining 500 cases is still recorded in work-in-process inventory — but then where is the product?

Our production supervisor comes up with the answer. It seems that our workers had some trouble starting up some of the new machines. Everything is fixed now, but for the first month of production every 40th jar of applesauce got smashed in the innards of the conveyor belts!

Thus, our output was only 19,500 cases and we spoiled 500 cases. We still expended the labor to produce 20,000 cases and we used all the material required to produce 20,000 cases, but at the end we only produced 19,500 cases.

Oh well, no use crying over spilled applesauce. But how should we account for the loss? Scrap the value of 500 cases of applesauce. Lower the value of work-in-process inventory and take a corresponding loss on the *Income Statement*.

Transaction: Scrap the value of 500 cases of applesauce from the work-in-process inventory. Take a loss on the *Income Statement* for this amount.

1 Reduce **INVENTORIES** on the *Balance Sheet* by the $5,100 value of the inventory to be scrapped (that is 500 cases times the standard cost of $10.20 each).

2 Charge $5,100 to **COST OF GOODS SOLD** for the loss in value of the inventory due to scrapping 500 cases of work-in-process inventory.

3 Remember that the resulting loss in the *Income Statement* must be reflected as a decrease in **RETAINED EARNINGS** in the *Balance Sheet*.

~

INVENTORY VALUATION WORKSHEET	RAW MATERIAL	WORK IN PROCESS	FINISHED GOODS
PRIOR INVENTORY VALUES	$181,400	$5,100	$198,900
I. Scrap 500 cases of applesauce from WIP inventory.	$0	$(5,100)	$0
INVENTORY VALUES AFTER THIS TRANSACTION	$181,400	$0	$198,900
		TOTAL INVENTORY	$380,300

Manufacturing Variances from Standard Cost

The most efficient type of cost accounting is one that makes use of predetermined costs, referred to as *standard costs*. This procedure consists of setting, in advance of production, what the unit cost *should* be, and upon completion of production, comparing the actual costs with these standard costs.

Any differences (either positive or negative) are then applied to the financial statements as a "variance" in order to reflect product cost reality.

Standard Costs

We at AppleSeed Enterprises use a standard costing system to value our inventory. See page 115. It is a convenient and accurate way to run the books and to account for what our products cost.

But, remember, the standard cost is what we *expect* our product to cost if all goes according to plan. That is, all must go *exactly* as expected (or excess money spent in one area must be saved in another) if our *actual cost* is to equal our standard cost.

In using a standard costing system, the various costs for materials, labor and overhead are booked into inventory at their *actual amounts*. But when product is placed in finished goods and then is sold, the transaction is performed "at standard."

The difference between the actual and the standard cost is then booked in the accounting records. These differences, if any, are called *manufacturing variances*. See the box below to learn the five major types of possible variances.

Types of Variances: For AppleSeed's product and production costs to be "at standard," that is, for no manufacturing cost variances to have occurred:

- We must produce 20,000 cases in a month — no more, no less. Otherwise we will have a *volume variance*.

- Our raw material must cost just what we have estimated them to be — no more, no less. Otherwise we will have a *purchase variance*.

- The amount of raw material used must be just as planned. Otherwise we will have a *yield variance*.

- We need no more or less direct labor and no overtime to produce our 20,000 cases. Otherwise we will have a *labor variance*.

- We don't have excess scrap produced in the production process. Otherwise we will have a *scrap variance*.

For AppleSeed's product and production costs to be at standard, that is, for no variances to have occurred:

1. We must produce exactly 20,000 cases in a month.

2. Our raw material must cost exactly what we have estimated.

3. The amount of raw material used must be just as planned.

4. We need no more or less direct labor and no overtime to produce our 20,000 cases.

5. We do not have excess scrap produced in the production process.

Most often, everything does not come out perfectly. We will then have to apply variances to our books. Remember, our production cost accounting relied upon standard cost. We used this standard cost to apply values to inventory and to cost of goods sold. If actual costs were different — and they always are, hopefully by just a little bit — we will have to adjust the books by entering variance amounts to our inventory value on the *Balance Sheet*.

Note that while it does not apply to AppleSeed production, there is one other kind of possible manufacturing variance, the **mix variance.** A multi-product company can make more (or less) of one product than planned. This production difference can result in more (or less) overhead "absorption" depending on the relative overhead contribution of the products actually produced. This "under" or "over absorption" is accounted for as a product mix variance.

In summary, **volume variances** can occur when we make more or less product than we had planned for. We must then spread our fixed costs and overhead over less product (resulting in a higher cost) or over more product (resulting in a lower cost).

Spending variances can occur when raw materials cost more or less than planned. Actual product cost reflects these differences.

Labor variances are very easy to understand. If it takes more man-hours to make our product than expected by the standard, then our product must cost more than planned.

~

If AppleSeed continuously books large manufacturing variances each month, we should modify our standard costs to make them conform more closely to reality.

Transaction 17. — Pay for Raw Material

Income Statement

NET SALES	$	-
COST OF GOODS SOLD	.	-
GROSS MARGIN		-
SALES & MARKETING		-
RESEARCH & DEVELOPMENT		-
GENERAL & ADMINISTRATIVE		-
OPERATING EXPENSE		-
INCOME FROM OPERATIONS		-
NET INTEREST INCOME		-
INCOME TAXES		-
NET INCOME	$	-

Cash Flow Statement

BEGINNING CASH BALANCE	$	-
CASH RECEIPTS		-
CASH DISBURSEMENTS		150,000 ❶
CASH FLOW FROM OPERATIONS		(150,000)
PP&E PURCHASE		-
NET BORROWINGS		-
INCOME TAXES PAID		-
SALE OF CAPITAL STOCK		-
ENDING CASH BALANCES	$	(150,000)

Balance Sheet

Assets

CASH ❷	$	(150,000)
ACCOUNTS RECEIVABLE		-
INVENTORIES		-
PREPAID EXPENSES		-
CURRENT ASSETS		(150,000)
OTHER ASSETS		-
FIXED ASSETS @ COST		-
ACCUMULATED DEPRECIATION		-
NET FIXED ASSETS		-
TOTAL ASSETS		(150,000)

Liabilities & Equity

ACCOUNTS PAYABLE ③	$	(150,000)
ACCRUED EXPENSES		-
CURRENT PORTION OF DEBT		-
INCOME TAXES PAYABLE		-
CURRENT LIABILITIES		(150,000)
LONG-TERM DEBT		-
CAPITAL STOCK		-
RETAINED EARNINGS		-
SHAREHOLDERS' EQUITY		-
TOTAL LIABILITIES & EQUITY	$	(150,000)

T17. Pay for some of the raw materials received in Transaction 11.

With our first month's production successfully placed in our finished goods warehouse, we throw a company picnic in celebration.

Halfway through the first hot dog, an important telephone call comes in. The president of Acme Apple and Jar Supply Incorporated, our apple and jar supplier, is on the line. He is calling to see how we are doing and when we plan to pay our bill for apples and jars. He suggests $150,000 or so would be appreciated.

Because we want to remain on good terms with this important supplier, we tell him, "The check is in the mail," and rush back to our offices to put it there.

Looking at our listing of current accounts payable, we note that we owe Acme $79,200 for apples, $184,000 for jars, and $33,200 for jar caps — a total of $296,400 outstanding.

Take out the checkbook and write a check for the $150,000 Acme has asked for.

Transaction: Pay a major supplier a portion of what is due for apples and jars. Cut a check for $150,000 in partial payment.

 Cut a check for $150,000 to pay the supplier. Increase **CASH DISBURSEMENTS** by that amount in the *Cash Flow Statement.*

 Lower **CASH** by $150,000 in the assets section of the *Balance Sheet.*

 Lower **ACCOUNTS PAYABLE** in the liabilities section of the *Balance Sheet* by $150,000 that we no longer owe since we just paid as described above.

Note: Actually paying for raw materials does not affect our inventory value in any way. Inventory value increased when we received the raw material and we created the accounts payable.

~

INVENTORY VALUATION WORKSHEET	RAW MATERIAL	WORK IN PROCESS	FINISHED GOODS
PRIOR INVENTORY VALUES	$181,400	$0	$198,900
I. Scrap 500 cases of applesauce from WIP inventory.	$0	$0	$0
INVENTORY VALUES AFTER THIS TRANSACTION	$181,400	$0	$198,900
		TOTAL INVENTORY	$380,300

Transaction 18. — Manufacture More Applesauce

Income Statement

NET SALES	$ -	
COST OF GOODS SOLD	1,530	
GROSS MARGIN	(1,530)	
SALES & MARKETING	-	
RESEARCH & DEVELOPMENT	-	
GENERAL & ADMINISTRATIVE	-	
OPERATING EXPENSE	-	
INCOME FROM OPERATIONS	(1,530)	
NET INTEREST INCOME	-	
INCOME TAXES	-	
NET INCOME	$ (1,530)	

Cash Flow Statement

BEGINNING CASH BALANCE	$ -	
CASH RECEIPTS	-	
CASH DISBURSEMENTS	9,020	
CASH FLOW FROM OPERATIONS	(9,020)	
PP&E PURCHASE	-	
NET BORROWINGS	-	
INCOME TAXES PAID	-	
SALE OF CAPITAL STOCK	-	
ENDING CASH BALANCES	$ (9,020)	

Balance Sheet

Assets

CASH	$ (9,020)	
ACCOUNTS RECEIVABLE	-	
INVENTORIES	197,670	
PREPAID EXPENSES	-	
CURRENT ASSETS	188,650	
OTHER ASSETS	-	
FIXED ASSETS @ COST	-	
ACCUMULATED DEPRECIATION	7,143	
NET FIXED ASSETS	(7,143)	
TOTAL ASSETS	181,507	

Liabilities & Equity

ACCOUNTS PAYABLE	$ 174,877	
ACCRUED EXPENSES	8,160	
CURRENT PORTION OF DEBT	-	
INCOME TAXES PAYABLE	-	
CURRENT LIABILITIES	183,037	
LONG-TERM DEBT	-	
CAPITAL STOCK	-	
RETAINED EARNINGS	(1,530)	
SHAREHOLDERS' EQUITY	(1,530)	
TOTAL LIABILITIES & EQUITY	$ 181,507	

T18. Manufacture another month's supply of our wonderful applesauce.

Things are progressing at our enterprise and the plant is churning out product. With this multiple transaction we will make another month's worth of applesauce and pay a few bills. Soon we will be ready to ship applesauce to our valued customers!

Shown at the bottom of the page are the series (K through Q) of Inventory Valuation Worksheet entries for the rest of the month. The table below translates these actions into transactions to post to AppleSeed's financial statements.

Transaction: Make entries in the *Income Statement, Cash Flow Statement,* and *Balance Sheet* as shown in the total column at below right. **Note:** For each separate worksheet entry (shown in columns K through Q below), the change in assets must always equal the change in liabilities.

WORKSHEET ENTRY	K	L	M	N	O	P	Q	TOTALS
COST OF GOODS SOLD							$1,530	$1,530
CASH DISBURSEMENTS			$9,020					$9,020
CASH			$(9,020)					$(9,020)
INVENTORIES	$166,200		$17,180	$7,143	$8,677		$(1,530)	$197,670
ACCUM. DEPRECIATION				$7,143				$(7,143)
CHANGE IN ASSETS	$166,200	$0	$8,160	$0	$8,677	$0	$(1,530)	$181,507
ACCOUNTS PAYABLE	$166,200				$8,677			$174,877
ACCRUED EXPENSES			$8,160					$8,160
RETAINED EARNINGS							$(1,530)	$(1,530)
CHANGE IN LIABILITIES	$166,200	$0	$8,160	$0	$8,677	$0	$(1,530)	$181,507

INVENTORY VALUATION WORKSHEET	RAW MATERIAL	WORK IN PROCESS	FINISHED GOODS
INVENTORY VALUES PRIOR TO THIS TRANSACTION	$181,400	$5,100	$198,900
K. Receive a month's raw material supply less labels (**T10**)	$166,200	$0	$0
L. Move a month's supply of raw materials into WIP. (**T12**)	$(171,000)	$171,000	$0
M. Pay hourly workers/supervisor for another month. (**T12**)	$0	$17,180	$0
N. Book manufacturing depreciation for the month. (**T13**)	$0	$7,143	$0
O. Book "all other" mfg. overhead for another month. (**T13**)	$0	$8,677	$0
P. Move 19,000 cases to finished goods @ standard cost. (**T15**)	$0	$(193,800)	$193,800
Q. Scrap 150 cases from WIP. (**T16**)	$0	$(1,530)	$0
INVENTORY VALUES AFTER THIS TRANSACTION	$176,600	$8,670	$392,700
	TOTAL INVENTORY		$380,300

Chapter 9.
Marketing and Selling

A wise old consultant once said to me, "Really, the only thing you need to be in business is a customer."

AppleSeed Enterprises, Inc., is ready to find customers for its super, new brand of applesauce. We will begin marketing our product and testing the receptiveness of the marketplace to a new supplier — us!

Next (unfortunately), we will suffer one major risk of doing business, the deadbeat customer.

~

Transaction 19. Produce product advertising fliers and T-shirt giveaways.

- Product pricing; break-even analysis.

Transaction 20. A new customer orders 1,000 cases of applesauce. Ship 1,000 cases at $15.90 per case.

Transaction 21. Take an order (on credit) for 15,000 cases at a discounted price of $15.66 per case.

Transaction 22. Ship and invoice customer for 15,000 cases of applesauce ordered in Transaction 21 above

Transaction 23. Receive payment of $234,900 for shipment made in Transaction 22. Pay the broker's commission.

Transaction 24. Oops! The customer from Transaction 10 goes bankrupt. Write off cost of 1,000 cases as a bad debt.

Transaction 19. — Produce Product Advertising

Income Statement

NET SALES	$	-
COST OF GOODS SOLD		-
GROSS MARGIN		-
SALES & MARKETING	103,250	❶
RESEARCH & DEVELOPMENT		-
GENERAL & ADMINISTRATIVE		-
OPERATING EXPENSE	103,250	
INCOME FROM OPERATIONS	(103,250)	
NET INTEREST INCOME		-
INCOME TAXES		-
NET INCOME	$	(103,250)

Cash Flow Statement

BEGINNING CASH BALANCE	$	-
CASH RECEIPTS		-
CASH DISBURSEMENTS		-
CASH FLOW FROM OPERATIONS		-
PP&E PURCHASE		-
NET BORROWINGS		-
INCOME TAXES PAID		-
SALE OF CAPITAL STOCK		-
ENDING CASH BALANCES	$	-

Balance Sheet

Assets

CASH	$	-
ACCOUNTS RECEIVABLE		-
INVENTORIES		-
PREPAID EXPENSES		-
CURRENT ASSETS		-
OTHER ASSETS		-
FIXED ASSETS @ COST		-
ACCUMULATED DEPRECIATION		-
NET FIXED ASSETS		-
TOTAL ASSETS		-

Liabilities & Equity

ACCOUNTS PAYABLE	$ 103,250	③
ACCRUED EXPENSES		-
CURRENT PORTION OF DEBT		
INCOME TAXES PAYABLE		-
CURRENT LIABILITIES	103,250	
LONG-TERM DEBT		-
CAPITAL STOCK		-
RETAINED EARNINGS	(103,250)	❷
SHAREHOLDERS' EQUITY	(103,250)	
TOTAL LIABILITIES & EQUITY	$	-

T19. Produce product advertising flyers and T-shirt giveaways.

The usual method of selling our type of product is through a food broker to a retail store and then ultimately to the consumer. Food brokers serve the purpose of manufacturers' representatives, convincing retailers to stock various brands of product. For their efforts, these brokers receive a commission of about 2% of all sales. They do not take title to the goods; they just smooth the way.

AppleSeed engages a topflight manufacturers' representative, SlickSales & Associates, to market its products. SlickSales and AppleSeed negotiate a sales commission of 2% of gross revenue to be paid to SlickSales for placing AppleSeed's applesauce with retailers.

SlickSales requests that AppleSeed prepare and then supply them with sales literature to be given to prospective customers. Everybody agrees that a direct mail promotion would be a good idea too.

We hire an advertising agency to design, print and mail a very fancy brochure to promote AppleSeed's applesauce products.

The agency also produces 10,000 AppleSeed Applesauce T-shirts to ship to supermarkets for use as a promotional giveaway.

Transaction: Our advertising agency submits a bill for designing, printing and mailing 4,500 very fancy brochures at $38,250 total cost. The 10,000 T-shirts cost $6.50 each for a total of $65,000. Book these amounts as an AppleSeed Enterprises marketing and selling expense.

1 Book brochure and T-shirt expenses totaling $103,250 under **SALES & MARKETING** expense in the *Income Statement*.

2 Lower **RETAINED EARNINGS** in the liabilities section of the *Balance Sheet* by this $103,250 selling and marketing expense.

3 Increase **ACCOUNTS PAYABLE** in the liabilities section of the *Balance Sheet* by the same amount for the bill we owe the advertising agency.

～

Product Costing, Break-Even, and Pricing-for-Profit

Profit is the difference between two large numbers: (a) sales, less (b) costs & expenses. Small changes in either can result in large swings in profit (loss). Volume, cost and price are all connected to ultimate enterprise profitability. *How?*

Marketing textbooks say that pricing decisions are best made in the marketplace. Price-setting should be based on a competitive understanding and on our competitive goals. Manufacturing costs should have little bearing on pricing decisions.

After we have set a competitive price, we should then look at our costs to see if an adequate profit can be made. If we can't make our desired profit selling our applesauce at a competitive price, then we have just two options: lower costs or exit the business.

Market Pricing

Who are AppleSeed's applesauce competitors? How does our product compare with their offerings? What do they charge for their applesauce? What should we charge to be competitive *and profitable?*

The chart below shows the wholesale and retail pricing structure for several brands of applesauce sold in our market. The chart translates the various markups (manufacturer's, wholesaler's and retailer's markups) into selling and cost prices at each level of distribution. Remember that a lower-level distributor's price is the next upper-level distributor's cost.

We decide to position AppleSeed's applesauce as a mid-priced brand of a very high quality. We think that at a retail price of $1.90 a jar (or $22.86 for a case of 12 jars), we offer good value. But can we make a profit at this selling price? A break-even analysis will help us answer this important question.

Review the volume and costs analysis on page 144. Then look at the break-even chart on page 145.

Break-Even Analysis

Financial types (such as AppleSeed's bankers) will ask the question, "How much will you have to sell to make a profit? "

Comparative Applesauce Prices in our Market

	MANUFACTURER'S SELLING PRICE *Base Price*	WHOLESALER'S SELLING PRICE *Plus 15% over manufacturer's price*	RETAILER'S SELLING PRICE *Plus 25% over wholesaler's price*
% OF MFG'S SELLING PRICE	100%	115%	143%
% OF RETAILER'S SELLING PRICE	70%	80%	100%
BRAND A	$15.21	$17.49	$21.86
BRAND B	$15.40	$17.71	$22.14
BRAND C	$16.58	$19.07	$23.84
APPLESEED ENTERPRISES' BRAND	$15.90	$18.29	$22.86

Appleseed Enterprises Proforma Annual Costs and Expenses
at Various Projected Production Volumes

	VARIABLE COST PER CASE	TOTAL FIXED COST PER YEAR	ANNUAL TOTALS @ ZERO CASES PER MONTH	ANNUAL TOTALS @ 5,000 CASES PER MONTH	ANNUAL TOTALS @ 10,000 CASES PER MONTH	ANNUAL TOTALS @ 15,000 CASES PER MONTH	ANNUAL TOTALS @ 20,000 CASES PER MONTH
Total Annual Variable Costs at Several Production Volumes							
+ MATERIAL COSTS	$8.550	—	$0	$513,000	$1,026,000	$1,539,000	$2,052,000
+ DIRECT LABOR	$0.615	—	$0	$36,900	$73,800	$110,700	$147,600
+ BROKER COM.	$0.318	—	$0	$19,080	$38,160	$57,240	$76,320
= TOTAL ANNUAL VARIABLE COSTS	$9.483	—	$0	$568,980	$1,137,960	$1,706,940	$2,275,920
Total Annual Fixed Costs (no change with increasing production volume)							
+ MFG. SUPERVISOR	—	$58,650					
+ DEPRECIATION	—	$85,714					
+ ALL OTHER MFG.	—	$104,124					
+ SG&A SALARIES	—	$251,160					
+ INTEREST	—	$100,000					
+ MARKETING	—	$223,250					
= TOTAL ANNUAL FIXED COSTS	—	$822,898	$822,898	$822,898	$822,898	$822,898	$822,898

Total fixed costs are the same at all production levels. That is why they are called "fixed costs." These fixed costs do not change if you make more or if you make less product.

Profit & Loss Statements at Several Production Volumes					
+ ANNUAL REVENUE @ $15.90 PER CASE	0	$954,000	$1,908,000	$2,862,000	$3,816,000
− TOTAL ANNUAL VARIABLE COSTS	0	$568,980	$1,137,960	$1,706,940	$2,275,920
− TOTAL ANNUAL FIXED COSTS	$822,898	$822,898	$822,898	$822,898	$822,898
= TOTAL ANNUAL PROFIT (LOSS)	$(822,898)	$(437,878)	$(52,858)	$332,162	$717,182

This revenue value, where increasing volume turns losses into profits, is called the company's *"break-even point."* The break-even point is that sales volume where revenues are exactly equal to costs plus expenses, and thus, the company neither makes a profit nor suffers a loss.

Your banker is sizing up the company's product and marketing efforts and gauging whether we can achieve a profitable sales volume. A break-even analysis focuses management on the inherent profitability (or lack thereof) of an enterprise.

Let's do a break-even analysis for AppleSeed. The table above shows AppleSeed's annual costs and expenses at various sales and production volumes. Some of AppleSeed's costs and expenses will not change with its volume of production and sales *(fixed costs)* and some will change *(variable costs)*.

Fixed Costs Fixed costs will be the same for AppleSeed month after month, whether the company makes 5,000 cases, 10,000 cases or even 20,000 cases per month. This fixed cost includes manufacturing costs and also SG&A expenses that are not related to volume. As shown in the table above, we can see that Apple-Seed's fixed costs are $822,898 per year.

Variable Costs Each time Apple-Seed sells a case of applesauce, it spends $9.483 in variable cost as shown in the table on the previous page. So, if the company sells 10,000 cases per month (that is, 120,000 cases per year), total variable cost will be $9.483 per case times 120,000 cases, for a total of $1,137,960 variable cost. If AppleSeed sells 20,000 cases per month, then the total variable cost will be doubled to $2,275,920.

AppleSeed's break-even chart below graphically represents the relationships shown in the table on the prior page

between: (a) total revenue, (b) fixed costs, (c) total variable costs and (d) profit (or loss) for production volumes from zero to 25,000 cases shipped per month. Apple-Seed turns a profit at a production and sales volume of about 10,700 cases per month. Profitability improves nicely as sales and production reach our 15,000 case per month target.

Note that the difference between total variable cost and total sales is often called *contribution* — the dollar amount that a level of sales "contributes" toward paying for fixed costs and expenses and any profit for the enterprise. The break-even point occurs when the contribution exactly equals all variable costs.

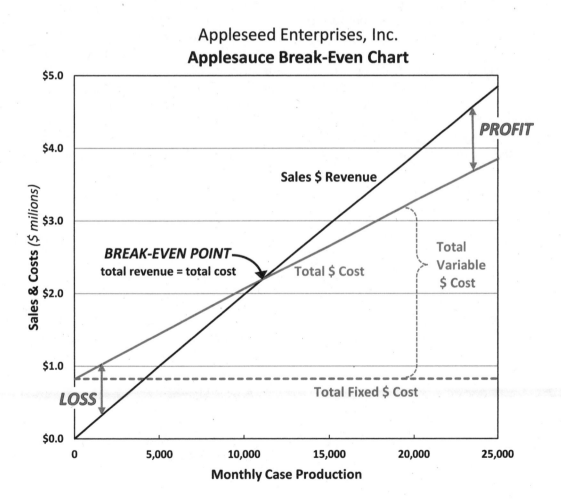

Appleseed Enterprises, Inc.
Applesauce Break-Even Chart

Price-Volume Curve

However, Appleseed certainly wants to be a profitable enterprise, not just a break-even one. To set an optimal price for our applesauce we need to construct a price-volume curve for our expected sales against our competitors in the marketplace.

If we raise prices, unit sales may fall. If we lower prices, absolute profits may fall if the lower price does not result in enough of a volume increase to compensate. The price-volume curve describes this relationship graphically.

To construct the graph we ask, "What would be the estimated sales volume if the product price was increased by 10% or by 20%?" We make similar volume estimates if the price was lowered. Along with the current selling price and volume estimates, we now have five data points on the curve. See sample graph at the top of the facing page plotting *cases sold* vs. *wholesale selling price* for our applesauce.

Most often these graphs are fairly linear with a downward slope. The higher the price, the lower the volume sold. If the line drops fast (small change in priced causes a large drop in volume), the demand is said to be "elastic." A shallow sloped line (large change in price causes a small drop in volume) describes an "inelastic" demand curve. Our curve has normal elasticity for our type of product.

Profit Maximization

Now, the fun part begins. How should we price our applesauce to generate maximum sales? How should we price our product for maximum profitability? The two prices are often slightly different due to the ratio of fixed versus variable costs. See sample graphs on the next page plotting *total revenue* and *total profit* vs. the *wholesale selling price*.

Total revenue peaks at a selling price of around $15.00 and maximum total profit at about $16.10 per case. We split the difference and set our list price at $15.90 but will discount to $15.66 for large orders (see Transaction 20 and Transaction 21). We'll see what happens!

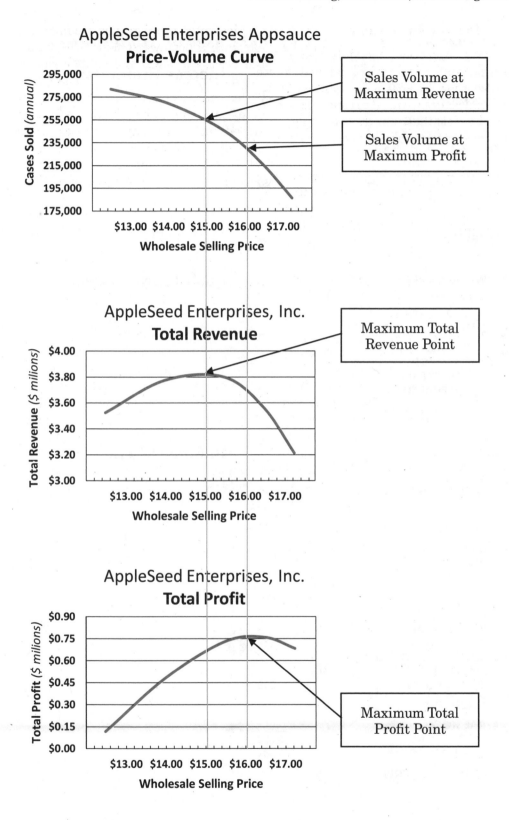

AppleSeed Enterprises Appsauce
Price-Volume Curve

Sales Volume at
Maximum Revenue

Sales Volume at
Maximum Profit

AppleSeed Enterprises, Inc.
Total Revenue

Maximum Total
Revenue Point

AppleSeed Enterprises, Inc.
Total Profit

Maximum Total
Profit Point

Transaction 20. — Ship 1,000 Cases of Applesauce

Income Statement

NET SALES	❶A	$ 15,900
COST OF GOODS SOLD	③B	10,200
GROSS MARGIN		5,700
SALES & MARKETING	❷A	318
RESEARCH & DEVELOPMENT		
GENERAL & ADMINISTRATIVE		
OPERATING EXPENSE		318
INCOME FROM OPERATIONS		5,382
NET INTEREST INCOME		
INCOME TAXES		
NET INCOME		$ 5,382

Cash Flow Statement

BEGINNING CASH BALANCE	$ -
CASH RECEIPTS	
CASH DISBURSEMENTS	
CASH FLOW FROM OPERATIONS	-
PP&E PURCHASE	
NET BORROWINGS	
INCOME TAXES PAID	
SALE OF CAPITAL STOCK	
ENDING CASH BALANCE	$ -

Balance Sheet

Assets

CASH		
ACCOUNTS RECEIVABLE	❶B	15,900
INVENTORIES	③A	(10,200)
PREPAID EXPENSES		
CURRENT ASSETS		5,700
OTHER ASSETS		
FIXED ASSETS @ COST		
ACCUMULATED DEPRECIATION		
NET FIXED ASSETS		-
TOTAL ASSETS		5,700

Liabilities & Equity

ACCOUNTS PAYABLE		$ -
ACCRUED EXPENSES	❷B	318
CURRENT PORTION OF DEBT		
INCOME TAXES PAYABLE		
CURRENT LIABILITIES		318
LONG-TERM DEBT		
CAPITAL STOCK		
RETAINED EARNINGS	④	5,382
SHAREHOLDERS' EQUITY		5,382
TOTAL LIABILITIES & EQUITY		$ 5,700

T20. A new customer orders 1,000 cases of applesauce. Ship 1,000 cases at $15.90 per case.

It's the moment we have all been waiting for — AppleSeed Enterprises' very first customer.

Your brother-in-law is the manager of a small convenience store chain. At the instigation of your spouse, he places an order for 1,000 cases to stock applesauce in his northwest region's stores.

Based on past experience, you trust your brother-in-law about as far as you can throw him ... and he weighs in at 240 lbs.

You accept the order but ask him to send a $15,900 prepayment check before you will ship. He says no. You decide to ship on credit and cross your fingers.

Transaction: Receive order for 1,000 cases of applesauce at a selling price of $15.90 per case. Ship product and send a $15,900 invoice to the customer.

1 (1A) Book your first sale of $15,900 as **NET SALES** on AppleSeed's *Income Statement.* (1B) Add an **ACCOUNTS RECEIVABLE** for the same amount in the *Balance Sheet.*

2 (2A) Book on the *Income Statement* the 2% commission ($318) for our broker as a **SALES & MARKETING** expense. (2B) Also book this $318 commission in **ACCRUED EXPENSE** on the *Balance Sheet.* The broker does not get paid until we do.

3 (3A) Reduce **INVENTORIES** on the *Balance Sheet* by $10,200 — 1,000 cases times standard cost of $10.20 for each case. (3B) Corresponding to the inventory reduction above, increase **COST OF GOODS SOLD** by $10,200 — the standard cost of 1,000 cases of applesauce.

4 Increase **RETAINED EARNINGS** on the *Balance Sheet* by $5,382 — the sale amount, less cost of goods, less the selling commission. That amount is AppleSeed's profit on the sale. □

~

Inventory Valuation Worksheet	RAW MATERIAL	WORK IN PROCESS	FINISHED GOODS
PRIOR INVENTORY VALUES FROM	$176,600	$8,670	$392,700
R. Ship 1,000 cases of applesauce at $10.20 standard cost/vase.	$0	$0	$(10,200)
INVENTORY SUBTOTALS AFTER THIS TRANSACTION	$176,600	$8,670	$382,500
		TOTAL INVENTORY	$567,770

Transaction 21. — Receive an Order

NET SALES	$	-	**Income Statement**
COST OF GOODS SOLD		-	
GROSS MARGIN		-	
SALES & MARKETING		-	
RESEARCH & DEVELOPMENT		-	
GENERAL & ADMINISTRATIVE		-	
OPERATING EXPENSE		-	
INCOME FROM OPERATIONS		-	
NET INTEREST INCOME		-	
INCOME TAXES		-	
NET INCOME	$	-	

BEGINNING CASH BALANCE	$	-	**Cash Flow Statement**
CASH RECEIPTS		-	
CASH DISBURSEMENTS		-	
CASH FLOW FROM OPERATIONS		-	
PP&E PURCHASE		-	
NET BORROWINGS		-	
INCOME TAXES PAID		-	
SALE OF CAPITAL STOCK		-	
ENDING CASH BALANCE	$	-	

CASH	$	-	**Balance Sheet**
ACCOUNTS RECEIVABLE		-	
INVENTORIES		-	
PREPAID EXPENSES		-	
CURRENT ASSETS		-	
OTHER ASSETS		-	
FIXED ASSETS @ COST		-	
ACCUMULATED DEPRECIATION		-	
NET FIXED ASSETS		-	
TOTAL ASSETS		-	
ACCOUNTS PAYABLE	$	-	
ACCRUED EXPENSES		-	
CURRENT PORTION OF DEBT		-	
INCOME TAXES PAYABLE		-	
CURRENT LIABILITIES		-	
LONG-TERM DEBT		-	
CAPITAL STOCK		-	
RETAINED EARNINGS		-	
SHAREHOLDERS' EQUITY		-	
TOTAL LIABILITIES & EQUITY	$	-	

Assets (label for upper balance sheet section)
Liabilities & Equity (label for lower balance sheet section)

T21. Take an order (on credit) for 15,000 cases of applesauce at $15.66 per case.

Our broker is beginning to do his job. We may soon receive a big order from one of the largest food retailers in the area. We have the goods in inventory, so we promise to ship promptly.

To close the deal, we authorize our broker to offer the prospective customer a 1.5% discount. The retailer agrees to purchase 15,000 cases at a discounted selling price of $15.66 per case ($15.90 list less the 24¢ discount).

Transaction: Receive an order for 15,000 cases of applesauce at a selling price of $15.66 per case, $234,900 for the total order.

Note: Receiving an order has no effect on the three major financial statements. Only when the product ordered is shipped to customers do you record a SALE and the associated COST OF GOODS.

∼

Transaction 22. — Ship 15,000 Cases of Applesauce

Income Statement

NET SALES	$	234,900
COST OF GOODS SOLD		153,000
GROSS MARGIN		81,900
SALES & MARKETING		4,698
RESEARCH & DEVELOPMENT		-
GENERAL & ADMINISTRATIVE		-
OPERATING EXPENSE		4,698
INCOME FROM OPERATIONS		77,202
NET INTEREST INCOME		-
INCOME TAXES		-
NET INCOME	$	77,202

Cash Flow Statement

BEGINNING CASH BALANCE	$	-
CASH RECEIPTS		-
CASH DISBURSEMENTS		-
CASH FLOW FROM OPERATIONS		-
PP&E PURCHASE		-
NET BORROWINGS		-
INCOME TAXES PAID		-
SALE OF CAPITAL STOCK		-
ENDING CASH BALANCES	$	-

Balance Sheet

Assets

CASH	$	-
ACCOUNTS RECEIVABLE		234,900
INVENTORIES		(153,000)
PREPAID EXPENSES		-
CURRENT ASSETS		81,900
OTHER ASSETS		-
FIXED ASSETS @ COST		-
ACCUMULATED DEPRECIATION		-
NET FIXED ASSETS		-
TOTAL ASSETS		81,900

Liabilities & Equity

ACCOUNTS PAYABLE	$	-
ACCRUED EXPENSES		4,698
CURRENT PORTION OF DEBT		-
INCOME TAXES PAYABLE		-
CURRENT LIABILITIES		4,698
LONG-TERM DEBT		-
CAPITAL STOCK		-
RETAINED EARNINGS		77,202
SHAREHOLDERS' EQUITY		77,202
TOTAL LIABILITIES & EQUITY	$	81,900

T22. Ship and invoice customer for 15,000 cases of applesauce ordered in Transaction 21.

Although we did lower our price to get this large order, our costs will remain the same. Thus we will garner a lower profit in this transaction than if we had sold at full list price.

AppleSeed's net sales amount will be $234,900 versus the $238,500 if we had sold at list price — a difference of $3,600 in lower sales.

Our gross margin (that is, sales less cost of goods sold) will be $81,900 versus $85,500 — again, a difference of $3,600 less margin.

In fact, this $3,600 difference in the original selling price will drop all the way to the bottom line as a lower profit. Discounts are dangerous profit-gobblers. Try to use them sparingly.

Transaction: Ship 15,000 cases of applesauce and send a $234,900 invoice to the customer.

1 (1A) Book sale of $234,900 as NET SALES on AppleSeed's *Income Statement*. (1B) Make a corresponding entry as an ACCOUNTS RECEIVABLE on the Balance Sheet.

2 (2A) On the *Income Statement* book COST OF GOODS SOLD for this sale of $153,000, equaling a $10.20 standard cost per case times 15,000 cases shipped. (2B) Reduce INVENTORIES on the *Balance Sheet* by this same amount.

3 (3A) Book on the *Income Statement* a SALES & MARKETING expense of $4,698 as the 2% selling commission for our broker. (3B) Also book this expense in ACCRUED EXPENSES on the *Balance Sheet*.

4 Increase RETAINED EARNINGS on the *Balance Sheet* by $77,202 — the sale amount less cost of goods sold less the selling commission.

~

Inventory Valuation Worksheet	RAW MATERIAL	WORK IN PROCESS	FINISHED GOODS
PRIOR INVENTORY VALUES	$176,600	$8,670	$382,500
S. Ship 15,000 cases of applesauce at $10.20 standard cost.	$0	$0	$(153,000)
INVENTORY VALUES AFTER THIS TRANSACTION	$176,600	$8,670	$229,500
		TOTAL INVENTORY	$414,770

Transaction 23. — Receive Payment

Income Statement

NET SALES	$	-
COST OF GOODS SOLD		-
GROSS MARGIN		-
SALES & MARKETING		-
RESEARCH & DEVELOPMENT		-
GENERAL & ADMINISTRATIVE		-
OPERATING EXPENSE		-
INCOME FROM OPERATIONS		-
NET INTEREST INCOME		-
INCOME TAXES		-
NET INCOME	$	-

Cash Flow Statement

BEGINNING CASH BALANCE	$	-
CASH RECEIPTS	❶A	234,900
CASH DISBURSEMENTS		4,698 ❷A
CASH FLOW FROM OPERATIONS		230,202
PP&E PURCHASE		-
NET BORROWINGS		-
INCOME TAXES PAID		-
SALE OF CAPITAL STOCK		-
ENDING CASH BALANCE	$	230,202

Balance Sheet

Assets

CASH ❸	$	230,202
ACCOUNTS RECEIVABLE		(234,900) ❶B
INVENTORIES		-
PREPAID EXPENSES		-
CURRENT ASSETS		(4,698)
OTHER ASSETS		-
FIXED ASSETS @ COST		-
ACCUMULATED DEPRECIATION		-
NET FIXED ASSETS		-
TOTAL ASSETS		(4,698)

Liabilities & Equity

ACCOUNTS PAYABLE	$	-
ACCRUED EXPENSES		4,698 ❷B
CURRENT PORTION OF DEBT		-
INCOME TAXES PAYABLE		-
CURRENT LIABILITIES		4,698
LONG-TERM DEBT		-
CAPITAL STOCK		-
RETAINED EARNINGS		-
SHAREHOLDERS' EQUITY		-
TOTAL LIABILITIES & EQUITY	$	4,698

T23. Receive payment of $234,900 for shipment made in Transaction 22 and pay the broker's commission.

Our big customer is very happy with our applesauce. He says that our brightly colored jars are "walking off the shelves." We're extremely happy that we decided to spend so much money on very fancy packaging.

Although it is true that "all you really need to be in business is a customer," what you really need is a customer who pays. With this transaction we will collect our first accounts receivable and turn it into cash.

Transaction: Receive payment of $234,900 for shipment that was made in Transaction 22. Pay the broker his $4,698 selling commission.

1 (1A) Book $234,900 in CASH RECEIPTS in the *Cash Flow Statement*. (1B) Decrease ACCOUNTS RECEIVABLE on the *Balance Sheet* by the same amount.

2 (2A) Issue a $4,698 check to our broker and record in CASH DISBURSEMENTS in the *Cash Flow Statement*. (2B) Lower ACCRUED EXPENSES by the amount paid the broker.

3 Increase CASH by $230,202 on the *Balance Sheet* (that is, $234,900 received less $4,698 disbursed).

Note: A customer's cash payment for goods in no way changes the *Income Statement*. The *Income Statement* recorded a sale when (a) we shipped the goods, and (b) the customer incurred the obligation to pay (our accounts receivable).

~

Transaction 24. — Write Off Shipment as a Bad Debt!

Income Statement

NET SALES	$	-
COST OF GOODS SOLD		-
GROSS MARGIN		-
SALES & MARKETING		(318)
RESEARCH & DEVELOPMENT		-
GENERAL & ADMINISTRATIVE		15,900
OPERATING EXPENSE		15,582
INCOME FROM OPERATIONS		(15,582)
NET INTEREST INCOME		-
INCOME TAXES		-
NET INCOME	$	(15,582)

2 A (SALES & MARKETING)
1 A (GENERAL & ADMINISTRATIVE)

Cash Flow Statement

BEGINNING CASH BALANCE	$	-
CASH RECEIPTS		-
CASH DISBURSEMENTS		-
CASH FLOW FROM OPERATIONS		-
PP&E PURCHASE		-
NET BORROWINGS		-
INCOME TAXES PAID		-
SALE OF CAPITAL STOCK		-
ENDING CASH BALANCE	$	-

Balance Sheet

Assets

CASH	$	-
ACCOUNTS RECEIVABLE		(15,900)
INVENTORIES		-
PREPAID EXPENSES		-
CURRENT ASSETS		(15,900)
OTHER ASSETS		-
FIXED ASSETS @ COST		-
ACCUMULATED DEPRECIATION		-
NET FIXED ASSETS		-
TOTAL ASSETS		(15,900)

1 B (ACCOUNTS RECEIVABLE)

Liabilities & Equity

ACCOUNTS PAYABLE	$	-
ACCRUED EXPENSES		(318)
CURRENT PORTION OF DEBT		-
INCOME TAXES PAYABLE		-
CURRENT LIABILITIES		(318)
LONG-TERM DEBT		-
CAPITAL STOCK		-
RETAINED EARNINGS		(15,582)
SHAREHOLDERS' EQUITY		(15,582)
TOTAL LIABILITIES & EQUITY	$	(15,900)

2 B (ACCRUED EXPENSES)
3 (RETAINED EARNINGS)

T24. Oops! Customer goes bankrupt. Write off as a bad debt the cost of 1,000 cases and reverse the sale. Sigh.

Remember back in Transaction 20 we shipped 1,000 cases of applesauce to your brother-in-law's company? You'll never guess what happened. They went bankrupt! Now he even wants a job.

We will never get paid. And because the goods have already been distributed and sold to applesauce lovers around the northwest, we will never get our product back either.

Transaction: Write off the $15,900 accounts receivable that was entered when you made the 1,000 case shipment. Also, reduce the amount payable to our broker by what would have been his commission on the sale. If we don't get paid, he doesn't either!

1 (1A) Book the bad-debt expense of $15,900 against GENERAL & ADMINISTRATIVE expense on the *Income Statement*. (1B) Reduce ACCOUNTS RECEIVABLE on the *Balance Sheet* by the $15,900 we will never collect. These entries reverse the sale we had made.

2 (2A) Book a "negative expense" of minus $318 in SALES & MARKETING expense on the *Income Statement*. (2B) Decrease ACCRUED EXPENSE on the *Balance Sheet* by the same amount. These entries reverse the commission that had been due our broker.

3 Reduce RETAINED EARNINGS on the *Balance Sheet* by $15,582, the sale amount we wrote off less the commission no longer due.

Note: Our out-of-pocket loss is really just $10,200 in the inventory value of the goods shipped.

Remember: In Transaction 20 we booked a profit from this sale of $5,382 — the $15,900 sale minus the $10,200 COST OF GOODS sold minus the $318 selling commission. Thus, if you combine the $15,582 drop in RETAINED EARNINGS booked in this transaction plus the $5,382 increase in RETAINED EARNINGS from Transaction 20, you are left with our loss of $10,200 from this bad debt.

~

Chapter 10.
Administrative Tasks

We've been busy making and selling our delicious applesauce. However, having been in business for three months, it's time to attend to some important administrative tasks.

~

Transaction 25. Pay this year's general liability insurance.

Transaction 26. Make principal and interest payments on three months' worth of building mortgage borrowing.

Transaction 27. Pay payroll-associated taxes and insurance benefit premiums.

Transaction 28. Pay some suppliers ... especially the mean and hungry ones.

Transaction 25. — Pay Insurance Premum

Income Statement

NET SALES	$	-
COST OF GOODS SOLD		-
GROSS MARGIN		-
SALES & MARKETING		-
RESEARCH & DEVELOPMENT		-
GENERAL & ADMINISTRATIVE		6,500 ❷
OPERATING EXPENSE		6,500
INCOME FROM OPERATIONS		(6,500)
NET INTEREST INCOME		-
INCOME TAXES		-
NET INCOME	$	(6,500)

Cash Flow Statement

BEGINNING CASH BALANCE	$	-
CASH RECEIPTS		-
CASH DISBURSEMENTS		26,000 ❶ A
CASH FLOW FROM OPERATIONS		(26,000)
PP&E PURCHASE		-
NET BORROWINGS		-
INCOME TAXES PAID		-
SALE OF CAPITAL STOCK		-
ENDING CASH BALANCES	$	(26,000)

Balance Sheet

Assets

CASH ❶ B	$	(26,000)
ACCOUNTS RECEIVABLE		-
INVENTORIES		-
PREPAID EXPENSES		19,500 ③
CURRENT ASSETS		(6,500)
OTHER ASSETS		-
FIXED ASSETS @ COST		-
ACCUMULATED DEPRECIATION		-
NET FIXED ASSETS		-
TOTAL ASSETS		(6,500)

Liabilities & Equity

ACCOUNTS PAYABLE	$	-
ACCRUED EXPENSES		- ③ B
CURRENT PORTION OF DEBT		-
INCOME TAXES PAYABLE		-
CURRENT LIABILITIES		-
LONG-TERM DEBT		-
CAPITAL STOCK		-
RETAINED EARNINGS		(6,500) ④
SHAREHOLDERS' EQUITY		(6,500)
TOTAL LIABILITIES & EQUITY	$	(6,500)

T25. Pay this year's general liability insurance.

During the first month we were in business many insurance brokers dropped by to try to sell us their wares.

We selected LightningBolt Brokers as our insurance agent. LightningBolt put together a package of building insurance, liability insurance and business interruption insurance that appeared to meet our needs.

We signed up for coverage and the broker said that she would send us a bill for the year, which we just got yesterday.

Transaction: With this transaction we will pay a full year's insurance premium of $26,000, giving us three months' prior coverage (the amount of time we have been in business) and also coverage for the remaining nine months in our fiscal year.

1 (1A) Issue a check for $26,000 to the insurance broker and book in **CASH DISBURSEMENTS** in the *Cash Flow Statement*. (1B) Lower **CASH** on the *Balance Sheet* by the amount of the check.

2 Book as a **GENERAL & ADMINISTRATIVE** expense on the *Income Statement* the $6,500 portion of the premium covering the last three months.

3 Book in **PREPAID EXPENSES** on the *Balance Sheet* the remaining $19,500 premium covering the next nine months.

Note: As time goes by, we will take this remaining $19,500 as an expense through the *Income Statement*. The transaction at that time will be to book the expense in the *Income Statement* and at the same time lower **PREPAID EXPENSES** in the *Balance Sheet*.

4 Reduce **RETAINED EARNINGS** in the *Balance Sheet* by the $6,500 loss due to the expense we have run through the *Income Statement*.

~

Transaction 26. — Pay Debt Principal and Interest

Income Statement

NET SALES	$ -	
COST OF GOODS SOLD	-	
GROSS MARGIN	-	
SALES & MARKETING	-	
RESEARCH & DEVELOPMENT	-	
GENERAL & ADMINISTRATIVE	-	
OPERATING EXPENSE	-	
INCOME FROM OPERATIONS	-	
NET INTEREST INCOME	(25,000)	③ A
INCOME TAXES	-	
NET INCOME	$ (25,000)	

Cash Flow Statement

BEGINNING CASH BALANCE	$ -	
CASH RECEIPTS	-	
CASH DISBURSEMENTS	25,000	❶ B
CASH FLOW FROM OPERATIONS	(25,000)	
PP&E PURCHASE	-	
NET BORROWINGS	(25,000)	❶ A
INCOME TAXES PAID	-	
SALE OF CAPITAL STOCK	-	
ENDING CASH BALANCES	$ (50,000)	

Balance Sheet

Assets

CASH	❶ C	$ (50,000)
ACCOUNTS RECEIVABLE		-
INVENTORIES		-
PREPAID EXPENSES		-
CURRENT ASSETS		(50,000)
OTHER ASSETS		-
FIXED ASSETS @ COST		-
ACCUMULATED DEPRECIATION		-
NET FIXED ASSETS		-
TOTAL ASSETS		(50,000)

Liabilities & Equity

ACCOUNTS PAYABLE	$ -	
ACCRUED EXPENSES	-	
CURRENT PORTION OF DEBT	-	
INCOME TAXES PAYABLE	-	
CURRENT LIABILITIES	-	
LONG-TERM DEBT	(25,000)	❷
CAPITAL STOCK	-	
RETAINED EARNINGS	(25,000)	③ B
SHAREHOLDERS' EQUITY	(25,000)	
TOTAL LIABILITIES & EQUITY	$ (50,000)	

T26. Make principal and interest payments on three months' worth of building debts.

Review the loan amortization schedule in Transaction 3. It shows how we must pay back the money we owe on the purchase of our building. Also, the fine print in the loan documentation says we must pay the principal and interest quarterly.

Three months have gone by since we got the loan, so interest and principal payments are now due. According to the amortization schedule, this year we owe a total of $100,000 in principal payments and also $100,000 in interest payments.

Transaction: Make a quarterly payment of $25,000 in principal and also a $25,000 interest payment on the building mortgage.

1 (1A) Lower RETAINED EARNINGS in the *Cash Flow Statement* by the $25,000 principal payment. (1B) Book in CASH DISBURSEMENTS for the $25,000 interest payment. (1C) Lower CASH on the *Balance Sheet* by the total $50,000 in cash that left the company.

2 Lower LONG-TERM DEBT on the *Balance Sheet* by the $25,000 principal payment made above.

3 (3A) Book the interest payment as a negative $25,000 under NET INTEREST INCOME on the *Income Statement*. (3B) Then book the resulting loss in RETAINED EARNINGS on the *Balance Sheet*.

Note: The interest payment entry on the *Income Statement* for this transaction is booked as a negative number since the account used to record the payment is INTEREST INCOME. If we had a category INTEREST EXPENSE on the *Income Statement* then interest payments would be booked as a positive number. Either way, RETAINED EARNINGS decreases by $25.000.

Got that? It's important to pay attention to the exact account meaning when determining whether an entry should be positive or negative.

~

Transaction 27. — Pay Payroll Taxes and Benefits

Income Statement

NET SALES	$	-
COST OF GOODS SOLD		-
GROSS MARGIN		-
SALES & MARKETING		-
RESEARCH & DEVELOPMENT		-
GENERAL & ADMINISTRATIVE		
OPERATING EXPENSE		-
INCOME FROM OPERATIONS		-
NET INTEREST INCOME		-
INCOME TAXES		-
NET INCOME	$	-

Cash Flow Statement

BEGINNING CASH BALANCE	$	-
CASH RECEIPTS		-
CASH DISBURSEMENTS		18,480	❶ A
CASH FLOW FROM OPERATIONS		(18,480)
PP&E PURCHASE		-
NET BORROWINGS		-
INCOME TAXES PAID		-
SALE OF CAPITAL STOCK		-
ENDING CASH BALANCE	$	(18,480)

Balance Sheet

Assets

CASH ❶ B	$	(18,480)
ACCOUNTS RECEIVABLE		-
INVENTORIES		-
PREPAID EXPENSES		-
CURRENT ASSETS		(18,480)
OTHER ASSETS		-
FIXED ASSETS @ COST		-
ACCUMULATED DEPRECIATION		-
NET FIXED ASSETS		-
TOTAL ASSETS		(18,480)

Liabilities & Equity

ACCOUNTS PAYABLE	$	-
ACCRUED EXPENSES		(18,480)	❷
CURRENT PORTION OF DEBT		-
INCOME TAXES PAYABLE		-
CURRENT LIABILITIES		(18,480)
LONG-TERM DEBT		-
CAPITAL STOCK		-
RETAINED EARNINGS		-
SHAREHOLDERS' EQUITY		-
TOTAL LIABILITIES & EQUITY	$	(18,480)

T27. Pay payroll-associated taxes and insurance benefit premiums.

We have some payroll-associated taxes and insurance benefit payments that are due for payment. We had better pay them! The government gets very nasty if we don't pay all withholding and FICA premiums when they are due.

These obligations are some of the few debts that cannot be erased by bankruptcy. Also, if the company does not pay these debts, the IRS often goes after officers of the company personally to collect the government's due.

Transaction: Pay payroll taxes, fringe benefits and insurance premiums. Write checks to the government and to insurance companies totaling $18,480 for payment of withholding and FICA taxes and for payroll-associated fringe benefits.

1 (1A) Book a CASH DISBURSEMENT of $18,480 in the *Cash Flow Statement.* (1B) Lower CASH on the *Balance Sheet* by the same amount.

2 Lower ACCRUED EXPENSES on the *Balance Sheet* by the $18,480 amount paid to the government and to various insurance companies.

Note: The *Income Statement* and RETAINED EARNINGS are not affected by this payment transaction. Because AppleSeed runs its books on an accrual basis, we already "expensed" these expenses when they occurred — not when the actual payment is made.

~

Transaction 28. — Pay Suppliers

Income Statement

NET SALES	$	-
COST OF GOODS SOLD		-
GROSS MARGIN		-
SALES & MARKETING		-
RESEARCH & DEVELOPMENT		-
GENERAL & ADMINISTRATIVE		-
OPERATING EXPENSE		-
INCOME FROM OPERATIONS		-
NET INTEREST INCOME		-
INCOME TAXES		-
NET INCOME	$	-

Cash Flow Statement

BEGINNING CASH BALANCE	$	-
CASH RECEIPTS		-
CASH DISBURSEMENTS		150,000	**❶**
CASH FLOW FROM OPERATIONS		(150,000)
PP&E PURCHASE		-
NET BORROWINGS		-
INCOME TAXES PAID		-
SALE OF CAPITAL STOCK		-
ENDING CASH BALANCE	$	(150,000)

Balance Sheet

Assets

CASH **❷**	$	(150,000)
ACCOUNTS RECEIVABLE		-
INVENTORIES		-
PREPAID EXPENSES		-
CURRENT ASSETS		(150,000)
OTHER ASSETS		-
FIXED ASSETS @ COST		-
ACCUMULATED DEPRECIATION		-
NET FIXED ASSETS		-
TOTAL ASSETS		(150,000)

Liabilities & Equity

ACCOUNTS PAYABLE **③**	$	(150,000)
ACCRUED EXPENSES		-
CURRENT PORTION OF DEBT		-
INCOME TAXES PAYABLE		-
CURRENT LIABILITIES		(150,000)
LONG-TERM DEBT		-
CAPITAL STOCK		-
RETAINED EARNINGS		-
SHAREHOLDERS' EQUITY		-
TOTAL LIABILITIES & EQUITY	$	(150,000)

T28. Pay some suppliers ... especially the mean and hungry ones.

Several of our raw material suppliers have telephoned recently and asked how we are doing ... and, by the way, when are we planning to pay their bills?

Because we are in a check-writing mood (and because we will shortly be asking them to send us more apples), we pay a chunk of those supplier bills.

Transaction: Pay suppliers a portion of what is due for apples and jars. Cut a check for $150,000 in partial payment.

1 Write a check for $150,000 to pay suppliers. Increase CASH DISBURSEMENTS by that amount in the Cash *Flow Statement.*

2 Lower CASH by $150,000 in the assets section of the *Balance Sheet.*

3 Lower ACCOUNTS PAYABLE in the liabilities section of the *Balance Sheet* by the $150,000 that we no longer owe, since we just paid as described above.

∼

Chapter 11.
Growth, Profit, and Return

With these transactions we will fast-forward through the rest of Apple-Seed's first year in business. We will determine our profit for the year, compute the income taxes we owe, declare a dividend and issue our first Annual Report to Shareholders.

Taxes and dividends — one bad, one good? Actually, without taxes, there would be no dividends. Dividends are paid out of retained earnings. If the business has earnings (and can thus pay dividends), then it will have to pay taxes. Taxes with earnings; no taxes with no earnings. No earnings, then no dividends. Thus, no taxes, no dividends.

But enough of this. Some really exciting events are taking place at our now not-so-little company. We have attracted the attention of a large nationwide food-processing conglomerate. The president of the conglomerate particularly likes our applesauce. She may make us an offer to buy the company! How much is it worth?

~

Transaction 29. Fast-forward through the rest of the year. Record summary transactions.

Transaction 30. Book income taxes payable.

Transaction 31. Declare a $0.375 per share dividend and pay to common shareholders.

- AppleSeed Enterprises, Inc. Annual Report to Shareholders

- What is AppleSeed worth? How to value a company.

Transaction 29. — Fast-Forward Summary

Income Statement

NET SALES	$ 2,804,760	
COST OF GOODS SOLD	1,836,000	
GROSS MARGIN	968,760	
SALES & MARKETING	212,895	
RESEARCH & DEVELOPMENT	26,000	
GENERAL & ADMINISTRATIVE	162,900	
OPERATING EXPENSE	401,795	
INCOME FROM OPERATIONS	566,965	
NET INTEREST INCOME	(75,000)	
INCOME TAXES	-	
NET INCOME	$ 491,965	

Cash Flow Statement

BEGINNING CASH BALANCE	$ -	
CASH RECEIPTS	2,350,000	
CASH DISBURSEMENTS	2,285,480	
CASH FLOW FROM OPERATIONS	64,520	
PP&E PURCHASE	-	
NET BORROWINGS	(75,000)	
INCOME TAXES PAID	-	
SALE OF CAPITAL STOCK	-	
ENDING CASH BALANCES	$ (10,480)	

Balance Sheet

Assets

CASH	$ (10,480)	
ACCOUNTS RECEIVABLE	454,760	
INVENTORIES	-	
PREPAID EXPENSES	(19,500)	
CURRENT ASSETS	424,780	
OTHER ASSETS	-	
FIXED ASSETS @ COST	-	
ACCUMULATED DEPRECIATION	64,287	
NET FIXED ASSETS	(64,287)	
TOTAL ASSETS	360,493	

Liabilities & Equity

ACCOUNTS PAYABLE	$ (82,907)	
ACCRUED EXPENSES	26,435	
CURRENT PORTION OF DEBT	-	
INCOME TAXES PAYABLE	-	
CURRENT LIABILITIES	(56,472)	
LONG-TERM DEBT	(75,000)	
CAPITAL STOCK	-	
RETAINED EARNINGS	491,965	
SHAREHOLDERS' EQUITY	491,965	
TOTAL LIABILITIES & EQUITY	$ 360,493	

T29. Fast-forward through the rest of the year. Record summary transactions for the remainder of the year.

AppleSeed Enterprises, Inc., has been in business for about three months now. We seem to have gotten the hang of recurding transactions and manipulating the *Income Statement, Cash Flow Statement* and *Balance Sheet*. It is fun.

With this series of entries, we will compress and summarize all the remaining transactions that took place in Apple-Seed's next nine months of operations. As you can see from the statements, we sold about $2.8 million in applesauce during the last nine months of the year and a total of $3.1 million for the whole year.

We also collected a little less than $2.6 million from customers during the year

and paid out a little over $2.7 million to suppliers, employees, etc. Significantly, we turned cash flow positive — that is, more cash receipts than cash disbursements — to the tune of over $64,520 during the last nine months of our fiscal year. Note that we were still cash flow negative by $136,538 for the whole year.

The bookings in this summary transaction close out our first year in business. Let's review the bottom line. INCOME FROM OPERATIONS amounted to $491,687. Subtract from this figure the interest paid on building debt and we have a total of $391,687 as our *pre-tax* profit for the year. A very nice showing. *Taxes next.*

Transaction: Book a series of entries in the *Income Statement, Cash Flow Statement* and the *Balance Sheet* summarizing transactions that take place in the remaining nine months of AppleSeed Enterprises' first fiscal year.

~

Transaction 30. — Book Income Taxes Payable

Income Statement

NET SALES	$	-
COST OF GOODS SOLD		-
GROSS MARGIN		-
SALES & MARKETING		-
RESEARCH & DEVELOPMENT		-
GENERAL & ADMINISTRATIVE		-
OPERATING EXPENSE		-
INCOME FROM OPERATIONS		-
NET INTEREST INCOME		-
INCOME TAXES		113,589
NET INCOME	$	(113,589)

① A

Cash Flow Statement

BEGINNING CASH BALANCE	$	-
CASH RECEIPTS		-
CASH DISBURSEMENTS		-
CASH FLOW FROM OPERATIONS		-
PP&E PURCHASE		-
NET BORROWINGS		-
INCOME TAXES PAID		-
SALE OF CAPITAL STOCK		-
ENDING CASH BALANCES	$	-

Balance Sheet

Assets

CASH	$	-
ACCOUNTS RECEIVABLE		-
INVENTORIES		-
PREPAID EXPENSES		-
CURRENT ASSETS		-
OTHER ASSETS		-
FIXED ASSETS @ COST		-
ACCUMULATED DEPRECIATION		-
NET FIXED ASSETS		-
TOTAL ASSETS		-

Liabilities & Equity

ACCOUNTS PAYABLE	$	-
ACCRUED EXPENSES		-
CURRENT PORTION OF DEBT		-
INCOME TAXES PAYABLE		113,589
CURRENT LIABILITIES		113,589
LONG-TERM DEBT		-
CAPITAL STOCK		-
RETAINED EARNINGS		(113,589)
SHAREHOLDERS' EQUITY		(113,589)
TOTAL LIABILITIES & EQUITY	$	-

②

① B

T30. Book income taxes payable.

Taxes are very simple.

For almost all corporations you just take pre-tax income and multiply it by the current Federal corporate tax percentage, currently 21% in the U.S. State corporate income tax rates vary. We will use 8% here. Then you take out your checkbook and write a check to the government for that amount. If you fail to send in the money on time or if you fudge the books and the IRS catches you, then you go to jail.

See, I told you taxes were simple. With this transaction we will compute and then book the income taxes we owe the government. We will actually pay them later on the tax due date.

Transaction: On a pre-tax income of $391,687, AppleSeed owes 21% in federal income taxes ($82,254) and 8% in state income taxes ($31,335), a total income tax bill of $113,587. We will not actually pay the tax for several months.

1 (1A) Book an **INCOME TAX** expense of $113,587 in the *Income Statement*. (1B) Lower **RETAINED EARNINGS** by the same amount in the *Balance Sheet*.

2 Book $113,587 worth of **INCOME TAXES PAYABLE** in the liabilities section of the *Balance Sheet*.

~

Transaction 31. — Book and Pay Dividend

Income Statement

NET SALES	$	-
COST OF GOODS SOLD		-
GROSS MARGIN		-
SALES & MARKETING		-
RESEARCH & DEVELOPMENT		-
GENERAL & ADMINISTRATIVE		-
OPERATING EXPENSE		-
INCOME FROM OPERATIONS		-
NET INTEREST INCOME		-
INCOME TAXES		-
NET INCOME	$	-

Cash Flow Statement

BEGINNING CASH BALANCE	$	-
CASH RECEIPTS		-
CASH DISBURSEMENTS		75,000	❶ A
CASH FLOW FROM OPERATIONS		(75,000)
PP&E PURCHASE		-
NET BORROWINGS		-
INCOME TAXES PAID		-
SALE OF CAPITAL STOCK		-
ENDING CASH BALANCES	$	(75,000)

Balance Sheet

Assets

CASH ❶ B	$	(75,000)
ACCOUNTS RECEIVABLE		-
INVENTORIES		-
PREPAID EXPENSES		-
CURRENT ASSETS		(75,000)
OTHER ASSETS		-
FIXED ASSETS @ COST		-
ACCUMULATED DEPRECIATION		-
NET FIXED ASSETS		-
TOTAL ASSETS		(75,000)

Liabilities & Equity

ACCOUNTS PAYABLE	$	-
ACCRUED EXPENSES		-
CURRENT PORTION OF DEBT		-
INCOME TAXES PAYABLE		-
CURRENT LIABILITIES		-
LONG-TERM DEBT		-
CAPITAL STOCK		-
RETAINED EARNINGS		(75,000)	❷
SHAREHOLDERS' EQUITY		(75,000)
TOTAL LIABILITIES & EQUITY	$	(75,000)

T31. Declare a $0.375 per share dividend and pay to the common shareholders.

This transaction will be our last for AppleSeed Enterprises this year, just before we close the books. The company has done well in its first year of operation and the board of directors decides to vote a dividend for common shareholders. The question is, how big a dividend?

Dividends are paid out of **RETAINED EARNINGS**, of which we have more than $250,000 as of the end of the year. We also have a very strong cash position, so we can afford to pay the dividend.

After much discussion, a $0.375 per share dividend is voted. With 200,000 shares outstanding, this dividend will cost the company $75,000; $56,250 to the investor group and $18,750 for you, the entrepreneur.

You go out and buy a small boat. What you really want is a 42-foot Hinckley.

Transaction: Declare and pay $0.375 per share dividend to AppleSeed's shareholders.

1 (1A) Book a **CASH DISBURSEMENT** (see note below) on the *Cash Flow Statement* for the $75,000 dividend payment. (1B) Reduce **CASH** on the *Balance Sheet* by the same amount.

2 Reduce **RETAINED EARNINGS** on the *Balance Sheet* by the dividend payment of $75,000.

Note: The *Cash Flow Statements* on these transaction spreads are abbreviated. That is, they do not have all the line items that a complete statement would have. The dividend payment should really be placed on a special line titled **DIVIDENDS PAID** rather than in **CASH DISBURSEMENTS**. Paying a dividend is not an operating expense and the cash disbursements line should be used for operating expenses only.

More: See Appendix D for a description of the structure of a more complete *Cash Flow Statement*.

Appleseed Enterprises, Inc. — Financial Statements

NET SALES	$ 3,055,560	100%	**Income Statement**
COST OF GOODS SOLD	2,005,830	66%	
GROSS MARGIN	1,049,730	34%	
SALES & MARKETING	328,523	11%	
RESEARCH & DEVELOPMENT	26,000	1%	
GENERAL & ADMINISTRATIVE	203,520	7%	
OPERATING EXPENSE	558,043	18%	
INCOME FROM OPERATIONS	491,687	16%	
NET INTEREST INCOME	(100,000)	-3%	
INCOME TAXES	113,587	4%	
NET INCOME	$ 278,100	9%	

BEGINNING CASH BALANCE	$ 0	**Cash Flow Statement**
CASH RECEIPTS	2,584,900	
CASH DISBURSEMENTS	2,796,438	
CASH FLOW FROM OPERATIONS	(211,538)	
PP&E PURCHASE	1,750,000	
NET BORROWINGS	900,000	
INCOME TAXES PAID	0	
SALE OF CAPITAL STOCK	1,550,000	
ENDING CASH BALANCES	$ 488,462	

CASH	$ 488,462	16%	**Balance Sheet**
ACCOUNTS RECEIVABLE	454,760	15%	
INVENTORIES	414,770	14%	
PREPAID EXPENSES	0	0%	
CURRENT ASSETS	1,357,992	45%	
OTHER ASSETS	0	0%	
FIXED ASSETS @ COST	1,750,000	58%	
ACCUMULATED DEPRECIATION	78,573	3%	
NET FIXED ASSETS	1,671,427	55%	
TOTAL ASSETS	3,029,419	100%	
ACCOUNTS PAYABLE	$ 236,297	8%	
ACCRUED EXPENSES	26,435	1%	
CURRENT PORTION OF DEBT	100,000	3%	
INCOME TAXES PAYABLE	113,587	4%	
CURRENT LIABILITIES	476,319	16%	
LONG-TERM DEBT	800,000	26%	
CAPITAL STOCK	1,550,000	51%	
RETAINED EARNINGS	203,100	7%	
SHAREHOLDERS' EQUITY	1,753,100	58%	
TOTAL LIABILITIES & EQUITY	$ 3,029,419	100%	

Assets / Liabilities & Equity

"Common Sized" statement analysis in red. *See page 188.*

Appleseed Enterprises Annual Report

To Our Shareholders:

I am happy to have this opportunity to report to you the results of AppleSeed Enterprises, Inc.'s first year of operation. Your company, in a very short time, has achieved its initial goal of becoming a recognized supplier of very high-quality applesauce.

Important Events

At the beginning of the year, Apple-Seed raised $1 million through a successful offering of its common stock. This capitalization has allowed us to purchase high-volume production machinery and to maintain sufficient inventory to break into the highly competitive applesauce industry.

Our production continues at over 20 thousand cases per month. As demand increases, we project that the current manufacturing facility can be operated at over twice these levels. Depending, however, on the weather conditions in the Northeast, raw material supply may limit our ability to reach increased levels of production.

Financial Results

In AppleSeed's first year of operation, our revenues exceeded $3 million. Apple-Seed's net income for the year was over $278,000, or $1.39 per share on 200,000 shares outstanding.

Our return on sales of 9.1% exceeds industry averages, as does our 15.9 % return on shareholders' equity. Return on assets was 8%. Our Balance Sheet remains strong. We end this year with over $488,000 in cash and cash equivalents.

AppleSeed continues to spend heavily in marketing and sales. We believe these investments will pay off handsomely in the future in significantly improved market position, especially in specialty segments of the applesauce industry.

During the coming year, we plan to introduce several new jar sizes and packaging configurations into the gift market. Product testing continues on specialty flavored and colored versions of our basic applesauce. A bright green sauce packaged in a shamrock-shaped jar will be introduced prior to St. Patrick's Day this year. We expect our new products to be well-received in the marketplace.

~

I thank our customers for their continuing confidence in our products and in our ability to serve their applesauce needs. I thank our shareholders for their continuing support and our employees for their productive efforts throughout AppleSeed's first year of operation.

Sincerely,

I. M. Rich

President and CEO

What's a Business Worth?

We've done a splendid job starting up an applesauce company. What do you think the business is worth now? A good question, one of interest to AppleSeed's shareholders. Let's look at several methods of company valuation.

Book Value Book value represents the value at which assets are carried on the "books" of the company. The book value of a company is defined as its total assets less its current liabilities and less any long-term debt. For AppleSeed Enterprises, Inc., book value is computed as $1,753,100 (that is, $3,029,419 in total assets less a total of $476,319 in current liabilities less some $800,000 in long-term debt outstanding).

Liquidation Value The liquidation value is what the company's assets would bring at a forced sale. Normally the liquidation value of a going concern has little relevance since the value of an operating business is much greater than its liquidation value.

For fun (?!) let's compute AppleSeed's liquidation value. Start with the company's book value and then subtract what would lower that amount if, for example, we could only get 10 cents on the dollar for inventory and 50 cents on the dollar for machinery. Using these assumptions, AppleSeed's liquidation value would be about $500,000. The bank would take it all.

Price-Earnings Multiple The company has 200,000 shares outstanding and earned a net income of $278,100 last year. Dividing net income by the number of outstanding shares gives a net income of $1.39 per share.

If we assume that companies like AppleSeed are currently selling at, let's say, 12 times earnings, then our company is worth $1.39 times this 12 multiple times 200,000 shares outstanding, equaling a value of over $3.3 million. Wow!

Market Value There is no market for AppleSeed's stock. The company is "closely held." Thus, there is no real "market value" for the company. Selling a private company is like selling a house. The business is worth what you can get for it.

Discounted Cash Flow The discounted cash flow method of valuation is the most sophisticated (and the most difficult) method to use in valuing the business. With this method you must estimate all the cash influxes to investors over time (dividends and ultimate stock sales) and then compute a "net present value" using an assumed discount rate (implied interest rate). There are just too many assumptions in this method to make it very useful in valuing AppleSeed. However, review the discussion in Chapter 21, Net Present Value, for a more detailed view on these calculations.

Alternative AppleSeed Enterprises Valuations

VALUATION METHOD	COMPANY VALUE
Book Value	$1,753.100
Liquidation Value	$504,807
Price-Earnings Multiple	$3,337,200
Market Value	sell to whom?
Discounted Cash Flow	too complex!

Section C.
Financial Statement
Construction and Analysis

About This Section

Congratulations! You have accurately kept the books of AppleSeed Enterprises, Inc., for the year. And a good year is was. What follows in this section are some techniques and details.

Journals and Ledgers We'll learn about the "books" that that accountants use to make transaction entries. Well, accountants once did use paper entry books and did atop high chairs. Now entries are made in computer memory. Some say that computers have made it easier to commit fraud. (When ledgers were paper books and entries were made with India ink, things were more difficult to fudge.)

Ratio Analysis Next we will review the common ways of analyzing financial statements to test the financial strength of the enterprise. We will review the liquidity of the company, how efficiently it uses its assets, how profitable it is and how effectively it is using "other people's money," that is, debt.

Accounting Policies We will review the different, but acceptable, ways to keep the company's books and why companies would want to use them. Note that some of these "creative accounting" techniques can be used to mask problems in the enterprise.

Cooking the books. Finally, we will discuss the ways of financial fraud and how to detect it. Some "tried and true" fraudulent techniques are important to understand whether you are an employee or an investor in the company.

Chapter 12.
Keeping Track with Journals and Ledgers

Financial accounting means recording each and every event (transaction) that has a financial impact on the enterprise. By keeping track of these activities just as they happen, the accountant can easily summarize the firm's financial position and then issue financial statements. Journals and ledgers are "the books" in which accountants scribble transaction entries.

The *General Journal* is a book (or a computer memory) in which all of a company's financial events are recorded in chronological order. Everything is there, there is nothing missing. Journal entries can (and must) be made if: (a) we know with reasonable certainty the amount of money involved, (b) we know the timing of the event, and (c) an actual exchange between the parties of cash, goods or some formal representation of value (such as stock) has occurred.

A *ledger* is a book of accounts. An account is simply any grouping of similar items that we want to keep track of. You can think of a ledger as a book with many pages. Each page of the ledger book represents one account.

The main benefit of a ledger system is that it allows us to determine how much we have of any item (account) at any point in time. Immediately after making a chronological journal entry, we update our ledger for each account that has changed as a result of that transaction.

Note that every time we make a journal entry, we will be changing the amount that we have in at least two accounts (ledger pages) in order to keep the *Balance Sheet* and the basic equation of accounting in balance:

$$\text{Assets = Liabilities + Equity.}$$

Any event having a financial impact on the firm affects this basic equation in some way or another. This basic equation

---

A journal is a book (or computer memory) in which all of a company's financial events are recorded in a chronological order. Everything is there, nothing is missing.

A ledger is a book of accounts. An account is any grouping of items of which we want to keep track. You can think of a ledger as a book with many pages. Each page of the ledger book represents one account.

---

equation summarizes the entire financial position of the firm. Furthermore, the equation must always stay in balance. To keep this equation in balance, a change in any one number in the equation must change at least one other number. Accountants call this system of making ledger changes in pairs the double-entry bookkeeping system.

Following are several of the account ledgers for AppleSeed Enterprises. Each ledger shows how our transactions have affected a single account. Note that at all times the ledgers present a current picture of AppleSeed's account balances.

The Cash Ledger shown below lists all transactions that affect the amount of cash in AppleSeed Enterprises' checking account. The ending cash balance on the Cash Ledger is the same amount as shown for the cash account on the *Balance Sheet* for the date of the last transaction. Shown following are additional AppleSeed Enterprises, Inc., ledgers.

AppleSeed Enterprises, Inc.
Cash Ledger

	TRANSACTION NUMBER & DESCRIPTION	INCOMING CASH (+)	OUTGOING CASH (-)	ENDING CASH BALANCE (=)
	Beginning of period balance			$50,000
T1.	Sell 150,000 shares at $10 each	$1,500,000		$1,550,000
T2.	G&A payroll checks		$3,370	$1,546,630
T3.	Borrowing to purchase building	$1,000,000		$2,546,630
T4.	Purchase building for $1.5 million		$1,500,000	$1,046,630
T5.	SG&A payroll		$7,960	$1,038,670
T6.	Pay payroll taxes to government		$9,690	$1,028,980
T7.	Make partial payment for machinery		$125,000	$903,980
T8.	Make final payment for machinery		$125,000	$778,980
T9.	Supervisor's payroll		$2,720	$776,260
T12.	Pay manufacturing payroll		$9,020	$767,240
T14.	Pay for jar labels		$20,000	$747,240
T17.	Partial payment to raw material suppliers		$150,000	$597,240
T18.	Pay manufacturing payroll		$9,020	$588,220
T23.	Receipts from customer, commission payment	$234,900	$4,698	$818,422
T25.	Pay insurance premiums		$26,000	$792,422
T26.	Pay mortgage principal and interest		$50,000	$742,422
T27.	Pay payroll taxes and benefit premiums		$18,480	$723,942
T28.	Pay hungry suppliers		$150,000	$573,942
T29.	Nine months' summary transactions (net)		$10,480	$563,462
T31.	Dividend payment		$75,000	$488,462

Financial Statements

Note that for each of AppleSeed's ledgers shown here, the right-most column shows the account value as of the completion of the transaction listed.

Ledgers should always be kept current. Then, when statements need to be prepared, the ledgers will always provide correct account values.

AppleSeed Enterprises, Inc.
Accounts Payable Ledger

TRANSACTION NUMBER & DESCRIPTION		TRANSACTION AMOUNT	ACCOUNTS PAYABLE
	Opening balance		$0
T10.	Receive labels	$20,000	$20,000
T11.	Receive two months' raw materials	$332,400	$352,400
T13.	Book a month's "all other" mfg. expense	$8,677	$361,077
T14.	Pay for labels received in T10	$(20,000)	$341,077
T17.	Partial payment to raw material suppliers	$(150,000)	$191,077
T18l.	Receive additional month's raw materials	$166,200	$357,277
T18p.	Book another month's "all other" mfg. expense	$8,677	$365,954
T19.	Book advertising flier and T-shirt expense	$103,250	$469,204
T28.	Pay hungry suppliers	$(150,000)	$319,204
T29.	Nine months' summary transactions (net)	$(82,907)	$236,297

AppleSeed Enterprises, Inc.
Inventory Ledger

TRANSACTION NUMBER & DESCRIPTION		BEGINNING INVENTORY	TRANSACTION	ENDING INVENTORY
	Opening balance			0
T10.	Receive applesauce jar labels	$0	$20,000	$20,000
T11.	Receive two months' inventory	$20,000	$332,400	$352,400
T12.	Pay manufacturing salaries	$352,400	$17,180	$369,580
T13.	Book depreciation and other mfg. overhead	$369,580	$15,820	$385,400
T16.	Scrap the value of 500 cases of applesauce	$385,400	$(5,100)	$380,300
T18.	Mfg another month's worth of applesauce	$380,300	$197,670	$577,970
T20.	Ship 1,000 cases of applesauce	$577,970	$(10,200)	$567,770
T22.	Ship 15,000 cases of applesauce	$567,770	$(153,000)	$414,770

AppleSeed Enterprises, Inc.
Accrued Expenses Ledger

	TRANSACTION NUMBER & DESCRIPTION	TRANSACTION AMOUNT	ACCRUED EXPENSES
	Opening balance		0
T2.	Payroll-associated taxes and benefits	$2,860	$2,860
T5.	Payroll-associated taxes and benefits	$6,830	$9,690
T6.	Pay payroll taxes and associated premiums	$(9,690)	$0
T9.	Payroll-associated taxes and benefits	$2,160	$2,160
T12.	Payroll-associated taxes and benefits	$8,160	$10,320
T18.	Payroll-associated taxes and benefits	$8,160	$18,480
T20.	Sales commission due	$318	$18,798
T22.	Sales commission due	$4,698	$23,496
T23.	Payment of sales commission	$(4,698)	$18,798
T24.	Reversal of sales commission due from **T20.**	$(318)	$18,480
T27.	Pay payroll taxes, fringe benefit, premiums	$(18,480)	$0
T29.	Nine months' summary transactions (net)	$26,435	$26,435

AppleSeed Enterprises, Inc.
Accounts Receivable Ledger

	TRANSACTION NUMBER & DESCRIPTION	TRANSACTION AMOUNT	ACCOUNTS RECEIVABLE
	Opening balance		$0
T20.	Applesauce sale - 1,000 cases @ $15.90	$15,900	$15,900
T22.	Applesauce sale - 15,000 cases @ $15.66	$234,900	$250,800
T23.	Payment received for **T22**	$(234,900)	$15,900
T24.	Bad debt from **T20** - write off receivable	$(15,900)	$0
T29.	Nine months' summary transactions (net)	$454,760	$454,760

Chapter 13.
Ratio Analysis

It is not so much the absolute numbers of sales, costs, expenses and assets that are important in judging the financial condition of an enterprise, but rather, the relationships between them.

For example:

- High cash available relative to the level of payables is a good indicator of how easily the company will be able to pay its bills in the future.

- Asset levels relative to sales volume indicates just how efficiently the company's investments in productive assets (machinery and inventory) can generate revenue.

- Gross margin as a percentage of sales determines how much the company is able to spend on various selling development and administrative activities and still make a profit.

Ratio analysis (that is, comparing one number on a company's financial statement with another number) is most useful when you wish to:

1. Compare year-to-year performance to determine if things are getting better or getting worse for the enterprise, or

2. Compare companies in an industry to see which is performing best given common constraints.

In this section, we will review AppleSeed Enterprises' first-year financial performance by analyzing the company's financial statements and the common ratio indicators of:

- **Liquidity**
- **Asset Management**
- **Profitability**
- **Leverage**

Finally, we will compare ratios across industries. Some businesses are naturally more profitable than others. Some require more capital; some require less.

The ratios computed on the following pages use AppleSeed Enterprises, Inc.'s *Income Statement* and *Balance Sheet* for the period from Transaction 1 through Transaction 31 shown in AppleSeed's Annual Report on page 178.

Common Size Statements:

Both the *Income Statement* and the *Balance Sheet* can be converted into "common size" statements for analysis. Common size statements present each item as a percentage of the statement's largest item.

Common Size Income Statement Normally, the largest item in the *Income Statement* is sales. Thus, when the *Income Statement* is converted into a common size statement, all items are presented as a percentage of sales. Reviewing the common size *Income Statement* focuses on the proportion of sales dollars absorbed by various cost and expense items.

AppleSeed's cost of goods sold is 34% of sales, our company's operating expense is 18%, net income is 8% and so forth. Not bad percentages for a company such as our little enterprise. See Apple-Seed's common size *Income Statement* shown on the facing page.

Common Size Balance Sheet To convert the *Balance Sheet* into a common size statement, all components are expressed as a percentage of total assets (or total liabilities & equity since they are the same amount). For example, Apple-Seed's current assets are 45% of total assets, long-term debt is 26% of total liabilities and equity and so forth.

Common size balance sheets help focus analysis on the internal structure and allocation of the company's financial resources. Common size statements are especially useful for the side-by-side analyses of several years of a company's performance, or when two companies of different size are being compared.

Appropriate year-to-year questions to ask are: "Why did we do better last year in this area than we did this year?" and "How well are we doing when we are compared to other companies in the industry?"

Appleseed Enterprises, Inc. — Financial Statements

Income Statement

NET SALES	$ 3,055,560	100%
COST OF GOODS SOLD	2,005,830	66%
GROSS MARGIN	1,049,730	34%
SALES & MARKETING	328,523	11%
RESEARCH & DEVELOPMENT	26,000	1%
GENERAL & ADMINISTRATIVE	203,520	7%
OPERATING EXPENSE	558,043	18%
INCOME FROM OPERATIONS	491,687	16%
NET INTEREST INCOME	(100,000)	-3%
INCOME TAXES	113,587	4%
NET INCOME	$ 278,100	9%

> Set NET SALES at 100% for a Common Size *Income Statement*

Balance Sheet

Assets

CASH	$ 488,462	16%
ACCOUNTS RECEIVABLE	454,760	15%
INVENTORIES	414,770	14%
PREPAID EXPENSES	0	0%
CURRENT ASSETS	1,357,992	45%
OTHER ASSETS	0	0%
FIXED ASSETS @ COST	1,750,000	58%
ACCUMULATED DEPRECIATION	78,573	3%
NET FIXED ASSETS	1,671,427	55%
TOTAL ASSETS	3,029,419	100%

Liabilities & Equity

ACCOUNTS PAYABLE	$ 236,297	8%
ACCRUED EXPENSES	26,435	1%
CURRENT PORTION OF DEBT	100,000	3%
INCOME TAXES PAYABLE	113,587	4%
CURRENT LIABILITIES	476,319	16%
LONG-TERM DEBT	800,000	26%
CAPITAL STOCK	1,550,000	51%
RETAINED EARNINGS	203,100	7%
SHAREHOLDERS' EQUITY	1,753,100	58%
TOTAL LIABILITIES & EQUITY	$ 3,029,419	100%

> Set TOTAL ASSETS and TOTAL LIABILITIES & EQUITY at 100% for a Common Size *Balance Sheet*

Liquidity Ratios:

The so-called liquidity ratios measure the ease with which a company can pay its bills when due. This ability is determined by whether the enterprise has cash in the bank or expects to generate cash (by sale of products and by the collection of accounts receivable), in sufficient amount to pay its bills as they become due.

There are periods of illiquidity in almost every company's life — when the company is unable to pay bills on time. Most often this situation is infrequent or only temporary and is usually no major problem. It's happened to all of us at one time or another.

However, if a company is illiquid on a regular basis, or for a long period of time, it is likely to find itself *busted, tapped-out, bankrupt.*

Everyone is interested in AppleSeed's ability to pay short-term debts, including its employees, suppliers and the bank that lent us money for our building. Even our customers care. They need a reliable supply of product.

Liquidity and profitability are different. It's possible — and indeed not all that uncommon — for a company to be profitable and illiquid at the same time. A company can show a profit on the *Income Statement* and still have very little cash on hand to pay its bills.

Profitability coupled with illiquidity can often occur in companies experiencing unexpected high growth. These companies need increased working capital to finance inventories and accounts receivable. Cash can be very tight. Happily, in these conditions, bankers love to lend money to those companies experiencing illiquidity due to rapid profitable growth.

Current Ratio The current ratio is one of the oldest and best-known measures of short-term financial strength. The ratio determines whether current assets (cash or assets that are expected to be converted into cash within a year) are sufficient to pay current liabilities (those obligations that must be paid within one year).

A current ratio for a general manufacturing company above 2.0 is considered good. It means that the company has twice the amount of current assets as it has current liabilities. A 1:1 ratio means that a company can just meet its upcoming bills. With a 2:0 ratio or better, there is a big financial cushion.

Quick Ratio The quick ratio is an even more conservative measure of liquidity than the current ratio. It is sometimes called the "acid test." The quick ratio is the company's "quick assets" (cash and accounts receivable) divided by current liabilities. Inventories are left out.

As shown in the computations here, AppleSeed Enterprises is quite liquid.

Appleseed Enterprises, Inc. — *Liquidity Ratios*

Balance Sheet

Assets

CASH	$ 488,462	A
ACCOUNTS RECEIVABLE	454,760	B
INVENTORIES	414,770	
PREPAID EXPENSES	0	
CURRENT ASSETS	1,357,992	C
OTHER ASSETS	0	
FIXED ASSETS @ COST	1,750,000	
ACCUMULATED DEPRECIATION	78,573	
NET FIXED ASSETS	1,671,427	
TOTAL ASSETS	3,029,419	

Liabilities & Equity

ACCOUNTS PAYABLE	$ 236,297	
ACCRUED EXPENSES	26,435	
CURRENT PORTION OF DEBT	100,000	
INCOME TAXES PAYABLE	113,587	
CURRENT LIABILITIES	476,319	D
LONG-TERM DEBT	800,000	
CAPITAL STOCK	1,550,000	
RETAINED EARNINGS	203,100	
SHAREHOLDERS' EQUITY	1,753,100	
TOTAL LIABILITIES & EQUITY	$ 3,029,419	

$$\textbf{Current Ratio} = \frac{Current\ Assets}{Current\ Liabilities} = \frac{C}{D} = \frac{\$1,357,992}{\$476,319} = 2.9$$

$$\textbf{Quick Ratio} = \frac{Cash + Receivables}{Shareholders'Equity} = \frac{A+B}{D} = \frac{\$488,462 + \$454,760}{\$476,319} = 2.0$$

Asset Management Ratios:

Assets are the financial engine of the enterprise. But how do we know that our assets are being used efficiently? Are we getting the biggest bang for our asset buck? Asset management ratios provide a tool to investigate how effective in generating profits is the company's investment in accounts receivables, inventory, and fixed assets.

Inventory Turn The inventory turn measures the volume of business that can be conducted with a given investment in inventory. AppleSeed "turns" its inventory four times each year. That is, AppleSeed needs to maintain an inventory value level of one-quarter of the total cost of its products sold (COGS) in a year.

Different types of businesses have dramatically different inventory turns. For example, a supermarket may turn its inventory 12 or more times a year while a typical manufacturing company turns its inventory twice.

Because inventory is built in anticipation of sales, inventory turn is especially sensitive to changes in business activity. If sales slow down, inventory can balloon and the inventory turn will decrease, a sign of pending trouble.

Asset Turn Ratio The asset turn ratio is a more general measure of efficient asset use. It shows the sales volume that a company can support with a given level of assets. Companies with low asset turn will require a large amount of capital to generate more sales. Conversely, a high asset turn means that the company can expand sales with a low capital investment.

Receivable Days Receivable levels (shown as collection days) is the average length of time the company's accounts receivable are outstanding — that is, how long between when the goods are shipped (on credit) and when the customer actually pays.

Credit sales create accounts receivable, shown in current assets on the *Balance Sheet*. These accounts receivable represent future cash in-flows into the business. The receivable days ratio (also known as the average collection period) just measures how fast, on average, the company gets this cash.

AppleSeed's sales terms state *"net 30."* This means that we expect the customer to pay us within 30 days after we ship our applesauce. As shown below, AppleSeed has a receivable days ratio of 54 days. Generally, companies average between 45 and 65 days receivables. Longer could be an indication of bad debts and possible write-offs.

Note that if AppleSeed could get its customers to pay faster — let's say in 35 days on average — and/or if it could get by on less inventory in stock (a higher turn), then a lot of cash would be "freed up" for other uses.

Appleseed Enterprises, Inc. — Asset Management Ratios

Income Statement

NET SALES	$ 3,055,560	**A**
COST OF GOODS SOLD	2,005,830	**B**
GROSS MARGIN	1,049,730	
SALES & MARKETING	328,523	
RESEARCH & DEVELOPMENT	26,000	
GENERAL & ADMINISTRATIVE	203,520	
OPERATING EXPENSE	558,043	
INCOME FROM OPERATIONS	491,687	
NET INTEREST INCOME	(100,000)	
INCOME TAXES	113,587	
NET INCOME	$ 278,100	

Balance Sheet

Assets

CASH	$ 488,462	
ACCOUNTS RECEIVABLE	454,760	**C**
INVENTORIES	414,770	**D**
PREPAID EXPENSES	0	
CURRENT ASSETS	1,357,992	
OTHER ASSETS	0	
FIXED ASSETS @ COST	1,750,000	
ACCUMULATED DEPRECIATION	78,573	
NET FIXED ASSETS	1,671,427	
TOTAL ASSETS	3,029,419	**E**

Liabilities & Equity

ACCOUNTS PAYABLE	$ 236,297
ACCRUED EXPENSES	26,435
CURRENT PORTION OF DEBT	100,000
INCOME TAXES PAYABLE	113,587
CURRENT LIABILITIES	476,319
LONG-TERM DEBT	800,000
CAPITAL STOCK	1,550,000
RETAINED EARNINGS	203,100
SHAREHOLDERS' EQUITY	1,753,100
TOTAL LIABILITIES & EQUITY	$ 3,029,419

$$\textbf{Inventory Turn} = \frac{Cost\ of\ Goods\ Sold}{Inventory} = \frac{B}{D} = \frac{\$2,005,830}{\$414,770} = 4.8\ \text{Turn}$$

$$\textbf{Asset Turn Ratio} = \frac{Annual\ Sales}{Assets} = \frac{A}{E} = \frac{\$3,055,560}{\$3,029,419} = 1.0\ \text{Turn}$$

$$\textbf{Receivable Days} = \frac{Receivables \times 365}{Annual\ Sales} = \frac{C \times 365}{A} = \frac{\$454,760 \times 365}{\$3,055,560} = 54\ \text{Days}$$

Profitability Ratios:

Profitability ratios are the common *"return on"* ratios: "return on sales," "return on assets" and so forth. Profitability ratios relate profits to some other piece of financial information such as sales, equity, or assets. These ratios measure aspects of management's operating efficiency; that is, management's ability to turn a profit given a level of resources.

Although the liquidity measures are most important indicators of short-term corporate health, profitability measures are most important in the long term.

In the long term, a business must consistently show a profit to remain viable and to provide its owners with a satisfactory return on their original investment.

Return on Assets The return on assets (ROA) ratio measures management's success in employing the company's assets to generate a profit.

Return on Equity The return on equity (ROE) ratio measures management's success in maximizing return on the owner's investment. In fact, this ratio is often called "return on investment," or ROI.

Return on Sales A company's return on sales (also called "profit margin") compares what is left over after all expenses and costs are subtracted from sales.

Gross Margin A company's gross margin (also called its "gross profit") measures how much it costs to make a company's products and, consequently, how much the company can afford to spend in SG&A and still make a profit.

Gross margin varies greatly between industries. For example, a retail business generally has a gross profit of around 25%. Computer software businesses can have a gross profit as high as 80% to 90% of sales. That means that for every dollar in sales, the computer software company spends only 10¢ to 20¢ to produce its product.

~

AppleSeed is doing rather well. An 8% return on sales (profit margin) is good for the industry. A 15% return on equity is fine too. The 8% return on assets is rather low, but not all that bad for AppleSeed's first year.

$$\textbf{Gross Margin} = \frac{Net\ Sales - COGS}{Net\ Sales} = \frac{A + B}{A} = \frac{\$3,055,550 + \$2,005,830}{\$3,005,560} = 34\%$$

Appleseed Enterprises, Inc. — Profitability Ratios

Income Statement

NET SALES	$ 3,055,560	A
COST OF GOODS SOLD	2,005,830	B
GROSS MARGIN	1,049,730	
SALES & MARKETING	328,523	
RESEARCH & DEVELOPMENT	26,000	
GENERAL & ADMINISTRATIVE	203,520	
OPERATING EXPENSE	558,043	
INCOME FROM OPERATIONS	491,687	
NET INTEREST INCOME	(100,000)	
INCOME TAXES	113,587	
NET INCOME	$ 278,100	C

Balance Sheet

Assets

CASH	$ 488,462	
ACCOUNTS RECEIVABLE	454,760	
INVENTORIES	414,770	
PREPAID EXPENSES	0	
CURRENT ASSETS	1,357,992	
OTHER ASSETS	0	
FIXED ASSETS @ COST	1,750,000	
ACCUMULATED DEPRECIATION	78,573	
NET FIXED ASSETS	1,671,427	
TOTAL ASSETS	3,029,419	D

Liabilities & Equity

ACCOUNTS PAYABLE	$ 236,297	
ACCRUED EXPENSES	26,435	
CURRENT PORTION OF DEBT	100,000	
INCOME TAXES PAYABLE	113,587	
CURRENT LIABILITIES	476,319	
LONG-TERM DEBT	800,000	
CAPITAL STOCK	1,550,000	
RETAINED EARNINGS	203,100	
SHAREHOLDERS' EQUITY	1,753,100	E
TOTAL LIABILITIES & EQUITY	$ 3,029,419	

$$\text{Return on Assets} = \frac{Net\ Income}{Inventory} = \frac{B}{D} = \frac{\$251,883}{\$3,029,419} = 8\%$$

$$\text{Return on Equity} = \frac{Net\ Income}{Shareholders'Equity} = \frac{A}{E} = \frac{\$251,883}{\$1,726,883} = 15\%$$

$$\text{Return on Sales} = \frac{Net\ income}{Net\ Sales} = \frac{C}{A} = \frac{\$251,883}{\$3,055,560} = 8\%$$

Leverage Ratios:

Leverage ratios (also called "safety" ratios) measure how much of the company's assets are financed with debt. These ratios:

1. Reveal the extent of a company's "equity cushion" available to absorb losses, and
2. Measure the company's ability to meet its short-term and long-term debt obligations.

Leverage is the use of other people's money ("OPM") to generate profits for yourself. By substituting debt (other people's money) for equity dollars (your own money), you hope to make more profit per dollar that you invest than if you had provided all the financing yourself.

Thus, debt "leverages" your investment. The leverage ratios measure the extent of this leverage. The reason leverage ratios are also called safety ratios is that too much leverage in a business can be risky ... unsafe to lenders. A lender may think of these ratios as safety ratios, while a business owner may think of them as leverage ratios.

Use too little financial leverage and the firm is not reaching its maximum profit potential for its investors. On the other hand, too much debt and the firm may be taking on a high risk of being unable to pay interest and principal if business conditions worsen. Using just the right amount of debt is a management call.

Debt-to-Equity Ratio This very important ratio shows how much debt the company has relative to its investor equity. Lenders want a low level of debt relative to the company's equity. It gives them comfort that the loan can be repaid (even out of shareholders' equity) if things go bad for the company.

Debt Ratio This ratio measures the amount of debt relative to the total assets of the corporation. The debt ratio is a measure of operating leverage.

AppleSeed's debt-to-equity and its debt ratio are relatively conservative for its type of business.

Appleseed Enterprises, Inc. — Leverage Ratios

Balance Sheet

Assets

CASH	$ 488,462
ACCOUNTS RECEIVABLE	454,760
INVENTORIES	414,770
PREPAID EXPENSES	0
CURRENT ASSETS	1,357,992
OTHER ASSETS	0
FIXED ASSETS @ COST	1,750,000
ACCUMULATED DEPRECIATION	78,573
NET FIXED ASSETS	1,671,427
TOTAL ASSETS	3,029,419 **A**

Liabilities & Equity

ACCOUNTS PAYABLE	$ 236,297
ACCRUED EXPENSES	26,435
CURRENT PORTION OF DEBT	100,000 **B**
INCOME TAXES PAYABLE	113,587
CURRENT LIABILITIES	476,319
LONG-TERM DEBT	800,000 **C**
CAPITAL STOCK	1,550,000
RETAINED EARNINGS	203,100
SHAREHOLDERS' EQUITY	1,753,100 **D**
TOTAL LIABILITIES & EQUITY	$ 3,029,419

$$\textbf{Debt to Equity} = \frac{Current + LT\ Debt}{Shareholders'Equity} = \frac{B+C}{D} = \frac{\$100,000 + \$800,000}{\$1,726,883} = 0.5$$

$$\textbf{Debt Ratio} = \frac{Current + LT\ Debt}{Total\ Assets} = \frac{B+C}{A} = \frac{\$100,000 + \$800,000}{\$3,029,419} = 0.3$$

Financial Ratios by Industry:

Just looking at a single ratio does not really tell you much about a company. You also need a standard of comparison, a benchmark. There are three principal benchmarks used in ratio analysis.

Financial ratios can be compared to:

1. Ratios of the company in prior years,
2. Ratios of another company in the same industry, and
3. Industry average ratios.

History The first useful benchmark is history. How has the ratio changed over time? Are things getting better or worse for the company? Is gross margin going down, indicating that costs are rising faster than prices can be increased? Are receivable days lengthening, indicating there are payment problems?

Competition The second useful ratio benchmark is comparing a specific company ratio with that of a competitor. For example, if a company has a significantly higher return on assets than a competitor, it strongly suggests that that company manages its resources better.

Industry The third type of benchmark is an industry-wide comparison. Industry-wide average ratios are published and can give an analyst a good starting point in assessing a particular company's financial performance.

Mostly, companies in the same industry have similar ratios, financial characteristics of the business that are primarily related to capital needs and available sources. However, some companies do perform better than others, and you can see it in their favorable financial ratios.

The table on the facing page, shows common ratio averages in various industries and what values are considered better or worse.

Favorable Liquidity Ratios
Apparel Manufacturing
Information Technology
Unfavorable Liquidity Ratios
Insurance
Software
High liquidity provides flexibility for a business and also makes it possible to ride out hard times.

∼

Favorable Asset Ratios
Airlines
Retail
Unfavorable Asset Ratios
Pharmaceuticals
Telecommunications
Some industries just must use (and thus need) a lot of capital. Growth could be limited without an easily available capital source.

∼

Favorable Profitability Ratios
Software
Hotels
Unfavorable Profitability Ratios
Supermarkets
Chemicals
There is not much room for error in businesses with low profitability. Companies with high profitability often have proprietary technology that makes it possible to charge high prices.

∼

Favorable Leverage Ratio
Software
Unfavorable Leverage Ratios
Supermarkets
Leverage comes with debt. Higher leverage can provide higher profitability but with high risk.

Financial Ratios by Industry

INDUSTRY	LIQUIDITY RATIO CURRENT RATIO	ASSET RATIOS INVENTORY TURN High Favorable	RECEIVABLE DAYS Low Favorable	ASSET TURN High Favorable	GROSS MARGIN High Favorable	PROFITABILITY RATIOS RETURN ON SALES High Favorable	RETURN ON ASSETS High Favorable	RETURN ON EQUITY High Favorable	LEVERAGE RATIO DEBT TO EQUITY
AIRLINES	1.9% ↗	16 ↗	23 ↗	0.8	59% ↗	3.5%	6.0%	11.6%	1.9
APPAREL MANUFACTURING	2.1 ↘	5 ↘	85	1.1	41%	1.8% ↗	5.7%	3.0%	0.9
BANKING	0.8	n/a	n/a	n/a	n/a	n/a	2.0% ↗	2.1% ↗	6.4 ↗
BROADCASTING	0.8	12	99	0.4	84% ↗	5.0%	5.7%	9.9%	1.2
CHEMICALS	1.0	9	91	0.5	19% ↘	1.7% ↗	4.3%	3.4%	1.9
COMPUTER MANUFACTURING	1.0	15 ↗	113 ↗	0.5	37%	8.2%	7.5%	11.0%	0.6
CONSTRUCTION EQUIPMENT	1.5	6	166 ↗	0.6	29% ↘	8.9%	10.0% ↗	21.2% ↗	2.0
FFINANCIAL SERVICES	1.1	n/a	n/a	0.1 ↗	40%	7.7%	2.2% ↗	6.9%	2.1
HOSPITAL & HEALTH CARE	1.7	13	58	1.0	n/a	3.8%	8.1%	4.6%	1.1
HOTELS	1.0	n/a	36	0.1 ↗	87% ↗	9.0%	11.3% ↗	16.2% ↗	2.5
INFORMATION TECHNOLOGIES	2.1 ↗	6	73	0.5	61%	3.4%	2.3% ↗	4.5%	0.6
INSURANCE	0.4 ↘	n/a	n/a	0.2 ↗	41%	3.4%	2.2% ↗	4.5%	0.6
OIL & GAS EXPLORATION	0.8	28 ↗	74	0.4	41%	11.8%	9.0%	11.5%	0.6
PHARMACEUTICLES	1.1	4 ↘	152 ↗	0.4	48%	11.4%	7.5%	10.5%	0.8
RESTAURANTS	0.8	18 ↗	36	0.7	55%	5.4%	8.7%	14.0% ↗	1.0
RETAIL	0.7	7	15 ↗	1.7 ↗	25% ↘	7.5%	9.0%	14.1% ↗	0.8
SOFTWARE	0.5 ↗	26 ↗	83	0.4	68% ↗	16.9% ↗	12.4% ↗	19.5% ↗	0.4 ↗
SUPERMARKETS	1.0	13	14 ↗	2.2 ↗	28% ↘	1.0% ↗	5.4%	7.5%	0.8
TELLICOMUNICATIONS	0.8	4 ↘	122 ↘	0.3 ↗	88% ↗	5.5%	4.6%	4.2%	0.9
UTILITIES	1.1	15	32	0.6	33%	6.0%	2.9%	1.7% ↘	1.8

FAVORABLE ↗   LESS FAVORABLE ↘

Note: Sometimes a high number for a ratio can demonstrate better performance; sometimes a low number is better. Here we have used up ↗ arrows and down ↘ arrows to indicate which industries have a better or worse average performance for a ratio type.

Adapted from *Almanac of Business & Industrial Ratios* by Leo Troy.

Chapter 14.
Alternative Accounting Policies

Various alternative accounting policies and procedures are completely legal and widely used but may result in significant differences in the values reported on a company's financial statements. Some people would call this chapter's topic "creative accounting."

All financial statements are prepared in accordance with Generally Accepted Accounting Principles (GAAP). But within these accepted principles are a variety of alternative policies and procedures that may be used.

Selection of one policy over another can depend upon management's judgment and upon circumstance. The financial books can look quite different depending upon which policy is chosen. These alternative accounting policies can be used creatively by management as the "cosmetics" of financial reporting.

The table below shows major alternative accounting policies in use today. Management, with assistance from their auditors, will select from this list of acceptable accounting principles those that best suit their particular enterprise and management philosophy. Generally, the alternative policies can be grouped into two main categories: those that are financially "aggressive" and those that are financially "conservative."

Conservative Policies

So-called conservative accounting policies tend to understate profits and lower inventory and other asset values. Many accountants think these actions take on a "conservative" posture for the business. Few expenses are capitalized, that is, (a) placing asset value on the *Balance Sheet* and amortizing it over time, rather than (b) classifying it as an expense immediately. Thus, expenses are higher and profits are lower in the short term, but more "solid" or conservative in the long term.

Aggressive Policies

The so-called aggressive accounting policies tend to inflate earnings and raise asset values, thus taking an "aggressive" financial posture. Reserves and allowances are low, which keeps profits high.

Alternative Accounting Policies and Procedures

ACCOUNTING POLICY	AGGRESSIVE APPLICATION	CONSERVATIVE APPLICATION
Revenue Recognition	At Sale *(Some risk remains)*	After Sale *(Buyer carries all Risk)*
Cost of Goods & Inventory Valuation Method	FIFO *(First-in, first-out)*	LIFO *(Last-in, first-out)*
Depreciation Method	Accelerated *(Faster)*	Straight-Line *(Slower)*
Reserves & Allowances *(Warranty, Bad Debt, Returns)*	Low Estimates *(Higher profit now)*	High Estimates *(Higher profit later)*
Contingent Liabilities	Footnote only *(Postpone bad news)*	Accrue When Known *(Take losses now)*
Advertising & Marketing Expenditures	Capitalize *(Write-off later)*	Expense *(Write-off now)*

Financial Statements

These selections of policy can lead to negative surprises, such as if returns or repairs were seriously under-estimated.

Neither conservative nor aggressive policies are "right" or "wrong." They are just different ways of viewing the same financial information. However, it is important when reviewing financial statements with the purpose of determining a company's financial condition, to understand the aggressive or conservative posture the company takes in compiling its books.

With conservative accounting policies, you can take comfort that the profits are real. With aggressive policies, profits may be overstated. *If, however, you see a company change its accounting policies from conservative to aggressive, watch out. This change may be a sign of big trouble ahead.*

GAAP does give management latitude to select certain accounting policies and procedures. However, these policies, once selected, must be used consistently and the year-to-year distortions are usually small. However, in periods of inflation, the difference between common inventory valuation methods can be large.

Inventory Valuation & Costing Methods

No, FIFO is not the name of a dog. It's one of the three methods that accountants may use to compute: (a) cost of goods sold for the *Income Statement* and (b) inventory value for the *Balance Sheet*.

Cost of goods sold is most often the single biggest deduction from sales revenue on the way to net profit. How best to value the inventory that makes up this large cost? GAAP offers three basic choices. In an inflationary period, or when costs of raw materials fluctuate, these three methods of inventory valuation will yield considerably different values. The three alternative valuation methods are:

Average Cost Method

Under the average cost method, the separate purchases of goods placed into inventory are summed to give the total inventory value and are averaged to give a cost of goods sold value. The average cost method is seldom used, offering no real convenience or added accuracy.

Effects of Inventory Valuation Method Choice on Inventory Valuation and Cost of Goods Sold (COGS)

	UNITS	PURCHASE PRICE	AVERAGE COST METHOD	LAST-IN, FIRST-OUT (LIFO)	FIRST-IN, FIRST-OUT (FIFO)
FIRST INVENTORY PURCHASE	1,000	$1,000			
SECOND INVENTORY PURCHASE	1,000	1,050			
THIRD INVENTORY PURCHASE	1,000	1,100			
FOURTH INVENTORY PURCHASE	1,000	1,150			
TOTAL INVENTORY	4,000	$4,300			
AVERAGE COST PER 1,000 UNITS		$1,075			
SALES REVENUE *(1,000 units @ $1.50)*			$1,500	$1,500	$1,500
COST OF GOODS SOLD			1,075	1,150	1,000
GROSS PROFIT			$ 425	$ 350	$ 500
STARTING INVENTORY VALUE			$4,300	$4,300	$4,300
LESS COST OF GOODS SOLD VALUE			1,075	1,150	1,000
ENDING INVENTORY VALUE			$3,225	$3,150	$3,300

Summary of FIFO vs. LIFO Financial Statement Effects

	LIFO	FIFO
COST OF GOODS	↑	↓
INVENTORY VALUE	↓	↑
PROFITS	↓	↑

FIFO Method

Under FIFO (first-in, first-out) methods of valuation, the costs of the earliest materials purchased are assigned to cost of goods sold and the costs of the more recent purchases are summed and allocated to yield ending inventory values.

This method conforms to the actual flow of goods in a factory with the most recent purchases placed at the back of the fridge, and also the oldest purchases placed in front to use before they spoil.

LIFO Method

Under the LIFO (last-in, first-out) method, costs of the latest purchases become cost of goods sold and the costs of the oldest purchases are assigned to inventory. When inventory costs are rising as in a period of inflation, using the FIFO method means higher profits (and higher taxes) than if the LIFO method were used.

The table on the previous page shows *Income Statement* and *Balance Sheet* effects of the three alternative inventory valuation and product costing methods in an inflationary period. Depending on the method used, gross profit can vary from a low of $350 with the LIFO method to a high of $500 with the FIFO method. The average cost method is in the middle of the muddle at $425 in gross profit.

All are "correct" values; they just result from applying different acceptable procedures. The table above summarizes the effects of FIFO and LIFO valuation.

While financial statements most often provide accurate, essential information, they do have limitations:

1. Some important corporate "assets" that are difficult to quantify (valued employees and loyal customers) are disregarded.

2. Only the historic values of tangible assets are presented, not current values.

3. Fallible estimates are made for many important items such as receivables collection, depreciation and the salability of inventory.

4. Profits shown on the *Income Sheet* and inventory values shown on the *Balance Sheet* can be significantly affected by accounting method choices.

Chapter 15.
Cooking the Books

The vast majority of audited financial statements are prepared fairly. They are assembled in accordance with GAAP and show sound fiscal controls and integrity of management. However, sometimes this is not the case and financial fraud is committed (and hidden): illegal payments made, assets misused, losses concealed, expenses under-reported, revenue over-recorded, and so forth.

The New Shorter Oxford English Dictionary has two definitions for the noun "cook." The first describes a person in the white hat behind the counter. The second definition is more appropriate to our discussion: "A person who falsifies or concocts something." So, the first cook *cooks* your lunch; the second cook *eats* your lunch.

"Cooking the books" means intentionally hiding or distorting the real financial performance or actual financial condition of a company.

~

This chapter will give you recipes for book-cooking. The goal here is not to make you able to prepare fraudulent financial statements by yourself. Leave this task to trained professionals. Rather, this discussion should make you better able to see the clues of fraud and remind you to be vigilant.

Managers most often cook the books for personal financial gain — to justify a bonus, to keep stock prices high and options valuable, or to hide a business's poor performance. The companies most likely to cook their books have weak internal controls and have a management of questionable character facing extreme pressure to perform.

Cooking is most often accomplished by moving items that should be on the *Income Statement* onto the *Balance Sheet* and sometimes vice versa. A variety of specific techniques can be used to raise or lower income, raise or lower revenue, raise or lower assets and liabilities, and thereby reach whatever felonious objective the businessperson desires. A simple method is outright lying by making fictitious transactions or ignoring required ones.

Cooking the books is very different from "creative accounting." It is creative to use accounting rules to best present your company in a favorable financial light. It is legal and accepted. Cooking the books is done for a deceptive purpose and is meant to defraud.

Income Statement Puffing up the *Income Statement* most often involves reporting some form of bogus sales revenue that results in increased profits. See *Box A* in the chart on the next page.

"Cooking the books" means intentionally hiding or distorting the real financial performance and/or financial condition of a company. Whether baked or pan-fried, this cooking is most often performed with a felonious purpose such as to defraud.

Techniques to Puff Up the Income Statement

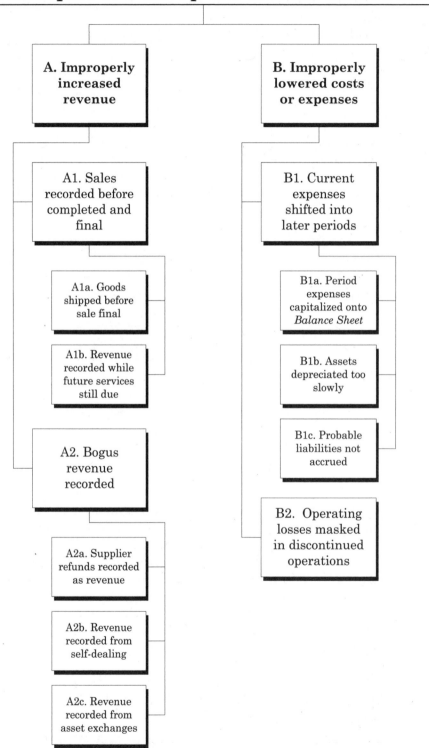

A. Improperly increased revenue

A1. Sales recorded before completed and final

A1a. Goods shipped before sale final

A1b. Revenue recorded while future services still due

A2. Bogus revenue recorded

A2a. Supplier refunds recorded as revenue

A2b. Revenue recorded from self-dealing

A2c. Revenue recorded from asset exchanges

B. Improperly lowered costs or expenses

B1. Current expenses shifted into later periods

B1a. Period expenses capitalized onto *Balance Sheet*

B1b. Assets depreciated too slowly

B1c. Probable liabilities not accrued

B2. Operating losses masked in discontinued operations

One of the simplest methods of cooking the books is padding the revenue; that is, recording sales before all the conditions required to complete a sale have occurred. The purpose of this action is to inflate sales and associated profits. A particularly creative technique is self-dealings such as increasing revenue by selling something to yourself *(Box A2b)*.

Revenue is appropriately recorded *only* after all these conditions are met:

1. An order has been received.

2. The actual product has been shipped.

3. There is little risk the customer will not accept the product.

4. No significant additional actions are required by the company.

5. Title has transferred and the purchaser recognizes his responsibility to pay.

The other common route to illegal reporting of increased profit is to lower expenses or to fiddle with costs. *(Box B)* A simple method to accomplish this deception involves shifting expenses from one period into another with the objective of reporting increased profits in the earlier period and hoping for the best in the later period.

Balance Sheet Most often both the *Balance Sheet* and the *Income Statement* are involved in cooking the books. A convenient cooking is exchanging assets with the purpose of inflating the *Balance Sheet* and showing a profit on the *Income Statement* as well! *(Box D1a)*

For example, a company owns an old warehouse, valued on the company books at $500,000, its original cost minus years of accumulated depreciation. In fact, the present value of the warehouse if sold would be 10 times its book value, or $5 million. The company sells the warehouse, books a $4.5 million profit and then buys a similar warehouse next door for $5 million.

Nothing has really changed. The company still has a warehouse, but the new one is valued on the books at its purchase price of $5 million instead of the lower depreciated cost of the original warehouse. The company has booked a $4.5 million gain, yet it has less cash on hand than it had before this sell-buy transaction.

Question: **How many sets of books does a company have?**

Answer: **Generally, companies keep *three different sets of books*, each serving a separate and legitimate purpose:**

1. One complete set of books for *financial reporting to the outside world* and to the owners of the business.

2. One modified set of financial statements focusing on *determining and defending tax liability*.

3. Other special presentation formats of financial information for management to use to *control the business operations*.

Techniques to Sweeten the Balance Sheet

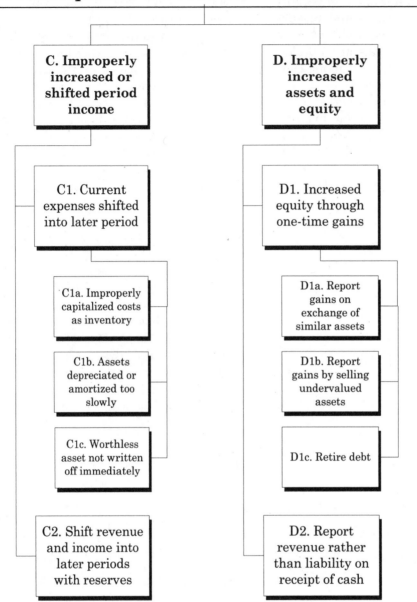

C. Improperly increased or shifted period income

D. Improperly increased assets and equity

C1. Current expenses shifted into later period

D1. Increased equity through one-time gains

C1a. Improperly capitalized costs as inventory

D1a. Report gains on exchange of similar assets

C1b. Assets depreciated or amortized too slowly

D1b. Report gains by selling undervalued assets

C1c. Worthless asset not written off immediately

D1c. Retire debt

C2. Shift revenue and income into later periods with reserves

D2. Report revenue rather than liability on receipt of cash

Why would a company exchange one asset for a very similar one ... especially if it cost them cash and an unnecessary tax payment? The only "real" effect of this transaction is the sale of an undervalued asset and booking of a one-time gain. If the company reports this gain as part of "operating income," the books have been cooked — income has been deceptively inflated. If the company purports that this one-time capital gain is reoccurring operating income, it has misrepresented the earning capacity of the enterprise.

~

Just as some people cheat on their tax returns, thinking they will not be caught, some companies "cook the books," hoping auditors and regulators will not catch them either.

Like "borrowing" $20 from the till until payday, and then not being able to repay the "loan," small illegalities can snowball into major fraud.

Remember, an auditor's job is only to systematically review the company's accounting and control procedures and then sample its business transactions to see whether appropriate policies and procedures are being followed in practice. But it is quite possible for a dedicated and corrupt management to mask transactions and deceive these auditors.

All fast-growing companies must eventually slow down. Managers may be tempted to use accounting gimmicks to give the appearance of continued growth. Managers at weak companies may want to mask how bad things really are. Managers may want that last bonus before bailing out. Maybe there are unpleasant loan covenants that would be triggered but can be avoided by cooking the books. A company can just be sloppy and have poor internal controls.

One key to watch for is management changing from a conservative accounting policy to a less conservative one, for example changing from LIFO to FIFO methods of inventory valuation or from expensing to capitalizing certain marketing expenses, easing of revenue recognition rules, lengthening amortization or depreciation periods.

Changes like these should be a red flag. There may be valid reasons for these accounting policy changes, but not many. Be warned.

Accounting Errors

A step less than fraudulent, but still bad, is an "error of principle," an accounting mistake in which an entry is recorded in the incorrect account, violating the fundamental principles of accounting. An error of principle is a procedural error, meaning that the value recorded was the correct value but placed incorrectly. An error of principle is different than failing to record the item in question ("error of omission") or recording the wrong value in the correct account ("error of commission"). These errors are referred to as input errors.

The complexities of business transactions, along with the human component of accounting, can lead to errors. Discovering these can take some detective work. Some errors can be considered a material error because it can affect how decisions are made. If a company discovers an error after reporting its finances and determines that the error significantly impacts the report, it typically issues a restatement.

Section D.
Business Expansion:
Strategy, Risk, and Capital

About This Section

Our startup enterprise has done well. The investors are happy with our progress and we can feel change jingle in our pockets. "AppleSeed" has become a well-recognized brand name and the demand for our products is strong.

It was not easy to raise the initial capital for our risky startup venture. Nevertheless, Great Aunt Lillian saw our potential, placed a bet and financed us. Now even Great Uncle Fred, skeptical before, is happy with their investment. In fact, at the company picnic he asked me to see him first if we needed money to expand!

Yes, we have come to that happy time in the history of a business — time to ask the questions: "Should we expand?" And if so, "How?" The rest of this book will deal with AppleSeed Enterprises' rapid growth.

Historical vs. Proforma Financials

Previous chapters show how to report a company's *historical* financial performance. Now we are going to look forward and predict the future. We will learn how to analyze alternative investment choices and make plans that will shape our company's future success.

In our analysis of future investment alternatives, we will be preparing so-called *proforma* financial statements. Proforma means "for form."

Proforma financial statements are in the exact same format as regular historical statements but are used to model the expected future performance of the company. Proforma financials (especially proforma cash flow statements) are useful tools to evaluate the impact of major capital investments by the company. They answer the question, "How might our financial future look if we make this investment?"

Qualitative & Quantitative Methods

The essence of business is to mobilize capital (money) to generate profit (more money). How successful we are often depends on making good capital investment decisions.

In this section, we discuss *qualitative* tools useful in analyzing business decisions: building decision trees, using strategic planning methods and understanding risk and uncertainty in any decision.

But it takes money to make money, and in the last chapter in this section, Ap-

"The chief determinant of what a company will become is the investments it makes today. **The generation and evaluation of creative investment proposals is far too important to be left to financial specialists; instead it is the ongoing responsibility of all managers throughout the organization."**

Prof. Robert C. Higgins
University of Washington
in *Analysis for Financial Management*

pleSeed Enterprises will sell additional equity and take on more debt to finance an aggressive expansion.

Then Section E will focus on the important *quantitative* tools (net present value (NPV), internal rate of return (IRR), and others) useful in selecting between alternative capital investments. Finally, in Chapter 22, we will take all that we have learned and apply it to AppleSeed Enterprises' business expansion.

Let's go! We will refocus and reconfirm our mission and vision of the future. We will discuss decision tree analysis, a structured way to assess the alternative pathways for AppleSeed's growth. Then we will select the best path to follow.

We will explore the strategic choices a business faces when investing for growth. No matter how good the proforma financial statements may look, a flawed strategy will lead to failure. We will look at the difference between risk and uncertainty, and how companies can deal with the potential negative consequences of their actions.

Finally, confident in our plans and in our future, we will raise capital by adding debt and additional equity to AppleSeed Enterprises' *Balance Sheet*.

Chapter 16.
Mission, Vision, Goals, Strategies, Actions, and Tactics

Developing optimal business strategies directed at reaching specific commercial and financial goals, is the highest level of planning and command in the organization.

We at AppleSeed Enterprises are going to make some important decisions. Sometimes deciding what to do is easy. Not much planning, analysis, or consultation is required to pick up a box of cornflakes on the way home from work. And we were running out of 1% milk anyway.

However, when a lot is riding on getting a business decision right, it is a good idea to be thoughtful and strategic. But what does strategy mean? How do we develop it?

Developing good strategy is a process. We ask some questions, test some assumptions, gather some information, look inward at our strengths and weaknesses, and look outward at our customers and the economic environment.

The process is "strategic" because we seek the best way to respond to our competitive environment given the resources available to us. The process is "planning" because we set goals and develop structured approaches to reach those goals. Strategic planning is a disciplined effort to produce fundamental decisions and actions that will shape and guide our organization toward our agreed-upon company goals.

- Strategy is systematically thinking things through and coming up with creative ways to reach business goals.

- Strategy is of the very highest importance to the success of the business and is thus the responsibility of top-level management.

- Strategy is always actionable. We plan and execute actions to implement strategy. Strategy is measurable and thus we will know if it works or not.

- Strategy is forward thinking. It is not about past actions but rather about shaping the future. However, strategy must also be in the moment and reflect the current environment facing the business.

- Strategy is systematic, realistic and inclusive. Strategy that is creative and unique will be more powerful.

- Strategy is constrained by the limited resources a company has available, but will optimally use all those available resources. Strategy capitalizes on a company's strengths but also will support its weaknesses.

Okay, got that! Now let's apply strategic thinking, strategic planning and strategic management to map a happy future for AppleSeed Enterprises.

Strategic Planning Hierarchy

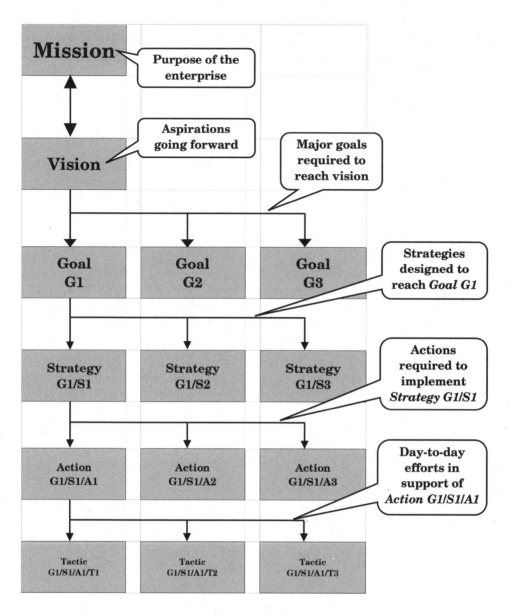

- Think of a company's **Mission**, **Vision**, and **Goals** as a hierarchy of *destinations*, and its **Strategies**, **Actions**, and **Tactics** as a hierarchy of *ways to get there*.

Strategic Planning Terms

- **Mission** The word *mission* comes from the Latin *missio,* meaning "sending away" a group to a foreign land and the business which the group is charged. A company's mission (or mission statement) describes the fundamental purpose of the organization or why we exist.

- **Vision** The word *vision* comes from the Old English word *witan,* meaning "to know," as in the power of anticipating that which will or may come to be. A company's vision is an expression of the business's aspirations going forward — what we desire to become.

- **Goals** The word goal comes from the Middle English word *gal,* meaning boundary; limit; the end point of a race. A company's goals are the three or four broad objectives the company sets for itself ... the key results to achieve.

- **Strategies** The word strategy comes from the Ancient Greek word *strategia*, meaning "office of general, command, generalship; to lead; to conduct." A company's strategies are high-level, long-term plans designed to accomplish specific goals. Each individual company goal may have several strategies required for implementation.

- **Actions** The word action comes from the Latin word *acto,* meaning "doing." Multiple coordinated actions are often required to best implement a strategy.

- **Tactics** The word tactic comes from the Greek word *taktikós,* meaning "fit for arranging or ordering." Tactics are day-to-day tasks that people in the company perform to accomplish an action in support of a strategy.

"Our plans miscarry because they have no aim. When a man does not know what harbor he is making for, no wind is the right wind."

Seneca the Younger
Roman philosopher and playwright, tutor and advisor of Nero

Let's apply these strategic planning terms and definitions to AppleSeed Enterprises. Ultimately, we'll answer the all-important question, "Are we doing the right things to reach our goals?" Then we can show our strategic plan to the Board of Directors to get their comments and sign-off on our plans for the future.

~

After a few meetings of the staff and some market research and then brainstorming sessions, this is what we have:

Mission Statement AppleSeed Enterprises' mission is to be a leading regional supplier of high-end specialty food products and provide a superior financial return to our shareholders.

Vision AppleSeed Enterprises' vision is to be recognized for its delicious and wholesome food products manufactured and marketed in an environmentally friendly manner.

Goal 1 Remain the premier supplier of gourmet applesauce in the region.

Goal 2 Become a premier supplier of other gourmet food products in the region.

Now, both of our goals will need separate strategies to make them real. Each of our strategies will need actions, and actions will need tactics to implement them. At each stage of the pyramid, we will assign responsibility, allocate resources, and measure results as we go forward.

Strategic planning is about predicting the future, and predicting the future is an inherently risky business, fraught with uncertainty. We will discuss business risk and uncertainty in the next chapter.

~

There are all sorts of cute techniques to assist managers in understanding their business environment and thinking strategically. Try a **SWOT** *analysis* (Strengths, Weaknesses, Opportunities and Threats), a **PEST** *analysis* (Political, Economic, Social and Technological) or a **STEER** analysis (Socio-cultural, Technological, Economic, Ecological and Regulatory). But don't get too carried away.

Chapter 17.
Risk and Uncertainty

AppleSeed Enterprises is planning for a major expansion. We will soon be making a significant investment with hope for a good return. However, things may go wrong. Ideally, we want a high return, but with a manageable and understood risk — that is what we call a "businessperson's risk."

Risk

What is risk? Can we understand the risks we face and take actions to lower them? A simple definition of risk is a business event that would generate a "negative surprise." A risk is something that we would regret if it occurred. In financial terms, risk is the probability of an investment's actual return being lower than expected.

We now have the two elements necessary to start us on a path of business risk management. How can we lower the potential financial downside of risk and/or lower the probability of its occurrence?

Risk can be both intrinsic (within ourselves) and extrinsic (from outside). Having to scrap a lot of product because of a quality problem is an intrinsic risk that could lead to very large business losses. A rival company unexpectedly introducing a competitive product that results in our lower sales revenue is an extrinsic risk.

If risk is the potential for a business loss, a business project may be deemed a high risk because either: (a) there is a high likelihood of a loss of any size, or (b) there is even a very small likelihood of a large loss. Almost every business action carries some degree of risk. High-risk actions require careful management because of their potential large negative consequences to the business.

Uncertainty

"Uncertainty" is different from risk. Uncertainty is not knowing what the future will bring. However, under the cloak of uncertainty, high risk can lurk. Thus, lowering uncertainty can lower risk too.

Uncertainty can be more dangerous than risk. Because we can often know the elements of risk, we can plan for risk and take measures to mitigate the negative consequences of risk. However, with uncertainty we are often flying blind. It is hard to lower uncertainty if you do not know what it is and thus what to do to lower it.

Threat

A threat is a potential event with a very low probability but a high negative impact. People buy insurance to protect themselves against threats such as their house burning down. Businesses can buy fire insurance too, but they cannot insure against an uncollectable debt caused by the business failure of their largest customer.

Note that specialized insurance instruments called "credit default swaps" were developed by the financial services industry to offer some protection against such unlikely, negative financial events as failure of a creditor. But as we now know (housing bubble crash), things have not gone very well with this type of insurance.

Bet Your Company Risk

Avoid taking a *"bet-your-company risk."* The potential negative consequences of such a risk are just too, too large. For example, a bet-your-company risk would be spending all your available resources on developing a risky new product. The company could fail if development were to be delayed or if sales were much lower than projected.

However, entrepreneurial companies usually must face *bet-your-company risks* as they start up and grow. Understanding and managing risk and uncertainty is especially important in these fledgling enterprises. Startups must be focused, innovative, responsive, and also very lucky to survive. Most often they are not that lucky, and they fail.

~

When planning AppleSeed's expansion we recognize that the future is uncertain and that financial projections are just that — projections. Our estimates of what may happen in the future are based on assumptions and on our ability to execute. Assumptions may prove not to be valid and future performance may not go according to plan. Sigh.

"The consequences of our actions are so complicated and so diverse, that predicting the future is a very difficult business indeed."

J.K. Rowling
British fantasy author of *Harry Potter and the Prisoner of Azkaban*

~

"The best way to predict the future is to invent it."

Alan Kay
American computer scientist known for his pioneering work on object-oriented programming and windowing graphical interface design

~

"It's tough making predictions, especially about the future."

attributed to **Yogi Berra**
American baseball player; actually, first said by **Niels Bohr**, Danish Nobel laureate

---

Chapter 18.
Making Decisions About
AppleSeed's Future

AppleSeed Enterprises' Board of Directors thinks that we can successfully expand our business and that now is a good time to do it. The Board has asked management — that's us — to prepare several alternative expansion plans for Board review.

The most astute member of the Board reminds us to think strategically. She recommends writing a strategic plan for the business and she counsels a judicious look at capital requirements and sources. First, however, we need to make some decisions.

Where do we want our company to be in five or 10 years? How will we get there from here? What level of risk are we comfortable with? How much money will we need to expand and where will we get it? What is our plan?

Let's generate ideas; let's brainstorm. Adding a new and complementary product line could be just the thing for us. Our trucks regularly deliver AppleSeed's gourmet applesauce to supermarkets and specialty stores around town. Adding more products on to the truck would be easy and economical. Gourmet potato chips could be a nice fit to increase our sales. We could buy that floundering, low-end potato chip company across town, Chips-R-Us, Inc., and then rebrand. Alternatively, we could just build a new factory from scratch.

Decisions, decisions! The question is how to expand our business. What follows are several useful methods to analyze AppleSeed's business expansion opportunities.

Decision Tree Analysis

Building a "decision tree" is a useful, thoughtful, and structured approach to making business decisions. A decision tree is an easy-to-understand graphic made up of a series of ordered forks (called nodes) that visualize a decision pathway. Drawing a decision tree is use-

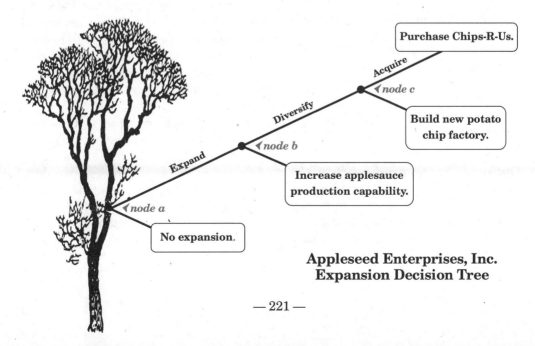

**Appleseed Enterprises, Inc.
Expansion Decision Tree**

ful in arraying all the key alternatives in a business decision. Then, just follow the decision tree to a decision!

Start at the lower-left base of the tree and follow through to each decision node. First, should AppleSeed expand, or not (*node a*)? Second, if we do expand, then should we diversify our product line beyond applesauce (*node b*)? Last, if we were to diversify into, say, potato chips, should we buy an existing company or build a new plant from scratch (*node c*)?

Each fork on the decision tree carries its own benefits and risks, costs, expenses and revenues. The decision tree structure helps us to systematically review pros and cons at each key stage of our decision.

Strategic Alternatives

Another way to analyze AppleSeed's expansion decision is to prepare a strategic alternatives table as shown here. AppleSeed could expand by selling new products or by entering new markets or both. These choices result in four strategic options:

PRODUCT LINE EXPANSION?

	NO	YES
MARKET EXPANSION? NO	*Option I.* Same product into the same market.	*Option II.* New product into the same market.
YES	*Option III.* Same product into a new market.	*Option IV.* New product into a new market.

Let's look at each option in detail:

Option I. Same product into the same market This option is the *status quo*. All growth would come from selling more of our applesauce into our existing markets. Because we want to expand rapidly, this option is not for us.

Option II. New product into the same market Expanding AppleSeed's product line to include gourmet potato chips and selling them through our existing retailers is an attractive and low-risk strategy. We are experts at manufacturing food products, and we understand the needs of our existing customers. Plus, they like us and would be happy to buy more products with our brand name.

Option III. Same product into a new market Selling into a new market could require costly new distribution methods. In addition, penetration could be time consuming. New markets can be risky. We lack experience with these customers.

Option IV. New product into a new market Simultaneously entering a new market with a new product is perhaps the riskiest of our four potential strategies, carrying the uncertainties of both the risks of product development and sales.

Overall, **Option II** seems to make the most sense for AppleSeed Enterprises, Inc. Potato chips it is!

Make vs. Buy Decision

Now, by expanding into a new product line, we will face a standard "make versus buy" strategic choice. See node c on the decision tree. Should we build our gourmet potato chip factory from scratch or should we buy an existing concern? We hear that a low-end potato chip company across town, Chips-R-Us, Inc., is not doing well and may be for sale for the cheap.

Purchase Alternative If we were to buy an existing company, we would have to refurbish their equipment to make our high-end product, but the cost would be less than starting from scratch. Chips-R-Us' capacity is not what we would want in the long term but would be adequate for a couple of years, and then we could expand.

"You will either step forward into growth or you step back into safety."

Abraham Maslow
American psychologist noted for his concept of the "hierarchy of human needs"

"Greenfield" Alternative Apple-Seed could start from scratch and build a new plant (on an empty "greenfield" site) with all new machinery. It will take a little longer to get going than if we bought Chips-R-Us, but the new plant would be perfect. How should we decide whether to build from scratch or make the acquisition?

Well, let's prepare some proforma cash flow statements that will allow us to compare the financial returns of the two alternatives under consideration. We will need to consider the dollar amounts and timing of a series of cash investments and the ultimate returns on these investments.

In Section E, we will review quantitative tools to help us and the Board of Directors compare the *purchase option* versus the *greenfield* option for Apple-Seed's expansion into potato chip manufacture and sales. Regardless of which option we choose, AppleSeed will need more capital to proceed. So, in the next chapter we will look at available sources and associated costs of new capital.

Chapter 19.
Sources and Costs of Capital

We've decided on an expansion strategy. But, AppleSeed does not have enough cash on hand to finance either an acquisition or major expansion of its business. However, we do have a very solid *Balance Sheet* with a 0.5 debt-to-equity ratio. Total debt is only one-half of our equity. (See the discussion of liquidity ratios on page 190.)

Our preliminary analysis of cash flows shows that AppleSeed will need $2 million for additional property, plant and equipment, plus more working capital to finance the expansion. We'll discuss how we prepared these projections in Chapter 22.

We are on good terms with the local bank. We could take on additional debt. Also, our venture capital investors have offered to purchase more stock in AppleSeed, that is, if the price is right.

More Debt for AppleSeed?

Banks will not lend unless they are almost positive that we will be able to repay what we owe. The amount of equity capital (stock) in the business acts as a safety cushion for the bank. The stockholders will lose everything before the bank would lose a penny. In general, debt is a cheap form of financing — if you can get it.

So, what will debt financing actually cost AppleSeed? Banks set their interest rate on loans with two components. They add the current "risk free" lending return from government bonds to a "risk premium" based on how risky they judge the company to be. For example, if government bonds are yielding 4% and our friendly loan officer sees us as a moderate risk justifying an additional 4% as a risk premium, then our total interest rate will be 8% for a loan.

More Equity for AppleSeed?

On page 178, we asked the question "What's the Business Worth?" The answer was only of academic importance for AppleSeed back then. Now things are different, and valuation is important. We want to sell more stock to help finance AppleSeed's expansion. But how much stock and at what price? The money raised will be added to AppleSeed's *Balance Sheet* and new shares will be issued.

We meet with our friendly venture capitalist and she says:

"We like what you have done and we can support your expansion plans. We're prepared to buy more stock, investing an additional $800,000 at a pre-money valuation of $2.5 million (and thus a post-money valuation of $3.3 million)."

Say what? Pre-money? Post-money? We mumble, "thanks and we'll get back to you." The next step is to crack an entrepreneurial finance textbook to figure out what our friendly VC is talking about.

Pre-Money Valuation

It all turns out to be rather simple. AppleSeed currently has 200,000 shares outstanding. (See Transaction 1 on page 91.) We own 50,000 founders' shares that we got for cheap at $1.00 per share. Our venture investors own 150,000 shares for which they paid $10.00 per share.

Currently, a conservative valuation for the company (based on a 12 times earnings multiple) would be about $3 million, or about $15.00 per share (computed as a $3.0 million value divided by 200,000 shares outstanding). This $3.0 million total value and $15.00 per share is what is meant as the "pre-money" valuation of the company, — the company's total estimated value before the sale of additional stock.

Post-Money Valuation

We're looking to raise $800,000 in new equity capital. Right after we raise this amount and place it into the company coffers (in our bank account and on the *Balance Sheet*), the so-called "post-money" value of the company will be:

$3,000,000 pre-money company value

+ 800,000 new investment

$3,800,000 post-money company value

Total pre-money and post-money valuations are intuitive. The post-money value of the company is just the pre-money value plus the amount of new money raised.

Now we come to the real point of negotiation with our friendly venture capitalist. How many new shares of stock does she get for investing $800,000 in AppleSeed new equity? And then, importantly, how much of the company will we still own after the financing?

Dilution

Remember, our Ms. Venture Capitalist has offered us $800,000 in new equity at a pre-money valuation of $2.5 million. We think that her valuation is on the low side and counter with an offer to issue stock with a $3.5 million pre-money valuation. Now we need to compute how many new shares we would issue to close this deal. We can determine how "dilutive" this offering will be to our ownership percentage. Dilution means how much less as a percentage of the total company we will own after we issue more shares.

Of the current 200,000 shares of stock outstanding for AppleSeed, we own 50,000 shares and the venture capitalists own 150,000 shares. Thus, we own 25% of the company and they own 75%. After the company issues more shares to the venture capitalists, we will still own our original 50,000 shares, but they will own 150,000 shares plus however many new shares the company needs to issue to induce the venture capitalists to trade the new stock for $800,000 in capital.

The negotiation we are having with our venture capitalist is over what pre-market valuation of the company to be used in computing the share price of the new offering. Look at the following table to see how pre-market valuation and the offering share price will affect both our and the venture capitalist's percentage ownership. (Note, the pre-money share price and the post-money share price are always the same. It is just how the math works.)

Equity Ownership & Dilution at Several Pre-Money Valuations

	PRE-OFFERING	DEAL A	DEAL B	DEAL C	DEAL D
INITIAL SHARES	200,000	200,000	200,000	200,000	200,000
PROPOSED PRE-MONEY VALUATION		$2,500,000	$3,000,000	$3,500,000	$4,000,000
SHARE PRICE (PRE- & POST-MONEY)		$12.50	$15.00	$17.50	$20.00
EQUITY $ TO BE RAISED		$800,000	$800,000	$800,000	$800,000
NEW SHARES TO BE ISSUED		64,000	53,333	45,714	40,000
+ OUR SHARES (INITIAL)	50,000	50,000	50,000	50,000	50,000
+ INVESTORS' SHARES (INITIAL)	150,000	150,000	150,000	150,000	150,000
+ NEW INVESTOR SHARES		64,000	53,333	45,714	40,000
= TOTAL SHARES		264,000	253,333	245,714	240,000
OUR % OWNERSHIP	25.0%	18.9%	19.7%	20.3%	20.8%

~

After much toing-and-froing, we split the value difference and agree on a share price of $15.00 with a $3.0 million pre-money value of the company. See details of the DEAL B in the table. In Transaction 32 on the following pages, we will issue stock and negotiate a line of credit.

Cost of Equity Capital

We know that the additional debt will cost AppleSeed interest at an 8% annual rate. But what does selling more equity cost? Well, there is no explicit "interest" rate attached to common stock, but venture investors do expect a very good return on their investment.

Before we closed the deal for the additional expansion equity, we did ask our venture capitalist what return she was expecting. She said she would be happy with a similar return to that received in the original investment. Investors paid $10.00 per share originally and we have estimated that the share price has increased to about $15.00 in two years. Therefore, this increase in value represents about a 22.5% annual return.

A 22.5% annual return is a lot higher than the 8% interest that the bank requires. But then, equity investors are taking a much higher risk. Note also that the bank would not have lent us money if we had not raised enough additional equity to keep our debt-to-equity ratio low and lowered the risk that the bank would lose capital if we were to default.

Weighted Average Cost of Capital

Most companies have several types and sources of capital. AppleSeed has both equity and debt in its capital structure, each costing a different amount. When making capital investment decisions it is useful to compute the "weighted average cost of capital" considering all the capital sources that the company employs.

See the capital structure table on this page. After the financing, 60% of AppleSeed's capital is equity with an estimated cost of capital of 22.5%. Further, 40% of AppleSeed's capital comes from debt, with half at an interest rate of 10% (mortgage rate from Transaction 3 on page 95) and the other half at 8% for the proposed new line of credit. Note that because interest is tax deductible as a business expense, the effective cost of debt capital is lower by the 34% expected tax savings (the 10% rate becomes a 6.6% cost; the 8% rate becomes a 5.3% cost).

AppleSeed's weighted average cost of capital (abbreviated WACC) is calculated by "weighting" the individual capital source costs by their percentage in the company's total capital structure.

Thus,

60% x 22.5%	=	13.5%	cost of equity
21% x 6.6%	=	1.3%	mortgage cost
19% x 5.3%	=	1.0%	credit line cost
100%		15.8%	WACC

We will see in the next section that this 15.8% return should be a minimum target for our expansion investments.

AppleSeed Enterprises Capital Structure Pre- & Post-Financing

	CAPITAL AS OF TRANSACTION 31 *(page 175)*	PROPOSED NEW FINANCING	TOTAL AFTER NEW FINANCING	% OF TOTAL CAPITAL
+ SHAREHOLDERS' EQUITY	$1,726,883	$800,000	$2,526,883	60%
+ MORTGAGE OUTSTANDING	$900,000		$900,000	21%
+ NEW CREDIT LINE		$800,000	$800,000	19%
= TOTAL CAPITAL	$2,626,883	$1,600,000	$4,226,883	100%
DEBT-TO-EQUITY RATIO	0.5		0.7	

Transaction 32. — Finance Expansion

Income Statement

NET SALES	$	-
COST OF GOODS SOLD		-
GROSS MARGIN		-
SALES & MARKETING		-
RESEARCH & DEVELOPMENT		-
GENERAL & ADMINISTRATIVE		-
OPERATING EXPENSE		-
INCOME FROM OPERATIONS		-
NET INTEREST INCOME		-
INCOME TAXES		-
NET INCOME	$	-

Cash Flow Statement

BEGINNING CASH BALANCE	$	0
CASH RECEIPTS		-
CASH DISBURSEMENTS		-
CASH FLOW FROM OPERATIONS		-
PP&E PURCHASE		-
NET BORROWINGS		100,000	**2** B
INCOME TAXES PAID		0
SALE OF CAPITAL STOCK		800,000	**1** B
ENDING CASH BALANCES	$	900,000

Balance Sheet

Assets

CASH	**3** $	900,000
ACCOUNTS RECEIVABLE		-
INVENTORIES		-
PREPAID EXPENSES		0
CURRENT ASSETS		900,000
OTHER ASSETS		0
FIXED ASSETS @ COST		-
ACCUMULATED DEPRECIATION		-
NET FIXED ASSETS		-
TOTAL ASSETS		900,000

Liabilities & Equity

ACCOUNTS PAYABLE	$	-
ACCRUED EXPENSES		-
CURRENT PORTION OF DEBT		100,000	**2** A
INCOME TAXES PAYABLE		-
CURRENT LIABILITIES		100,000
LONG-TERM DEBT		-
CAPITAL STOCK		800,000	**1** A
RETAINED EARNINGS		-
SHAREHOLDERS' EQUITY		800,000
TOTAL LIABILITIES & EQUITY	$	900,000

T32. Finance expansion! Sell 53,333 shares of Appleseed's common stock ($1 par value) for $15 per share and draw down $100,000 from a new line of credit.

This stock sale transaction is similar to that shown in Transaction 1. We have exchanged a percentage ownership in the company for capital.

In that transaction the stock price was only $10.00 per share, and thus for every $100,000 we raised we exchanged 10,000 shares of stock worth almost 5% of the company.

Because the stock price is higher now at $15.00 per share, we will only transfer 6,666 shares (2.6% of the company) to raise that same $100,000.

Flush with this new equity and to add some borrowing flexibility, we negotiated a line of credit with the local bank.

A line of credit is a flexible, short-term business loan where the bank agrees that AppleSeed can borrow (a "draw down") up to a prearranged maximum loan balance, but only if and when the money is needed. Interest is not charged on the part of the line of credit that is unused, and money is available without having to reapply every time we draw down money from the line.

Transaction: Our friendly venture capitalist has happily agreed to finance our expansion into gourmet potato chip manufacture. She purchases 53,333 shares of common stock at $15.00 per share for a total of $799,995 and throws in a $5 bill to make our accounting easier.

Our friendly banker is impressed that we were able to sell more stock and offers us a line of credit that matches the $800,000 additional equity we raised. Interest is paid of 0.666% per month (8% per year) on the outstanding balance only. We draw down $100,000 to seal the deal.

① (1A) Issuing stock creates a liability for the company. Apple-Seed "owes" the new stockholders a portion of its assets, so increase CAPITAL STOCK on the *Balance Sheet* by $800,000.
(1B) In the *Cash Flow Statement* add the $800,000 from this stock sale to SALE OF CAPITAL STOCK.

② (2A) We have established an $800,000 line of credit but have only taken down $100,000 to-date. Thus, add this amount to CURRENT PORTION OF DEBT in the liabilities section of the *Balance Sheet*. (2B) Add in the *Cash Flow Statement* this $100,000 as NET BORROWINGS.

③ The total of $900,000 in cash received from the stock sales plus new borrowings is added to CASH on the *Balance Sheet*.

Section E.
Making Good Business Investment Decisions

About This Section

Capital investment decisions are among the most important that management can make. Often capital is a company's scarcest resource, and using our capital wisely is essential for success. Capital investments are long-term bets to build a better future. More than any other business action, capital investment decisions will define the company and its ultimate value.

Faced with limited capital resources, management must decide which capital projects are economically feasible. Management must select projects that will contribute the most to increasing the company's value. This process of evaluating, comparing, and selecting projects is called "capital budgeting."

Budgeting

Budget, from the French *bougette*, or purse, refers to a list of all planned expenses and revenues. It is a plan for saving and spending.

~

Capital budgeting is a systematic approach to determining whether a company's planned major capital investments are worth pursuing. Capital budgeting is concerned with the justification of capital expenditures. Capital budgeting analysis can provide a rationale to select between alternative projects by answering the question "Which proposed project will most increase the company's value over time?"

~

This section will introduce you to the quantitative tools necessary to make good capital investment decisions. Then in the last chapter, Chapter 22, we will apply all this new knowledge to evaluate our expansion plans and to prepare a capital budget for AppleSeed Enterprises.

Long-term projects usually spend cash (i.e., negative cash flow) early in the project's lifetime and harvest rewards (i.e., positive cash flow) later. Different projects can have very different cash flows both in dollar amounts and in timing. To compare project values, we will use numeric techniques that consider the "time value of money."

First, the analysis requires estimating the size and timing of all incremental cash flows from the project. These future cash flows are then "discounted" to estimate their *present value (PV)*. These present values (both investments and returns) are then summed to get the so-called *net present value (NPV)* of the project in today's dollars. NPV is the estimated value added to the company by executing the project. Generally, the project

---

But beware! Having a quantitative basis for evaluating business decisions can provide objectivity. However, the rigid methodologies used can force potentially flawed assumptions and projections that will compromise the analysis. Just because resultant numbers look precise and accurate does not mean they are meaningful. Don't forget the maxim *"garbage in; garbage out."*

---

that has the highest NPV is selected to go forward.

A *discount rate* is used in NPV calculations. This rate is like an interest rate, but in reverse. A commonly used discount rate for capital budgeting is the company's *weighted average cost of capital (WACC),* which considers the company's financing mix. An additional rate increment is added if the project carries a higher risk than that of the company as a whole. This discount rate is sometimes called the "hurdle rate," the company's minimum acceptable return on capital invested.

It is best to look at quantitative project evaluation tools as just one of several useful decision-making resources. Careful strategy selection, management intuition, and study of historic precedent go well with quantitative measures such as NPV in making capital budget decisions.

Just "eyeballing" a set of numbers provides as much guidance as an overly precise computation, especially when the required input variables are not predictable with much accuracy. Some practitioners have gone so far as to say that most detailed quantitative analysis is not as important as good management judgment and thoughtful strategy.

Using *both* quantitative and qualitative measures is important in making business decisions about the future of the company. However, no matter how good the "numbers" may look, sound strategies are absolutely essential. No matter how high the computed NPV for a capital project, if the company's basic strategies are defective, the capital project will fail to reach its goals.

Chapter 20.
Time Value of Money

Capital budgeting decisions require analyzing business cash flows often spanning years. Accounting for the *time value of money* is essential in these analyses. More on capital budgeting in Chapter 21.

~

"A bird in the hand (today) is worth two in the bush (tomorrow)." Now you know most of what you need to know about the time value of money. It is intuitive.

Everybody would rather have a dollar in his or her pocket today than to receive a dollar far into the future. Finance types say that today's dollar is worth more — that it has more value — than a dollar received tomorrow. The rest of this chapter will answer the questions "Why so?" and "How much?"

The three main reasons for this time difference in value are:

1. **Inflation** Inflation does reduce purchasing power (value) over time. With 5% per year inflation, a dollar received a year from today will only buy 95¢ worth of goods then.

2. **Risk** There is always the chance that the promise of a dollar in the future will not be met, and you will be out of luck. The risk could be low with a CD at an FDIC insured bank; or the risk could be high if it is your brother-in-law who is promising to repay a personal loan.

3. **Opportunity Cost** If you loan your dollar to someone else, you have lost the opportunity to use it yourself for a time. That opportunity has a value to you today that makes today's dollar worth more than tomorrow's.

The three concepts — inflation, risk and opportunity cost — are the drivers of *present value* (PV) and *future value* (FV) calculations used in capital budgeting.

The mathematics of present value and future value calculation are a bit more difficult than the addition and subtraction we have used in the *Balance Sheet, Income Statement* and *Cash Flow Statement*. However, if you only understand the concepts — but not all the math — you will still get 95% of the way to understanding.

There is a special vocabulary used to discuss capital budgeting and the time value of money. Just as with the three major financial statements, there are new words to learn (or perhaps, old words with new specific meanings). It is a necessary short ride and not all that complex.

All will become clear. *Trust me.*

Values, Rates and Time

Values are measured in currency. We will use U.S. dollars. Other places use different currency. Some interesting value types are present value, future value,

---

"A bird in the hand is worth two in the bush."

Proverb first found in English in
The Life of St. Katharine of Alexandria, John Capgrave, 1450

Present Value (PV) **Present value calculations are used in business to compare cash flows (cash spent and received) at different times in the future. Converting cash flows into present values puts these different investments and returns onto a common basis and makes capital budgeting analysis more meaningful and useful in decision-making.**

discounted value, terminal value, net present value and so forth. But note that in financial calculations spanning time, currency value can be looked at from two different perspectives: as so-called "nominal" dollars or as so-called "real" dollars.

Nominal dollars are just the actual amount spent in dollars taken out of your wallet. *Real dollars,* on the other hand, are adjusted for inflation.

Why bother calculating both? Well, when you take out inflation (i.e., convert from "nominal dollars" into "real dollars") the price difference becomes much more comparable and easier to explain. See Appendix A for more details.

~

Rates are measured in percentages and with an associated time period (for example, 5% per year). The period could be a month or a day or even continuous. Some interesting rates are *inflation rate, interest rate, discount rate,* and *hurdle rate.* Specialized rates include *internal rate of return, risk premium* and *return on investment*. Details follow.

Capital Budgeting

In capital budgeting, different projects require different investment and will have different returns over time. In order to compare projects "apples to apples" and "oranges to oranges" on a financial basis, we will need to convert their cash flows into a common and comparable form. That common form is *present value* (PV).

Simply put, a little bit of cash that is invested today followed by lots of cash returned soon would be a *really good* financial investment. However, lots of cash invested today followed by a little bit of cash returned in a long time would be a *bad* investment.

Capital budgeting analysis is as simple as that. All the complex *net present value* (NPV) and *internal rate of return* (IRR) calculations are just details. Nevertheless, details can be important.

In the next chapter we will take what we have learned and apply it to understanding net present value (NPV) analysis. It is the most powerful and widely used analytic technique in capital budgeting.

Summary: PV and FV

Present value (PV) is the current value of a future sum of money or stream of cash flows given a specified rate of return. Future cash flows are discounted at the discount rate, and the higher the discount rate, the lower the present value of the future cash flows. Determining the appropriate discount rate is the key to properly valuing future cash flows, whether they be earnings or obligations.

Present value is the concept that states an amount of money today is worth more than that same amount in the future. In other words, money received in the future is not worth as much as an equal amount received earlier.

Money not spent today could be expected to lose value in the future by some implied annual rate, which could be inflation or the rate of return if the money was invested. Calculating present value involves assuming that a specific rate of return could be earned on the funds over the time period

FV calculation allows investors to predict, with varying degrees of accuracy, the amount of profit that can be generated by different investments. The amount of growth generated by holding a given amount in cash will likely be different than if that same amount were invested in stocks, so the FV equation is used to compare multiple options.

Determining the FV of an asset can become complicated, depending on the type of asset. In addition, the FV calculation is based on the sometimes invalid assumption of a stable growth rate. If money is placed in a savings account with a guaranteed interest rate, then the FV is easy to determine accurately. However, investments in the stock market or other securities with a more volatile rate of return can present greater difficulty.

Equations?!

The equations on the following pages are not all that daunting. But if you are having trouble, just read the words and try to understand the concepts.

The actual manual computations can become cumbersome. But, Microsoft Excel spreadsheet functions make computation of PV and FV easy. Later in this chapter we will describe their use.

Present Value (PV) & Future Value (FV)

- The most commonly applied model of the "time value of money" is compound interest. *Compounding* is the process of computing the future value of money you have today given a certain interest rate.

- Use this formula to determine how much money **FV** *(future value)* you will have in your savings account after **y years** if you deposit an amount **PV** *(present value)* now and receive interest at a rate of **i** per year.

$$FV = PV \times (1 + i)^y$$

- So, if the amount you deposit **PV** is $100.00 and the interest rate **i** is 4% per year and you leave the money in the bank for **y** years (7), you will be able to withdraw a total of $131.59 in seven years as **FV**.

$$FV = \$100.00 \times (1 + 0.04)^7 = \$131.59$$

- Now, if you want to compute the present value **PV** of a future value **FV** to be received in **y years** using the discount rate of **d** *per year*, then you would rearrange the equation above as:

$$PV = \frac{FV}{(1 + d)^y}$$

- Note, *discounting* is the process of computing the present value of money to be received in the future. Discounting future project cash flows *(future values)* into *present values* will be important when we financially evaluate alternative capital projects. More later.

Interest, Discounting and Rates

- Think of **interest** as the "rent" you must pay to borrow and use someone else's money.

- **Interest rates** are analogous to miles-per-hour speed measures. Both interest and speed measures have a numeric amount applied in a unit of time.

  "Sixty miles per hour" means that if you are traveling at that rate, in an hour you will go sixty miles. An interest rate of 4% per year means that if you deposit $100 in a bank account you will be able to withdraw $104 in a year or withdraw $132 in seven (7) years.

- **Discounting** is the process of finding the *present value* today of cash projected to be received at some future date. The projected amount of cash in the future is reduced using a discount rate for each unit of time between now and the future.
  Got that?

- Think of *discounting* as computing interest but going backwards. In discounting (going backwards), you use a *discount rate* instead of using an *interest rate* (going forward).

- So, $132 projected to be received seven years (7) in the future would be discounted back to a value $100 using a 4% annual discount rate. Both amounts are in "nominal" dollars, the currency of the day.

Financial Statements

Computing PV and FV with Excel®

Present value (PV) and future value (FV) can be computed using the formulas shown on the prior pages, with financial calculators, or most easily with computer spreadsheet applications such as Excel from Microsoft. See the sample spreadsheet below.

	A	B	C	D E	F	G	H	I	J
1									
2		Monthly Payments on a $10,000 Car Loan at 10% Annual interest rate							
4				Excel function =PV ([rate], [nper], [pmt])					
6		0.83%	[rate]	% interest rate per period (10%/12).					
7		48	[nper]	total number of monthly payments					
8		($253.63)	[pmt]	$ payment eash month					
10				PV(.0083,48,-253.63)					
11			$10,000	= PV(B6,B7,B8)					
13			$10,000	Total Principle Payments					
14			$2,174	Total Interest Payments					
15			$12,174	Total Payments					
16									
17		Future Value of Total Car Loan Payments Discounted to Origination							
19				Excel function =FV ([rate], [nper], [pmt],[pv])					
21		$10,000	[pv]	present $ value of future payments					
23				FV(.0083,48,-253.63,10000)					
24			$0	= FV(B6,B7,B8,B21)					

Excel has extensive help screens to guide use of financial functions. In the following chapter we will use the Excel net present value (NPV) function in making capital investment decisions.

Chapter 21.
Net Present Value (NPV) and
Internal Rate of Return (IRR)

We're going to invest cash now with high hopes of a large future return. But will the anticipated payback be enough to cover our initial investment given the project's high risk? Further, would any of our alternative projects provide us with a better financial return? *Answering these questions is the essence of capital budgeting.* **Net present value (NPV)** *analysis provides "gold standard" answers.*

~

The NPV of a proposed project is the present value (PV) of future cash flows from the project minus today's value of invested cash. In NPV analysis, relevant cash inflows and outflows are discounted to compute the present value for each and then added. The resultant NPV is an estimate of how much the project will increase the wealth of the company.

If NPV is positive, the project will add that value. A project with a negative NPV should seldom be pursued. If we must choose between several project alternatives, the project with the highest NPV will provide the highest value to the company. The higher the NPV, the better.

As you will see in the next few pages, actually computing NPV is a piece of cake. All the heavy lifting is done by computer spreadsheets. The hardest part of an NPV analysis is estimating the right cash flows to use in the formulas.

The very foundation of NPV analysis is the accurate forecasting of cash flows associated with a capital project. These pro-forma cash flow projections answer the questions "What initial investment will be required for this project?" and then "How will this project impact the company's future total cash flows?"

But beware: Application of these concepts and formulas without understanding their limits will often lead to erroneous and misleading results. Also, the mistaken impression of accuracy given by computation of seemingly overly precise variables can give a false confidence in proforma projections. And don't forget strategy. No matter how high an NPV, if a company's strategies are defective, its capital investment projects will most likely fail.

~

Later in the chapter, we'll discuss other analysis techniques used in capital budgeting, including IRR, ROI and payback period. But most often, all you will need is NPV. In the next chapter, we will apply NPV analysis to our planned business expansion at Appleseed Enterprises!

Cash Flow Forecasting

Accurately estimating the amounts and timing of all the project cash inflows and outflows can be tricky. Forecasting cash flows requires a detailed understanding of the business and the project being analyzed, its input variables, and expected outcomes.

We must estimate the amount and timing of original investments, changes in working capital, and in ongoing costs and expenses. We must understand customers' needs and wants, and market conditions to properly forecast revenues. In addition, current and future financial environment, expected rates of inflation, project risk, and tax considerations each play a part in NPV computations. Moreover, each of these elements of cash flow must be sequenced so that the NPV analysis will properly account for the time value of money. It is a lot to ask. See the box at the bottom of this page for Warren Buffett's take on NPV analysis!

Selecting a Discount Rate

Selecting the appropriate discount rate is also difficult. The minimum discount rate would be equal to the company's weighted average cost of capital. Any project must return that amount or it will dilute the value of the company. Then a "risk premium" should be added if there is increased risk in the project relative to the inherent risk associated with the company's overall business.

Venture capitalists add a risk premium of 30% or more to startup company projects. A modest risk premium of 5% to 15% might be more appropriate for an expansion project for an established company. Developing an NPV versus discount rate analysis may be helpful. See page 252-253.

Sensitivity Analysis

Not all the input variables in a capital budgeting analysis are equally important. For example, sales forecasts are almost always critical variables. Costs +/- 10% for a high gross-profit product may not be all that important.

Performing a "sensitivity" analysis can help identify the key variables in a capital budgeting analysis. In a sensitivity analysis, variables are systematically changed to see how the resultant NPV or IRR is affected. If changing an assumption results in a big change in the computed project value, then it is an important variable to get right. If changing an assumption results in just a small change, then it is less important.

In "scenario analysis," you might want to look at all your financial assumptions from a conservative perspective and see how cash flows are affected. For example, assume that everything will cost more and take longer to accomplish than your original projections. Often it is useful to prepare three sets of proforma statements: one with conservative (pessimistic) assumptions, one with realistic assumptions (most probable), and one with optimistic assumptions.

NPV Guidelines

Here are some operating guidelines for cash flow forecasting and NPV analysis:

1. **Cash flow forecasting** The total cash flows used in NPV analysis should come from well-prepared proforma financial statements developed for the project.

2. **Count ALL incremental cash flows** Incremental cash flows are those that arise from the project, from sales, costs, expenses, capital investment, increase in working capital, or other sources.

   Opportunity costs count too. If an existing asset or employee will be part of the project, then these costs should be included in the project's cash flow.

3. **Count ONLY incremental cash flows** Don't include sunk costs.

"Our advice: Beware of geeks bearing formulas."

Warren Buffett
Commenting on financial models and the financial collapse of 2008

We have already spent that money and they should not be a part of the forward-looking decision process.

Accounting conventions used in *balance sheet* and *income statement* construction can mask the value of a project. Cash flow and profits are not the same. Being profitable does not necessarily mean the project has a positive cash flow.

4. **Use nominal dollars in cash flow projections** A portion of the selected discount rate used in NPV calculations accounts for inflation. We must use nominal dollars in our forecasts so as not to double-count. See Appendix B, Nominal vs. Real Dollars.

5. **Account for time** Capital budgets often show initial cash outflow (the investment) and then a future cash inflow (the return). When analyzing cash flow, take into account that a dollar spent today is worth more than a dollar received in the distant future.

The discounted value of a future cash flow is determined by reducing its value by the appropriate discount rate for each unit of time (period) between when the cash flow is to be valued and the actual time of the cash flow in the future.

6. **Don't include costs of financing** In capital budgeting, the costs of financing should not be in the cash flow projections. Remember, part of the discount rate used in NPV computations includes a cost-of-capital estimate.

7. **Account for risk** Not all projects have the same risk. A project that is riskier should generate a higher expected return. A portion of the discount rate used in the NPV computation deals with risk degree.

8. **Understand assumptions** Numeric tools used to evaluate capital projects often can provide valuable insights, but misapplied, they are worthless. Understand the assumptions upon which these calculations rest.

Microsoft Excel makes the computation part of NPV and IRR analysis easy. However, estimating cash flows and NPV discount rates can still be problematic. Nevertheless, using spreadsheet functions to perform sensitivity analyses quickly on key variables can greatly add to the value of analyses.

Using Spreadsheets

To compute NPV or IRR, the cash flow inputs are entered as an array (a sequence of spreadsheet cells) and the financial functions are computed using the formulas shown here. Be sure to review all the "help" screens available for each function to understand their application.

NPV(rate,value1,value2, ...) *Rate* means the selected discount rate over one period. *Value* represents the array of each cash outflow or cash inflow equally spaced at the end of each period.

IRR(values,guess) *Values* represents an array of cells that contain the numbers for which you want to calculate the IRR. The optional *guess* input is an estimate of the resultant IRR. The spreadsheet uses an iterative technique starting with the guess to calculate the IRR.

Other spreadsheet functions are available for modified internal rate of return (MIRR) calculations using a lower discount rate for cash inflows and also for calculations to be used with projects with irregular cash flows (XNPV and XIRR).

Net Present Value (NPV) Formula

- The "net present value" (NPV) of a proposed project is the sum of all the project's projected cash flows over time discounted by an appropriate rate to bring them to a present value. If the NPV of a project is positive, the project is projected to increase the value of the business by that amount.

- Shown here is an annotated version of the standard **Net Present Value (NPV)** equation. It is not very daunting once you get the hang of the concepts and work through some examples. Anyway, spreadsheets will do all the heavy lifting.

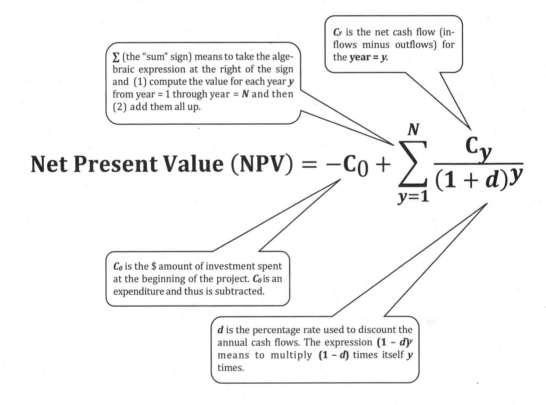

C_y is the net cash flow (inflows minus outflows) for the **year = y**.

Σ (the "sum" sign) means to take the algebraic expression at the right of the sign and (1) compute the value for each year y from year = 1 through year = N and then (2) add them all up.

$$\text{Net Present Value (NPV)} = -C_0 + \sum_{y=1}^{N} \frac{C_y}{(1+d)^y}$$

C_0 is the $ amount of investment spent at the beginning of the project. C_0 is an expenditure and thus is subtracted.

d is the percentage rate used to discount the annual cash flows. The expression $(1 - d)^y$ means to multiply $(1 - d)$ times itself y times.

Net Present Value (NPV) Example

- Using the sample capital project cash flows in this table, we will calculate the NPV for the project.

CASH FLOWS	START	YEAREND YEAR 1	YEAREND YEAR 2	YEAREND YEAR 3
– Initial Investment (C_0)	$C_0 = \$725$			
+ Cash Inflow in Year		$500	$800	$950
– Cash Outflow in Year		$200	$350	$450
= Net Cash Flow for Year	($725)	$C_1 = \$300$	$C_2 = \$450$	$C_3 = \$500$

Array the equation for three years including the initial investment (C_0):

$$\mathbf{NPV} = -\mathbf{C_0} + \frac{C_1}{(1+d)^1} + \frac{C_2}{(1+d)^2} + \frac{C_3}{(1+d)^3} +$$

Then substitute variables for cash flow amounts and use a discount rate of, say, 12%, and solve:

$$NPV = -\$750 + \frac{\$300}{1 + 0.12} + \frac{\$450}{(1 + 0.12)(1 + 0.12)} + \frac{\$500}{(1 + 0.12)(1 + 0.12)(1 + 0.12)} = \$257$$

- Using the Excel function gives the same result:

	A	B	C	D	E	F	G	H	I
1									
2		**Net Present Value (NPV) Example**							
4					Excel function =NPV (rate,[value1], [value2], ...)				
6		12%	rate		discount rate				
8		($725)	[value1]		C_0 initial $ investment (beginning year 1 outlay)				
9		$300	[value2]		C_1 $ returned year-end 1				
10		$450	[value3]		C_2 $ returned year-end 2				
11		$500	[value4]		C_3 $ returned year-end 3				
13					NPV(.12,300,450,500) - 725				
14		$257	=NPV(B6,B9,B10,B11) + B8						

Internal Rate of Return (IRR)

- The **internal rate of return (IRR)** of a project is the discount rate that makes the present value of future cash flows equal to the initial investment. Thus, the IRR is that point where NPV = $0.

- A project's NPV is *higher* when using a low discount rate because the computed value of future cash flows is higher if discounted less. A project's NPV is *lower* when using a high discount rate because the computed value of future cash flows is lower if discounted more.

- See the following graph. Using a discount rate of 12%, we computed NPV = $257 for our sample project. With a 5% discount rate, the NPV would be over $400. With a 35% discount rate, the NPV would be negative — the project would cost us more than it would bring in. The IRR in this example is 30% (where NPV = $0).

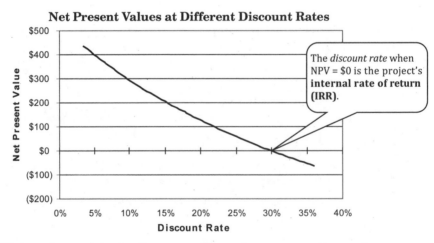

Net Present Values at Different Discount Rates

The *discount rate* when NPV = $0 is the project's **internal rate of return (IRR)**.

- IRR is often misunderstood as the annual profitability of the project investment. This level of return is only if cash flows from the project can be invested at the same rate as the IRR — seldom the case.

NPV vs. IRR?

- NPV and IRR measure two different, but complementary, aspects of capital use. The two methods of evaluating capital investments each have inherent advantages and disadvantages. See the table below.

Net Present Value (NPV) vs. Internal Rate of Return (IRR) in Capital Budgeting

	NPV	IRR
ADVANTAGES	— **NPV** is a direct measure of expected value-added to the company from executing the project. — Comparing the value of alternative projects is easy with **NPV** analysis: just pick the project with the highest **NPV.**	— **IRR** is a popular capital budgeting tool because it shows the efficiency of capital use in an easy-to-understand percent return format. — Computing **IRR** is valid without having to estimate a discount rate.
DISADVANTAGES	— **NPV** requires an assumed input discount rate (capital cost plus risk premium), which may be difficult to estimate.	— **IRR** computes only a percent return, not a value, and thus disregards project scale and is not a measure of ultimate worth to the company. — **IRR** can make a small project appear more attractive than a large project. In fact, a very small project could have a very high **IRR** but also have a low and very unattractive **NPV.** — **IRR** assumes cash flow returns are invested at an often unrealistically high rate (the **IRR**). MIRR (modified internal rate of return) analysis solves this problem.

Other Measures

Finance types regard NPV as the all-around best measure of value-added from a capital project, but there is also a place for IRR in determining how efficiently capital is employed. NPV and IRR measure two different, complementary aspects of capital use. NPV and IRR can be used together in making capital budgeting decisions.

What follows are other common capital budgeting techniques — some with flaws, others helpful, but complex.

Return on Investment (ROI) There is no standardized way of computing ROI. Many organizations use ROI to mean several different analytical techniques. Thus, ROI measurement is flexible but also subject to confusion. Use the well-defined NPV and IRR instead.

Payback Period Payback period refers to the period required for the return on an investment to *repay* the sum of the original investment. Shorter payback periods are obviously preferable to longer payback periods (assuming all else being equal).

Payback period as a measurement is easy to compute and is intuitively understandable. However, payback period computations ignore the time value of money and ignore any cash flows occurring after the payback period ends. As a method of capital budgeting analysis, payback period has serious limitations.

Real Option Analysis Real option analysis allows for go/no-go decisions during a project. The flexibility to slow down, or to even stop a project if necessary, lowers risk to the company. This lowered risk adds initial value to the project over another project that could not be stopped. Real option analysis can be quite complex but is very useful for large capital projects.

Monte Carlo Analysis A Monte Carlo analysis is a complex multivariable NPV calculation that first assigns various probability values to capital project variables and then simulates many outcomes using the brute force of computing power. The Monte Carlo analysis output is a probability distribution histogram showing the volatility and sensitivity in a project's NPV. It is a very powerful technique but requires sophistication to apply.

Summary

Generally, when comparing projects, the project with the highest NPV should be accepted. The IRR of the project is the discount rate where the NPV equals zero and the discounted costs of the project equal discounted returns. Generally, if a project's IRR is greater than the company's hurdle rate, it should be accepted.

Capital budgeting using NPV and IRR measures allows management to select rationally from alternative projects with very different cash flows.

Different capital projects have different cash flows in both dollar amounts and time. NPV analysis makes comparing the financial worth of alternative projects possible in a standardized way. NPV accounts for the time value of money by calculating the present value of future project cash flows. NPV is a direct measure of expected value-added to the company from executing the capital project.

Chapter 22.
Making Good Capital
Investment Decisions

At the last board meeting, our esteemed directors approved AppleSeed's plans for a major product line expansion into gourmet potato chips. Now we are weighing two alternative capital projects designed to meet that goal:

1. **"Greenfield" Option** Building a new plant from scratch, or

2. **"Purchase" Option** Acquiring an existing business, Chips-R-Us, Inc.

In this chapter, we'll prepare a cash flow forecast for both alternatives and then perform an NPV analysis to help us select the best capital project for Apple-Seed going forward.

Projecting Sales

Projecting sales is a good place to start when preparing a cash flow forecast. So here we go. See the graph below.

Proforma Revenue Estimates

AppleSeed's purchase of Chips-R-Us would allow us to continue selling their low-end branded product while we start up our gourmet potato chip product line. Alternatively, if we build a potato chip plant from scratch we won't be selling anything for a year or so. The profitability of the current Chips-R-Us brand is lower than what we expect to receive from our new gourmet potato chips, but at least we would be receiving some income while we launch our own branded product.

~

Now that we have sales forecasts, let's estimate cash flows for the two alternative capital projects.

Estimating Cash Flows

Cash flow forecasts are constructed from estimates of three major "cash-using" and "cash-generating" business elements:

1. **Cash from operations,**

2. **Capital spending,** and

3. **Increase in working capital.**

The following two pages detail cash flow forecasts for AppleSeed's alternative capital projects. Here is how we arrived at these numbers.

Cash from Operations Estimating the cash from operations begins with preparing proforma *Income Statements* for each of the years being analyzed. We start by projecting incremental sales expected from the capital project and then match those sales with the incremental costs and expenses necessary to generate those sales. These costs and expenses are

Appleseed Enterprises Inc. Expansion Alternatives—Purchase Option
Cash Flow Analysis (in $ thousands)

Purchase Option	Initial	Year 1	Year 2	Year 3	Year 4	Year 5	Year 6	Year 7
1. Cash Flow from Operations (added to cash flow)		$120	$230	$465	$656	$788	$920	$1,035
Depreciation (added back to cash flow)		131	150	160	198	195	182	168
Taxes (subtracted from cash flow)		(24)	(58)	(140)	(223)	(268)	(313)	(352)
2. Capital Spending:								
Purchase assets of Chips-R-Us, Inc. including old factory building and equipment	(1,125)							
Repair old Chips-R-Us factory building		(275)	(150)	(50)	(50)	(10)	(10)	(10)
Refurbish old potato-chip-making machines		(200)	(75)	(5)	(5)	(5)	(5)	(5)
Purchase and install new fancy packaging machinery		(75)	0	0	0	0	0	0
Purchase and install state-of-the-art QC laboratory		(50)	0	0	0	0	0	0
Repair old delivery trucks and decorate with distinctive potato chip art		(25)	(25)	(5)	(5)	(5)	(5)	(5)
Enlarge factory to increase production capacity		0	0	(200)	(100)	0	0	0
Purchase/install additional potato-chip-making machines		0	0	0	(500)	(100)	0	0
3. Increases in Working Capital (subtracted from cash flow)		(300)	(88)	(138)	(156)	(131)	(138)	(125)
4. Terminal Value of Business (estimated 8x cash flow)		0	0	0	0	0	0	5,813
Sum of Cash Flows and Terminal Value	($1,125)	($698)	($15)	$88	($185)	$463	$631	$6,519
PV of Annual Cash Flows Discounted at 15.8%	($1,125)	($603)	($11)	$56	($103)	$223	$262	$2,335

Net present value (NPV) for purchase option @15.8% Discount Rate = $1,034

Cumulative Cash Flows	($1,125)	($1,823)	($1,838)	($1,750)	($1,935)	($1,472)	($841)	$5,679

Lowest Cumulative Cash Flow (in year 4) = ($1,935)

Total Capital Spending = ($3,080)

Appleseed Enterprises Inc. Expansion Alternatives—Greenfield Option
Cash Flow Analysis (in $ thousands)

Greenfield Option	Initial	Year 1	Year 2	Year 3	Year 4	Year 5	Year 6	Year 7
1. Cash Flow from Operations (*added to cash flow*)		$0	$50	$250	$400	$681	$850	$1,000
Depreciation (*added back to cash flow*)		216	238	235	219	201	185	170
Taxes (*subtracted from cash flow*)		0	(13)	(75)	(136)	(232)	(289)	(340)
2. Capital Spending:								
Build large new factory building specifically designed for potato chip processing	(2,150)	0						
Purchase and install high-capacity potato-chip-making machinery		(600)	(250)	(100)	0	0	0	0
Purchase and install new fancy packaging machinery		(75)	0	0	0	0	0	0
Purchase and install state-of-the-art QC laboratory		(50)	0	0	0	0	0	0
Purchase new delivery trucks and decorate with distinctive potato chip art			(50)	(75)	(25)	0	0	0
3. Increases in Working Capital (*subtracted from cash flow*)		0	(63)	(188)	(250)	(181)	(169)	(150)
4. Terminal Value of Business (*estimated 8x cash flow*)		0	0	0	0	0	0	5,439
Sum of Cash Flows and Terminal Value	($2,150)	($509)	($87)	$48	$208	$470	$577	$6,119
PV of Annual Cash Flows Discounted at 15.8%	($2,150)	($440)	($65)	$31	$116	$226	$239	$2,191

Net present value (NPV) for greenfield option @15.8% Discount Rate = $148

	Initial	Year 1	Year 2	Year 3	Year 4	Year 5	Year 6	Year 7
Cumulative Cash Flows	($2,150)	($2,659)	($2,746)	($2,699)	($2,491)	($2,021)	($1,443)	$4,676

Lowest Cumulative Cash Flow (in year 2) = ($2,746)

Total Capital Spending = ($3,375)

AppleSeed's Make vs. Buy Estimated Cash Flows

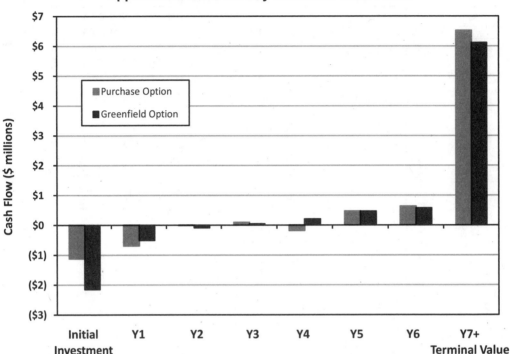

then subtracted from sales. (Note: We must add back the depreciation charges since these charges are included as a cost in the *Income Statement* but do not lower cash in the period. (See pages 27 and 125 for more explanation.) Finally, we will subtract any taxes paid, thus yielding an estimated *cash from operations* for each year.

Capital Spending Next we must estimate for both capital projects the amount and timing of cash to be invested in property, plant and equipment. With the greenfield option we will have large capital expenditures for land, a new building, and new machinery. If we purchase Chips-R-Us, we will need capital to refurbish both the plant and old machinery to bring them up to our high standards. Also, we will purchase additional potato-chip-making machines to expand Chips-R-Us' production capacity.

The costs to buy land and construct a new building will be high in the greenfield

option. Purchasing Chips-R-Us is less expensive, but their existing factory will need extensive refurbishment.

Increases in Working Capital Now we need to forecast the additional working capital (primarily accounts receivable and inventory) required to support our expanded business. It takes money to make money, and the more we sell the more working capital we will need.

Because purchasing Chips-R-Us will result in earlier and higher sales, we will need more early working capital with that alternative capital project.

~

There is one last, but very important projection we must make before we compute NPV: the "terminal value" of both our proposed capital projects.

Terminal Value Forecasting cash flows beyond a certain period is often too uncertain and impractical for an NPV analysis. So *terminal values* are often added

Financial Comparison of AppleSeed's Expansion Alternatives

✓ checks show the superior alternative.

	ACQUIRE CHIPS-R-US, INC.	BUILD FROM SCRATCH
NET PRESENT VALUE (NPV)	✓ $1,034,000	$148,000
INTERNAL RATE OF RETURN (IRR)	✓ 25%	17%
LOWEST CUMULATIVE CASH	✓ ($1,935,000)	($2,746,000)
TOTAL CAPITAL SPENDING	✓ ($3,080,000)	($3,375,000)

to the last year's cash flow forecast to estimate and account for the long-term value of the capital project as an ongoing business.

The terminal value can be thought of as the price of the whole capital project's business if it were sold as an ongoing concern. Note that for many projects the terminal value can be a major part of the value added by the whole project, especially when starting a new business or making a major business expansion.

In our NPV comparisons, we have estimated terminal values conservatively at eight times the projected after-tax income for each expansion alternative.

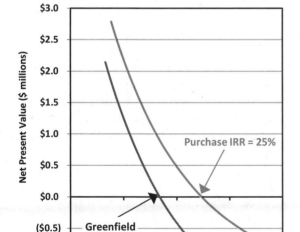

Purchase IRR vs. Greenfield IRR

Purchase IRR = 25%

Greenfield IRR = 17%

Note that although the terminal values are large for both alternatives, the amount received is projected seven years out in our analysis and thus is highly discounted. This amount is still significant, but not so overwhelming.

Computing NPV and IRR

We've carefully projected cash flows for both of AppleSeed's expansion alternatives. See the detailed projections on pages 252 and 253.

Now we must select a discount rate before we can perform NPV computations. Neither the purchase option nor the greenfield option seems riskier than the other. Also, neither would add a significantly greater risk to our business than what we already have. Thus, using AppleSeed's average weighted cost of capital (WACC) of 15.8% seems reasonable for our NPV comparison. (See page 227 for a discussion of AppleSeed's WACC.)

The next step is for us to go to the computer, feed the numbers into an Excel spreadsheet, and let the electrons fly.

~

Voila! The table at the top of this page summarizes the results of our comparative cash flow forecasts and NPV calculations. Our computed NPV of the purchase alternative capital project is significantly higher than that of the greenfield alternative. The IRR is higher for the Chips-R-Us purchase as well.

Further, the amount of cash we will need at one time (lowest cumulative cash) is significantly lower for the purchase alternative than for the greenfield option. Capital spending is about the same, plus or minus 10% or so.

Financially, the purchase of Chips-R-Us makes the most sense for AppleSeed's expansion into the potato chip market. Note that even though the greenfield alternative "only" has an NPV of $148,000, it still would have been an attractive project and would return value to Apple-Seed. However, because the purchase alternative offers the higher NPV of $1,034,000, it makes good financial sense to choose that alternative.

~

We present our NPV and IRR analysis to AppleSeed's board and they agree that purchasing Chips-R-Us is the way to go. I call Chips-R-Us' owner and invite him to dinner to finalize the negotiations. We won't go to a fancy place because I don't want him to think we have a lot of money to spend.

Over dinner, we settle on a price of $1.25 million, just as we have projected in our NPV analysis. We will only be purchasing assets, leaving Chips-R-Us liabilities for them to liquidate. I call our lawyers and ask them to work on the purchase-and-sale agreement. Then I call our accountant and ask her the best way for AppleSeed to book this acquisition. She mumbles something about new regulations that she needs to review and says she'll get back to us on FASB Rule 141(R).

Acquisition Accounting

FASB has regulations to be used in accounting for business combination. In 2009 they promulgated new rules — the so-called "acquisition" method of busi-ness combination. So that's what we will use to account for AppleSeed's legal take-over of Chips-R-Us.

Using this acquisition method, all the acquired tangible assets of Chips-R-Us will be recorded on AppleSeed's books at fair market value on the date we acquire them. Fair market value is defined by FASB as "the price that would be received to sell an asset or paid to transfer a liability in an orderly transaction between market participants at the measured date."

We are going to have an appraiser come out and value the land, factory, and equipment we will be purchasing. The inventory value we can figure out ourselves. Also, there will be significant one-time legal and accounting fees associated with the acquisition. These additional acquisition expenses will be run through the *Income Statement* as incurred.

Most of the assets we are purchasing from Chips-R-Us are tangible "bricks and mortar" assets, which are easy to value. But we are also purchasing "intangible" assets such as customer lists, trade names, supply contracts, trade secrets, recipes for potato chip making, and such — hard to quantify directly but FASB Rule 141(R) shows how!

Any excess we pay for Chips-R-Us over and above the fair market value of net assets recorded on our *Balance Sheet* will be reported as "goodwill." Goodwill will just sit on our books until it is "impaired" and no longer valuable, then we will have to write it off (amortize) through the *Income Statement* and take a loss for the amount.

Note that amortization of intangible assets is similar to the process of depreciation for tangible assets, written off each year according to a formula.

~

Transaction 33 on the following pages completes our acquisition of Chips-R-Us and starts AppleSeed on its great adventure as a larger business.

With the addition of potato chips to our applesauce product offering, perhaps we should change our name from Apple-Seed Enterprises, Inc., to something a little more flashy like Amalgamated Gourmet Food Products Corporation — *AG-FPC* for short. What do you think?

Transaction 33. — Acquire a Business

Income Statement

NET SALES	$ -	
COST OF GOODS SOLD	-	
GROSS MARGIN	-	
SALES & MARKETING	-	
RESEARCH & DEVELOPMENT	-	
GENERAL & ADMINISTRATIVE	35,000	❷ A
OPERATING EXPENSE	35,000	
INCOME FROM OPERATIONS	(35,000)	
NET INTEREST INCOME	-	
INCOME TAXES	-	
NET INCOME	$ (35,000)	

Cash Flow Statement

BEGINNING CASH BALANCE	$ -	
CASH RECEIPTS	-	
CASH DISBURSEMENTS	-	
CASH FLOW FROM OPERATIONS	-	
PP&E PURCHASE	1,250,000	❶ A
NET BORROWINGS	-	
INCOME TAXES PAID	-	
SALE OF CAPITAL STOCK	-	
ENDING CASH BALANCES	$ (1,250,000)	

Balance Sheet

Assets

CASH	❶ B	$ (1,250,000)	
ACCOUNTS RECEIVABLE		-	
INVENTORIES		-	
PREPAID EXPENSES		-	
CURRENT ASSETS		(1,250,000)	
OTHER ASSETS	❶ D	50,000	
FIXED ASSETS @ COST		1,200,000	❶ C
ACCUMULATED DEPRECIATION		-	
NET FIXED ASSETS		1,200,000	
TOTAL ASSETS		$0	

Liabilities & Equity

ACCOUNTS PAYABLE		$ 35,000	❷ B
ACCRUED EXPENSES		-	
CURRENT PORTION OF DEBT		-	
INCOME TAXES PAYABLE		-	
CURRENT LIABILITIES		35,000	
LONG-TERM DEBT		-	
CAPITAL STOCK		-	
RETAINED EARNINGS		(35,000)	❷ C
SHAREHOLDERS' EQUITY		(35,000)	
TOTAL LIABILITIES & EQUITY		$0	

T33. Buy Chips-R-Us Inc.'s assets and treat this business combination as an acquisition under FASB Rule 141(R).

We've done it! Chips-R-Us is ours! But after the euphoria subsides we realize that there is a lot of work to do. As a good start, let's adjust the books to account for this momentous purchase. Then we'll drive over to our new plant and begin to learn how to make the world's best potato chips.

Transaction: Purchase certain assets of Chips-R-Us for $1.25 million and combine the business into our financial statements as an acquisition as per FASB Rule 141(R). The appraised fair market value of the purchased assets is $1.20 million, leaving a $50,000 balance as the intangible asset, goodwill. Write a check to the owners of Chips-R-Us for $1.25 million. Receive from our appraiser, lawyers and accountants, bills totaling $35,000 for professional services performed on our behalf. *Gasp.*

1 (1A) Record the $1.25 million payment as a **PP&E PURCHASE** in the *Cash Flow Statement* and (1B) lower **CASH** by that amount on the *Balance Sheet*. (1C) Add the $1.2 million appraised value of the purchased assets to **FIXED ASSETS @ COST** on the *Balance Sheet*. (1D) Finally, add the remaining $50,000 spent to **OTHER ASSETS** on the *Balance Sheet* as "goodwill."

2 (2A) Charge **GENERAL & ADMINISTRATIVE** expense in the *Income Statement* for $35,000 for the professional services bills and also (2B) add that amount to **ACCOUNTS PAYABLE** in the liabilities section of the *Balance Sheet*. (2C) This expense has lowered net income, so subtract the amount from **RETAINED EARNINGS** as well.

From the Management *(i.e., the Author)*: It has been a pleasure navigating the financial statements of our company, AppleSeed Enterprises, Inc. with you.

Mail us at ***info@mercurygroup.com*** with any comments, questions, corrections, or just to say hello. We promise, to answer every one! **:-)**

Conclusion

We've come a long way. Our fears of both accounting and financial reporting have melted away. We've learned the vocabulary; we've learned the structure. We know what FASB means and we appreciate the importance of GAAP.

Your goal was to gain knowledge of accounting and finance, to assist you in your business dealings. You wanted the power that comes from understanding financial manipulations. You have done it. I was happy to help, but you did all the work, the heavy lifting.

～

You now understand:

- How an enterprise can be rapidly growing, highly profitable and out of money all at the same time and why this state of affairs is fairly common. (page 57)
- That accrual has nothing to do with the Wicked Witch of the West. (page 3)
- When in the course of business affairs, a negative cash flow is a sign of good things happening and when it's a sign of impending catastrophe. (page 66)
- How discounts drop right to the bottom line as lost profits and why they are so very dangerous to a company's financial health. (page 153

- The important difference between liquidity and profitably. (pages 190)
- Those expenditures that are costs and those that are expenses. (pages 9-10)
- Depreciation's differing effect on income and on cash. (pages 27, 112)
- Why product cost always depends on volume. (pages 113-115)
- Limits of the common costing systems and when to apply (and, more importantly, when to ignore) the accountant's definition of cost. (page 132)
- Three common — and different — definitions of what a business is worth. (page 178)
- Why assets must always equal liabilities plus shareholders' equity (worth) on the *Balance Sheet.* (page 16-17)
- Why working capital is important and what business actions leads to more and what actions lead to less. (page 36)
- The difference between cash in the bank and profit on the bottom line and how the two are interrelated. (page 78)
- How many sets of books a company actually keeps. (page 207)

Congratulations! You have learned just enough about accounting and financial reporting to "speak the language" and understand the "numbers of business." Well done!

- Why some qualitative business analysis tools are as important as the numbers. (page 234)

- The difference between risk and uncertainty and which is worse. (pages 219-220)

- The difference between pre-money and post-money company valuations when you sell stock. (pages 225-226)

- Why a dollar in your pocket today can be worth a lot more than a dollar received tomorrow. (page 235)

- Why a development investment made today must return a much greater sum to the coffers of the company in later years. (page 235)

- Which business financing is more expensive, equity or debt? (page 234)

- The necessity (and limitation) of forecasting cash flows over time when making capital investment decisions. (page 141)

- When to use NPV analysis and when to use IRR and why it is important in capital investment decision making. (page 247)

and more...

We have come a long way. We can appreciate my young accountant's poetic remark:

"It's just so symmetrical, so logical, so beautiful and it always comes out right."

It always comes out right!

Appendixes

The following appendixes don't fit into the pedagogical narrative of the rest of this book, but are interesting and informative nonetheless. Read each for a further understanding of financial accounting.

The extensive **Index** to this volume starting on page 289 will be a helpful reference. Internet search methods are discussed on page 293. There is a wealth of information on the web.

~

Appendix A.
Short History of Business Fraud and Speculative Bubbles

The Spanish-born American philosopher George Santayana said, "Those who cannot remember the past are condemned to repeat it." To save you, the potentially poor reader, from financial ruin, what follows is a rogue's gallery of financial frauds to avoid. First, here are a few investing rules that help you avoid frauds:

1. ***Demand Explanations*** Do not invest in arcane schemes with promoters who will not explain the investments clearly. Make sure you understand exactly where the investment returns will come from and at what risk.

2. ***No QB*** Beware the "quick buck" or getting "something for nothing." Promises of "too-good-to-be-true" returns are just that.

3. ***References!*** Always do reference checking before investing. Charlatans spend much time, money, and effort in trying to appear legitimate. Beware. Do not be fooled.

Unfortunately, just following these three rules doesn't guarantee you will never be fleeced. So, do not "put all your eggs in one basket." That way, even if you are duped, not everything is lost. Diversify your investments.

Ponzi Schemes

In a Ponzi scheme, gullible investors are enticed to purchase arcane investments that promise fantastic returns. Early investors are paid off with money raised from later victims, until no more money can be raised.

Ponzi schemes are doomed to collapse because there are no underlying earnings —just recycling of money. However, not all investors lose. The first investors can gain if they manage to get out in time.

Charles Ponzi (1919) With $200 in borrowed capital, the "Ponzi scheme" namesake, Charles Ponzi, opened his Securities Exchange Company at 27 School Street in Boston on the day after Christmas in 1919.

Ponzi claimed to invest in an arbitrage of international postage return coupons and promised a 50% return in 45 days and a 100% return in 90 days. Early investors did get these spectacular returns. Actually, Ponzi was paying off the early investors by using money received from new investors.

For a time, Ponzi was the toast of the Northeast. His investment company was a great success. In 1920, Ponzi bought a grand house in Lexington, a wealthy suburb of Boston, and even a local bank, the Hanover Trust Bank.

However, Ponzi's operation collapsed in August 1920 when, based on a tip from a local newspaper, federal agents raided Ponzi's corporate headquarters and the Massachusetts Attorney General put him in jail. In a little more than eight months,

---

"You only find out who's swimming naked when the tide goes out."

Warren Buffett
commenting on seeing financial fraud when markets collapse

Ponzi had collected $10 million from more than 10,000 investors. In bankruptcy, investors received just 37 cents on the dollar.

At trial, Ponzi pleaded guilty to federal charges of mail fraud and was sentenced to five years in federal prison, serving three years. When released from federal prison and facing state charges, Ponzi jumped bail and fled to Florida, where he set up a real estate business and began selling "prime Florida property" (i.e., swamp land) to gullible investors. Eventually, Ponzi spent nine years in a Massachusetts prison and then was deported back to Italy.

Bubbles

Bubbles are fueled by speculators who are willing to pay even greater prices for already overvalued assets sold to them by the speculators who bought them in the preceding round.

Each financial bubble in history has been different, but they all involve a mix of fundamental business and psychological forces. In the beginning stages, an attractive return on a stock or commodity drives prices higher and higher. People make questionable investments with the assumption that they will be able to sell later at a higher price to a "greater fool." Unrealistic investor expectations take hold and become self-fulfilling until the bubble "pops" and prices fall back to a more reasonable underlying value.

Why do bubbles sometimes last so long? One reason is that nobody likes to be a "party pooper" and people are getting rich. In addition, there is nothing inherently illegal about profiting during a bubble. The only problem is getting out before the collapse. Whoever owns the overpriced asset when the bubble pops is the loser, just as the last person standing in a game of musical chairs.

Tulip Bulbs (1630s) One of the most famous market bubbles took place in the 17th century in Holland where tulip bulbs were traded for small fortunes. Flowers and bulbs became coveted luxury items and status symbols.

The most spectacular and highly sought tulip bulbs would grow flowers with vivid colors, lines and flames on the petals, especially those infected with a rare type of mosaic virus causing a variegated pattern. Spectacular single bulbs went for as much as 5,000 Dutch guilders, a truly remarkable sum given that Rembrandt received only about one-third that amount for painting The Night Watch in 1642.

Good bulbs were scarce. It took seven years to grow a tulip bulb from seed and there was no guarantee that the resulting flower would be as good as the parent. If divided, bulbs would breed true, but dividing bulbs could occur only every two years.

Tulips bloom in April and May for only about a week, and bulbs can be uprooted and moved safely only from June to September. Thus "spot market" purchases for actual bulb delivery occurred only during these months.

"Flame" Tulip

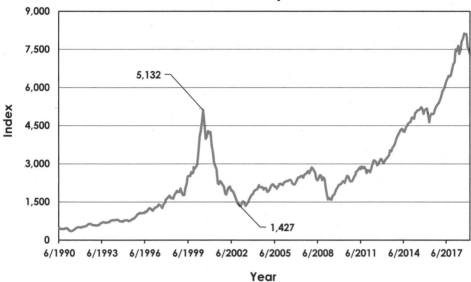

NASDAQ Composite Index

In early 1636, Dutch traders, meeting in local taverns, created a type of formal "futures market" where contracts to buy bulbs at the end of the season were bought and sold. Contract price of rare bulbs continued to rise all throughout the year. However, in February 1637, prices for tulip bulb contracts collapsed abruptly and the trade of tulip contracts and of bulbs ground to a halt. Bulbs then fetched less than a penny on the dollar.

In fact, no actual deliveries of bulbs were ever required to satisfy these futures contracts. The Dutch Parliament passed a decree that contracts could be voided for a small fee — perhaps the first government "bailout" of a speculative bubble!

Technology Stocks (1995–2001) The "dot-com" bubble was a speculative stock market bubble of the late 1990s, collapsing in 2001. The period was marked by the emergence of new Internet-based companies commonly referred to as "dot-coms." stocks and widely available venture capital created an over-exuberant environment. Many of the start-up dot-com businesses dismissed standard business models and focused on increasing market share at the expense of the bottom line. Companies became grossly overvalued.

In March 2000, the NASDAQ Composite Index peaked at over 5,000, more than double its value of just a year before. In the next two years the market crashed to less than 1,500, and almost $5 trillion in market value evaporated. See the graph of NASDAQ prices above. The Index recovered, but it took 15 years.

U.S. Housing Crisis (2008–2010) The U.S. housing price bubble burst in 2007, with house prices dropping everywhere. On average, house prices across the United States had increased by an unsustainable 143% in the prior decade, driven by easy loans and speculative feelings of buyers and bankers that prices would rise forever. Who knew?

Investing in bubbles can be quite profitable if you can get out before the bubble bursts. Many people did not get

Phoenix, AZ House Price Index
12/1995 = 100

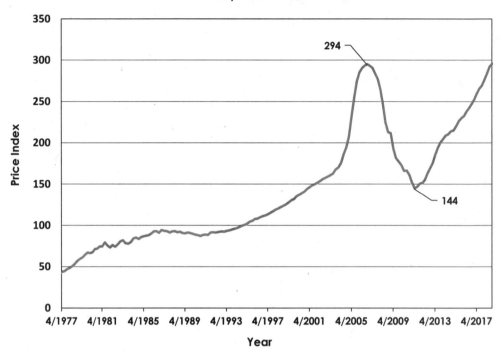

out in this crisis, and many lost their homes to foreclosure.

Phoenix, Arizona homes were particularly hard hit, losing over 50% of their value peak-to-valley. Prices have recovered, but it took over 10 years after the crash.

Bitcoin (2017-2018) Here we go again. The cryptocurrency Bitcoin soared in value the winter of 2017 and promptly fell back to earth in the spring of 2018. Why? Who knows? Possible explanations for bizarre bubble behavior (only seen in hindsight, sigh) include:

1. "Greater Fool Theory" where a fool overpays hoping to sell later to a "greater fool" at a profit.

2. Participants extrapolating from past rising prices projecting similar rises in the future, even to totally unreasonable heights.

3. Everybody is doing it, so let's follow the herd and continue the party.

4. People playing with other people's money with little to lose and perhaps big gains thru commissions and fees.

Whatever the reason, these speculative bubbles seem to regularly occur in all economies.

Bubbles are not caused by fraudulent activity as much as by human avarice and frailty. However, swindles and accounting fraud often come to light just after bubbles pop. Often nobody is looking and few care while the good times roll. Highly leveraged frauds often run out of cash and collapse when bubbles pop.

Garden-Variety Fraud

Most large business frauds are deceptively simple. Some people with power and high positions lie, cheat, and steal. Often accountants and regulators do not

"... A speculative bubble is a social epidemic whose contagion is mediated by price movements."

Robert Shiller
Yale University economics professor and Nobel Laurate

catch the crooks until real damage has been done. Some of the more amazing recent frauds are discussed here.

Salad Oil Scandal (1963) Anthony "Tino" De Angelis was a Bayonne, New Jersey–based commodities trader who bought and sold vegetable oil for his company, Allied Crude Vegetable Oil Refining Corporation.

Tino master-minded a scam where ships apparently full of salad oil (but mostly filled with water with only a few feet of salad oil on top) would arrive at the New Jersey company docks. Inspectors would confirm that the ships were full of oil (but only by looking at the top of the tanks) and would release to Tino's company millions of dollars in loans on the supposed delivery of this new inventory.

The swindle collapsed when Tino got greedy and tried to corner the world's salad oil market by buying futures contracts using this fraudulently borrowed money. More than 50 banks including Bank of America, American Express, and many international trading companies lost over $1 billion in today's dollars. Tino ended up with a seven-year jail sentence.

Enron (2001) A Houston-based energy trading company, Enron Corporation was the seventh largest company (revenues of over $100 billion) in the United States in 2000. Then the bottom fell out and Enron filed for bankruptcy protection in 2001.

What happened? Willful corporate fraud through "institutionalized, systematic, and creatively planned" accounting fraud said the federal indictments. Sen-

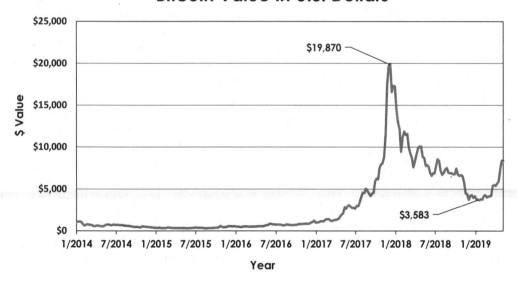

Bitcoin Value in U.S. Dollars

> **"...there must be a vast fund of stupidity in human nature, or else men would not be caught as they are, a thousand times over, by the same snares ... while they yet remember their past misfortunes, they go on to court and encourage the causes to what they are owing, and will again produce them."**
>
> Cato the Younger *(95–46 BC)*
> Roman Orator

ior Enron corporate officials, including the company's chief financial officer, set up "limited partnership" shell companies to mask debt liabilities. Then Enron, the parent company, would sell assets between the shell companies, book revenue, and then report sham profits.

The company's stock price hit $90 per share in the summer of 2000, and insiders started to sell. The stock eventually dropped to less than 20 cents per share. More than $60 billion in company stock value and more than $2 billion in employee pension plan funds were lost.

Enron founder and chairman, Ken Lay, was convicted of fraud, but died of a heart attack before being sentenced. Former Enron CEO Jeffrey Skilling is currently serving a 24-year sentence for fraud. Andrew Fastow, the former chief financial officer and some say mastermind behind the company's complicated financial schemes, got off easy with only a six-year prison sentence; his wife went to prison for a year as an accomplice to tax fraud. Watch out when your spouse asks you to sign that joint federal tax return!

Arthur Anderson LLP, the once-large worldwide accounting firm, was Enron's accountant. In 2002, the firm was convicted of obstruction of justice for shredding documents related to its audit of Enron. Then, as a convicted felon, Anderson could no longer provide CPA services to public companies. The firm collapsed.

In 2001, Arthur Anderson employed 85,000 people worldwide and 28,000 people in the United States, and had revenues exceeding $9.3 billion. Today, the firm has a single office in Chicago with 200 employees.

WorldCom (2002) Before its 2002 bankruptcy filing, WorldCom had become the second-largest long distance telephone company in the United States. (AT&T was then the largest.) The company grew primarily by buying smaller telecommunications companies, but a general business slowdown put a damper on further acquisitions and its business.

To cover up declining earnings, senior management directed underreporting of costs (interconnection expenses with other tele-communications companies) and booking bogus accounting entries to overstate revenues. By the time the scheme collapsed, WorldCom's assets were overinflated by almost $11 billion. The company's stock plummeted from over $60 per share to less than a buck.

Bernard Ebbers, WorldCom's infamous chairman and CEO, was convicted of fraud and filing false documents to regulators. He is serving a 25-year prison term at Oakdale Federal Correctional Complex in Louisiana. The earliest date that Bernie (Inmate #56022054) can be released is July 2028, at which time he will be 85 years old. Five other former WorldCom executives are also serving time.

Sarbanes-Oxley

As you can see from our examples, the early 2000s were a particularly ripe time for fraud of the "garden variety." The United States Congress was outraged! Outraged by so much executive malfeasance! Something had to be done!

So, Congress passed a law, the "Public Company Accounting Reform and Investor Protection Act of 2002," called "Sarbanes-Oxley" for short, named after the bill's primary sponsors Senator Paul Sarbanes (D-MD) and Representative Michael G. Oxley (R-OH). The bill passed the House 423–3 and the Senate 99–0. President George W. Bush signed it into law stating it was the "most far-reaching reforms of American business practice since the time of Franklin D. Roosevelt."

The law has 11 sections outlining new rules and regulations for the financial reporting of public companies and the behavior of their senior executives and the accounting firms that audit them.

Under the new law, making or certifying misleading financial statements exposes senior corporate officials to substantial civil and criminal penalties. Now, CEOs and CFOs must personally certify that company financial statements "do not contain any untrue statement of a material fact or omit to state a material fact necessary to make the statements made, in light of the circumstances under which such statements were made, not misleading with respect to the period covered by the report." Got that? Don't you feel safer already?

Sarbanes-Oxley has been criticized as just too much paperwork. Other commentators praise the law as essential to maintain the integrity of our capitalistic system. But, it has proved hard to keep fraudsters at bay. Witness the following.

Theranos (2002-2018) Founded in 2002 by Elizabeth Holmes, a beautiful Stanford dropout. The medical test equipment start-up, Theranos, experienced a spectacular rise before its ultimate downfall. At its height, the company had a market capitalization of over $9 billion and 800 employees. Holmes then owned 50% and was ranked in *Forbes Magazine* as one of the richest women in the world.

Holmes attracted "the most illustrious board in U.S. corporate history" including former Secretaries of State George Schultz and Henry Kissinger, James Mattis, retired U.S. Marine Corps General and later Secretary of Defense under U.S. President Donald Trump, former U.S. Senators Bill Frist (R-TN), Sam Nunn (D-GA), and a few other wise old men apparently mesmerized by Holmes' beauty. Also, the company formed business agreements with Walmart, the Cleveland Clinic, Capital Blue Cross, Caritas, and others adding credibility.

It was all a big fraud. The technology did not work, and Holmes lied to investors about its promise. Holmes and her ex-lover, venture capitalist and Theranos COO and President Ramesh "Sunny" Balwani have been charged with nine counts of wire fraud and two counts of conspiracy to commit wire fraud and are awaiting trial in the U.S. District Court in San Jose, California. They face up to 20 years in prison.

Paradoxically, Holmes' father, Christian Rasmus Holmes IV, was a vice president at Enron.

What goes around, comes around.

Appendix B.
Nominal vs. Real Dollars

In financial calculations spanning time, currency value can be looked at from two different perspectives. It's important when doing historical analysis or making financial projections to understand these two views of value.

One way to look at currency is as pieces of paper — you know, the ones in your wallet. A paper dollar today is the same piece of paper as a dollar tomorrow. These dollars are called *"nominal dollars,"* or *"current dollars."* Their value is in the money of the day, today

In nominal dollars, a McDonald's Big Mac cost 50¢ 20 years ago and it costs $3.75 today. Nominal dollars and current prices are just the dollars that Dad took out of his wallet to buy you that Big Mac 20 years ago or the dollars that you spent today to buy one for your son. However, prices tend to increase over time primarily due to inflation. Sometimes it is useful to look at "values" of goods in the past (or expected values in the future) rather than at their actual cost way back when in nominal dollars.

From this inflation-corrected perspective, we will use *"real dollars,"* also called *"constant dollars."* Real dollars are nominal dollars that have been adjusted to take out (or add back in) the effects of inflation.

Why bother? Well, it is very difficult to analyze financially the price of today's Big Mac at $3.75 with a 20-years-ago Big Mac at 50¢. It is basically the same burger. And thus, when you take out inflation (i.e., convert from nominal dollars into real dollars) the price difference becomes much more comparable and explainable.

Money Illusion

The term *money illusion* refers to the tendency of people (old people?) to think of currency in nominal rather than real terms. People remember and pay more attention to the numerical or face value of money (nominal dollars) than they do to its relative purchasing power (real dollars). Thus, Dad keeps talking about those 50¢ Big Macs just as Granddad kept telling us about a 10¢ breakfast of scrambled eggs, bacon and coffee. Whatever.

Nominal vs. Real Dollars

- In economic parlance, "nominal" dollars are the face value of currency, whereas "real" dollar values have been corrected for inflation relative to some base year.

- All financial statements are reported in **nominal dollars.** If the company sold $100 in widgets in 1995 and $110 in widgets in 2006, then these numbers will be shown under the respective years in financial reports. So, sales were slightly up. Right?

- Not really in value terms. If we looked at sales in the two periods in **real dollars** (that is, corrected for inflation from 1995 to 2006), we would see that real sales were down in value (purchasing power).

- To convert a nominal dollar amount from "year y" into real dollar purchasing power in another "year x," use the following formula. In the Consumer Price Index (CPI) issued by the Commerce Department, 1983/4 is selected as the base year equal 100.

  Accounting for inflation between 1995 and 2006, we would need to sell $132.28 worth of widgets in 2006 to equal the $100 value of our sales performance back in 1995.

  $$\textbf{Real Dollars}_x = \textbf{Nominal Dollars}_y \left(\frac{\textbf{CPI}_x}{\textbf{CPI}_y}\right)$$

- Using our example and with the $CPI_{1995} = 152.4$ and the $CPI_{2006} = 201.6$, then

  $$2006 \text{ Real Dollars} = \$100 \times \left(\frac{201.6}{152.4}\right) = \$132.28$$

Real Dollars (Constant Dollars)

- **Real dollars** (also called *constant dollars*) are amounts that have been adjusted to account for the impact of inflation. **Nominal dollars** (also called *current dollars*) are the actual dollars paid or received at the time without any adjustments.

- The following graph shows the selling price of a pound of OREO® Brand Cookies for each year from 1980 to 2018 in nominal dollars and also the value of the cookies in real dollars.

  The nominal price consumers paid for a pound of cookies increased from $1.49 in 1980 to $3.68 in 2018. That is more than double the price. However, much of this price rise is due to inflation during the 38-year period. See the price (nominal and real) graph below.

Price of OREO Brand Cookies 1980 to 2018

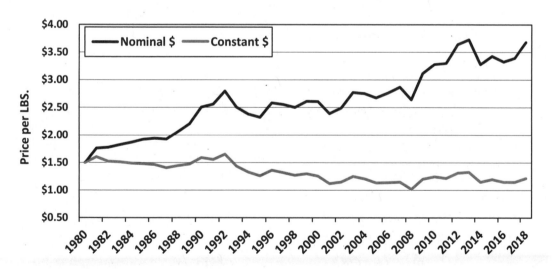

- The data table on the next page shows the relationship between nominal dollars, the CPI, and inflation-adjusted real dollars.

Price of OREO Brand Cookies from 1980 to 2018

YEAR	A. PRICES IN NOMINAL DOLLARS	B. PRICES IN 1980 REAL DOLLARS	CONSUMER PRICE INDEX (CPI)	YEAR	A. PRICES IN NOMINAL DOLLARS	B. PRICES IN 1980 REAL DOLLARS	CONSUMER PRICE INDEX (CPI)
1980	$1.49	$1.49	82.4	2000	$2.61	$1.25	172.2
1981	$1.76	$1.60	90.9	2001	$2.39	$1.11	177.1
1982	$1.78	$1.52	96.5	2002	$2.49	$1.14	179.9
1983	$1.82	$1.52	100.0	2003	$2.77	$1.24	184.0
1984	$1.87	$1.48	103.9	2004	$2.75	$1.20	188.9
1985	$1.92	$1.47	107.6	2005	$2.68	$1.13	195.3
1986	$1.94	$1.46	109.6	2006	$2.76	$1.13	201.6
1987	$1.93	$1.40	113.6	2007	$2.87	$1.14	207.3
1988	$2.06	$1.44	118.3	2008	$2.64	$1.01	215.3
1989	$2.20	$1.46	124.0	2009	$3.11	$1.20	214.5
1990	$2.51	$1.58	130.7	2010	$3.28	$1.24	218.0
1991	$2.56	$1.55	136.2	2011	$3.30	$1.21	224.9
1992	$2.80	$1.64	140.3	2012	$3.64	$1.31	229.6
1993	$2.50	$1.43	144.5	2013	$3.73	$1.32	233.0
1994	$2.38	$1.32	148.2	2014	$3.28	$1.14	236.7
1995	$2.32	$1.25	152.4	2015	$3.43	$1.19	237.0
1996	$2.58	$1.36	156.9	2016	$3.33	$1.14	240.0
1997	$2.55	$1.31	160.5	2017	$3.40	$1.14	245.1
1998	$2.50	$1.26	163.0	2018	$3.68	$1.21	251.0
1999	$2.61	$1.29	166.6				

Column A. *Price in Nominal Dollars* shows the actual amount consumers paid for a one-pound bag of OREO Brand Cookies in the year indicated.

CPI Column shows the Consumer Price Index for each year. CPI has been normalized by the United States Commerce Department so that 1983/84 prices are designated as 100.

Column B. *Price in Real Dollars* show the value of a one-pound bag of OREO Brand Cookies as adjusted for inflation using the equation on the prior page and the CPI value of 1980 as a base.

For example, although consumers in 1996 would have to pay $2.58 for a pound of cookies in nominal dollars, the actual value of that amount in 1980 real dollars (that is, discounting for inflation from 1989 through 1996) would be only $1.36, a 15¢ less than the nominal price in 1980.

~

Inflation over time can cause dramatic differences in real and nominal dollar amounts. Analysis of present, past, or future economic and business conditions must properly account for inflation to understand the sweep of financial history.

Appendix C.
Nonprofit Accounting and Financial Statements

Important functions of for-profit financial statements are to: (a) correctly compute a company's profit and any tax liability in a period, and (b) report these results to owners and the government.

Nonprofit financial statements have a different purpose. There are no traditional owners of a nonprofit entity (just constituencies). But the government is still very interested in nonprofit financials and reporting. The nonprofit status for an organization provides a large tax break for the organization's activities as well as personal income tax deductions for donors.

Much of for-profit and nonprofit accounting and financial statements are the same. We will describe here the major differences. *Hint, the biggest differences between these two organizational types is in the specific definitions of revenue and profit (surplus) and when and how they are recorded and reported.*

The Nonprofit World

Almost all nonprofit organizations are state-chartered corporations and must register as such with the Secretary of State in the locale where they are organized. (The American Red Cross and the Boy Scouts of America are federally chartered.)

All nonprofit organizations must have a public purpose (mission) and they do not have "owners" in the traditional sense. They are held as a public trust and governed by a voluntary board of directors. Note that while all nonprofits do not pay taxes, only some nonprofits, "501(c)(3) public charities" offer tax deductions to their donors.

By law, no individual director or staff member of a nonprofit can benefit personally from any net profits (called *surplus* in nonprofit language) generated by the organization. On the other hand, in for-profit companies, profits belong to the owning shareholders.

Public Charities
(501(c)(3) Organizations

Not all nonprofit organizations can accept tax-deductible contributions. Only so-called "public charities" can. 501(c)(3) refers to the section of IRS tax code describing public charities.

These charities include most organizations active in the arts, education, health care, and human services. Religious congregations are also considered public charities, but for constitutional reasons they are not required to register with the IRS.

For all cash, check, or credit card donations, the nonprofit organization must provide the donor a written communication as a record of the contribution. Bank records (canceled checks, or credit card statements) are sufficient provided they show the date, the name of the charity, and the amount of the payment.

Nonprofit
Statement of Activities

The nonprofit *Statement of Activities* is analogous to the *Income Statement* of for-profit companies. The *Statement of Activities* shows money coming into the organization (revenue) and money going out (expenses).

Nonprofit Financial Statements

Statement of Activities *(Income Statement)* ②

		Without Restrictions	With Restrictions	TOTAL
Revenue ①	CONTRIBUTIONS & GIFTS	$ -	$ -	$ -
	PROGRAM SERVICES REVENUE	-		-
	GRANTS & CONTRACTS	-		-
	OTHER REVENUE	-		-
	TOTAL REVENUE	$ -	$ -	$ -
Expense ③	FUNDRAISING	-		
	PROGRAM SERVICES	-		
	GRANTS & CONTRACTS			
	MANAGEMENT & GENERAL	-		
	OPERATING EXPENSE		-	$ -
	CHANGE IN NET ASSETS			- ④
	BEGINNING NET ASSETS			-
	ENDING NET ASSETS			$ -

Statement of Cash Flows ⑦

BEGINNING CASH BALANCE	$ -
CASH RECEIPTS	-
CASH DISBURSEMENTS	-
CASH FLOW FROM OPERATIONS	-
PP&E PURCHASE	-
NET BORROWINGS	-
INVESTMENT INCOME	-
ENDING CASH BALANCES	$ -

Statement of Financial Position *(Balance Sheet)* ⑤

Assets	CASH	$ -
	ACCOUNTS RECEIVABLE	-
	INVENTORIES	-
	PREPAID EXPENSES	-
	PLEDGES RECEIVABLE	-
	INVESTMENTS	-
	NET FIXED ASSETS	-
	TOTAL ASSETS	$ -
Liabilities & Net Assets	ACCOUNTS PAYABLE	$ -
	ACCRUED EXPENSES	-
	CURRENT PORTION OF DEBT	-
	LONG-TERM DEBT	-
	TOTAL LIABILITIES	$ -
	W/O DONOR RESTRICTIONS	- ⑥
	WITH DONOR RESTRICTIONS	-
	TOTAL NET ASSETS	$ -
	TOTAL LIABILITIES & NET ASSETS	$ -

The money left over when you subtract expenses from revenue for a nonprofit organization is called "surplus" or, more formally stated, the organization's **CHANGE IN NET ASSETS** over a specified time period. The term, **NET ASSETS** is unique to nonprofit accounting and is analogous to a for-profit-company's shareholders' equity on the *Income Statement.*

See the three main nonprofit financial statement formats on the facing page. A fourth statement, unique to nonprofit reporting, the *Statement of Functional Expenses,* is shown on page 279.

Nonprofit Revenue Types

① Nonprofit revenue is all the money coming into the organization during the period (plus pledges to contribute in the future). Revenue is shown on the *Statement of Activities* and categorized by type:

CONTRIBUTIONS & GIFTS are recorded in the *Statement of Activities* when cash is received from a donor or a promise (pledge) to give cash in the future is made by the donor.

Pledges are formal and specific donor promises to give. Pledges to nonprofit organizations are handled in a very special way. They are recognized as revenue when the pledge is made, not when money is actually received.

Contributions and gifts (and pledges, when funded) are often tax deductible by the donor when given to 501(c)(3) public charities.

PROGRAM SERVICES REVENUE is recorded when the nonprofit organization provides a product or service to a client for a fee. This transfer of product or service for money is often called an "exchange transaction." The nonprofit organization exchanges its products or services for cash paid by the receiver of the products or services.

Just because goods and services are purchased from a nonprofit organization, does not mean that the nonprofit organization is jeopardizing its nonprofit status. Nonprofit organizations often sell goods and services that support their public mission. The nonprofit organization may even generate an increase in **NET ASSETS** (surplus) in the transaction, analogous to profit for a for-profit company. More later.

GRANTS & CONTRACTS is revenue from institutional donors such as governmental agencies, other charitable organizations, and foundations. These grants and contracts are usually: (a) for a specific stated purpose, (b) to be performed in a specific period of time, and (c) directly related to the recipient nonprofit organization's skills and charitable mission.

OTHER REVENUE is revenue received from sources other than those listed as separate line items. If revenue from a source type is large, it really should have its own line on the *Statement of Activities.* Membership fees, ticket sales, auction proceeds, revenue from special events, advertisement sales, contributed goods or services (at fair market value), and so forth, are examples of other types of revenue included here.

Nonprofit Revenue Restrictions

② Revenue is classified on the *Statement of Activities* in two groupings, depending on whether any use restrictions are placed on the contribution by the donor:

Without Donor Restrictions (unrestricted revenue). The organization can use this revenue for any mission purpose at the discretion of the Board of Directors.

With Donor Restrictions (restricted revenue). The organization can only use this revenue for the specific purpose (and time period) specified by the donor (and accepted by the board). Prior to changes in nonprofit accounting practice (2017), endowments (only interest received can be spent, never the principal) were a separate category. Now it is just thrown into the restricted revenue bucket.

Nonprofit Expenses

③ Expenses shown on the *Statement of Activities* are grouped into specific categories:

FUNDRAISING expenses are expenditures to solicit contributions, gifts, contracts, and grants.

PROGRAM SERVICES expenses are expenditures to deliver goods and services to clients in support of mission. Salaries and wages are often the biggest expense here.

GRANTS & CONTRACTS expenses are expenditures to fulfill the requirements of government and foundation contracts in support of the organization's mission.

MANAGEMENT & GENERAL expenses are sometimes called overhead. Expenditures for occupancy, utilities, general management, accounting, legal, and other keeping the doors open necessities.

Net Assets

④ Note the change, beginning, and ending **NET ASSETS** lines at the bottom of the *Statement of Activities*.

CHANGE IN NET ASSETS is simply the difference between the nonprofit organization's revenues and expenses for the period, often called surplus. This amount is analogous to profit in a for-profit company.

BEGINNING NET ASSETS is the accumulated annual changes in net assets since the nonprofit's inception — sum of **UNRESTRICTED NET ASSETS** and **RESTRICTED NET ASSETS** — shown on all the organization's prior year's *Statements of Activities*.

ENDING NET ASSETS is simply the sum of the beginning net assets at the start of the accounting period plus the net assets

generated by the organization in the current period. The double line designates a final total.

ENDING NET ASSETS will be shown as **TOTAL NET ASSETS** on the *Statement of Financial Position* for this accounting period and will be shown on the *Statement of Activities* as the **BEGINNING NET ASSETS** at the start of the next accounting period.

NOTE: The net assets of nonprofit organizations and profits of for-profit companies differ in that net assets belong to the organization itself and may *only be used* by the organization in support of its public mission. In contrast, all the profits made by a for-profit company belong to its shareholders (owners).

These profits are available for distribution as dividends to these shareholders. But since nonprofit organizations have no "owners" they can make no such distributions and all surplus is retained by the organization to be used in furtherance of its mission.

Statement of Financial Position

⑤ The *Statement of Financial Position* for a nonprofit organization shows the organization's financial strength at a single point in time, commonly reported at the end of a year. It is analogous to a for-profit company's *Balance Sheet*.

The statement presents: (a) assets — what the organization owns. (b) liabilities — what the organization owes others, and (c) net assets — what the organization's is worth.

⑥ **NET ASSETS** can be thought of as a special obligation of the organization to be used to serve its mission; and represents its unspent wealth (revenue minus expenses) accumulated since the founding of the organization. **NET ASSETS** are presented on the statement separately by restriction category.

Statement of Cash Flows

⑦ The nonprofit organization's *Statement of Cash Flows* is like a checkbook register and is structured just the same as that of a for-profit enterprise. You record the payments (cash outflows) and deposits (cash inflows) for a period of time.

Nonprofit Statement of Functional Expenses

This IRS required statement, unique to nonprofits, presents the organization's expenses in greater detail than on the *Statement of Activities*. A matrix format is used showing natural expenses in rows (salaries, benefits, supplies, and so forth),

Nonprofit Statement of Functional Expenses ⑩

	Program A	Program B	Program C	Management & General	Fundraising	Indirect Overhead	Total Expense
Salaries & Benefits	$	$	$	$	$		$
Rent & Utilities							
Supplies							
Contractors & Consultants							
Depreciation							
Direct Overhead							
all other							
Total Expense	$	$	$	$	$	$	$
Contributions & Gift Revenue	$	$	$	$	$	$	$
Grants & Contract Revenue							
Total Program Revenue	$	$	$				
Surplus *(Total Revenue - Total Expense)*	$	$	$				

Program Services ⑧ Support Services ⑪ ⑨ ⑫ ⑬ ⑭

versus functional expenses in columns (specific programs and internal indirect program support services).

Programs

Most nonprofit organizations administer several stand-alone, though most often interrelated, programs. It is often useful to look at their financials separately and the *Statement of Functional Expenses* does just that.

⑧ **Functional Expense Groups** Reporting by these groupings shows the organization's expenditures by major programs. Is the organization's spending congruent with its mission? Is it putting its money where its mouth is?

⑨ **Natural Expense Groups** Reporting by these groupings shows the organization's expenditures by the type of expense — how it spends its money to get desired results. Is this allocation of expenses the most efficient and effective mix?

Overhead

Overhead expenses are often viewed with suspicion by donors and other funders as a potential waste of money. However, these expenses are real (rent, utilities, audits, finance, staff training and so forth) and are required in a well-managed organization.

Classification of overhead as support services, direct overhead and indirect overhead, provides more information and additional clarity to these important and necessary expenses.

⑩ **Support Service Allocations** Some overhead expenses are best thought of as organization-wide, such as the CEO's salary. Others can be assigned to a specific program as direct overhead, such as occupancy, the space costs used by the program.

⑪ **Indirect Overhead** Indirect overhead is an expense type that is difficult to assign to a specific project or functional expense group.

⑫ **Direct Overhead** Direct overhead can be assigned but is really of an "all-other" type and does not fit into a natural expense group.

⑬ **Revenue by Program** As it prepares budgets, the board must decide and then earmark and allocate what unrestricted contribution and gift revenue monies will be used in which projects. As monies come in, they are listed here by function. Grants and contact revenue is easy to list by program.

⑭ **Surplus by Program** Revenue minus expense equals surplus. Is the organization generating a surplus in all its programs? Is one program showing a large loss, and can we justify this loss? This data line summarizes the SURPLUS generated by separate programs.

Fund Accounting

Since restricted revenue must be earmarked for the donor's stated gift purpose, nonprofit organizations account separately for expenses by each program funded. This requirement adds complexity to a nonprofit's accounting that is not found in for-profit organization.

When a nonprofit organization accepts restricted revenue, it forms a commercial "contract" with the donor requiring it to spend the revenue as described in the contract. Auditors and the IRS require that the nonprofit organization document this restricted use in its books.

Performance Measurement: Ratios, Benchmarks, & Trends

Most of the financial ratios described in Chapter 13 are applicable to nonprofit organizations as well. Follows a discussion of ratios specifically useful to nonprofits.

Fundraising Expense Ratio is the FUNDRAISING expense divided by the TOTAL REVENUE. Values of 10% to 30% are normal, depending on the type of solicitation as well as the type of organization and its aggressiveness.

Return on Revenue is the standard profitability ratio computed as increase in NET ASSETS divided by TOTAL REVENUE for a period. I know, I know, nonprofit organizations do not generate profits like for-profit companies do. However, nonprofits have the analogous increase in CHANGE IN NET ASSETS (revenue minus expenses) and call it a surplus. Achieving a surplus will be necessary to grow the size and scope of the organization.

Consistent surplus generation by a nonprofit organization is an indicator of strong financial management. Break-even results do not allow for breathing room for when things do not go according to plan. Surplus provides that cushion to ride out a slow donation period or to seize a strategic opportunity.

Revenue Reliance Ratio measures how many of your eggs are being carried in one basket. Reliance on just a single income source is risky because it could go away and leave you with nothing to fall back on.

Lower overall risk to the organization's long-term viability is found with a broad base of support from individuals, foundations, and government agencies through contributions and gifts, program services revenue, contracts, and grants.

Self-Sufficiency Ratio measures the PROGRAM SERVICES REVENUE divided by TOTAL REVENUE. A high ratio means the organization generates enough revenue on its own through program services to sustain itself without gifts and grants.

Overhead Ratio is the percentage of a nonprofit's TOTAL EXPENSES that is devoted to its FUNDRAISING plus MANAGEMENT & GENERAL expenses. There is no "right" percentage here, 15% to 30% is common. Organizations have different strategies of operation and function in different realms.

Donors scrutinize this fundraising ratio. However, we all can agree that the fund-raising and administrative expenses are essential to sustaining the organization. How much to spend, however, is a continuing debate.

～

Nonprofit organizations must decide how to measure performance to mission and to the financial performance of actions in support of the mission. In for-profit companies, there is a single ultimate measurement — profits. Things are not so simple for nonprofit organizations.

Key questions to ask and then to answer are:

1. Overall, how healthy is our organization today? Is it healthier today than it was three years ago? Why or why not?

2. Are our programs sustainable, that is, generating the resources required to meet today's needs without compromising the future?

This book focuses mostly on financial measures of success. Note that an organization faithfully adhering to its mission, but operating with sloppy resource (financial) management, is failing. However, also note that a beautifully run financial operation that strays from its mission is also failing.

Most important decisions made by nonprofit organizations are based, in some material way, on accounting decisions.

Efficient and effective stewardship of monies received in support of mission is the gold standard by which to measure all performance in nonprofits.

Key Performance Indicators

KPIs are quantifiable measurements as well as qualitative written descriptions of a nonprofit organization's health and success. An organization's KPIs are usually benchmarked against peer organizations and commonly recognized business-model ratios.

Different types of nonprofit organizations will use different KPIs. For example: contribution & gift revenue growth compared to fundraising expense, visitor and membership data for a museum, enrollment data for a day care center, number of patients served for a clinic, and so forth.

Graphic "dashboards" are an ideal way to concisely present these KPIs to stakeholders of the organization. Dashboards are a simple, often colorful, graphic representation of KPIs. With dashboards, performance to mission can be seen at a glance and historical trends — both favorable and unfavorable — are obvious. Dashboard presentations convey financial and operating information in an easy to understand and difficult to ignore or misinterpret format, riveting attention to what is truly important.

Form 990

IRS Form 990 *Return of Organization Exempt from Income Tax* is the annual government tax filing required by all nonprofit organizations. Nonprofits do not pay income taxes, but they do provide donors with income tax deductions, so the IRS wants to make sure that everything is on the up-and-up.-

Information in the four major nonprofit financial statement is required plus salary information of the highest paid officers of the nonprofit organization. The form is signed by the organizations CEO or treasurer under penalty of perjury. The I.R.S. is serious.

Additional Resources

See the author's nonprofit finance and governance books:

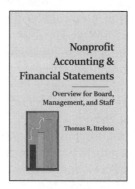

Nonprofit Accounting & Financial Statements: Overview for Board, Management, and Staff, 2nd Edition, 256 pages, 2017. ISBN-13: 978-0-9971089-6-5

A Picture Book of Nonprofit Financial Statements, 60 pages, 2017 ISBN-13: 978-0-9971089-4-1

Web site An excellent web site providing nonprofit accounting and finance guidance is published by the Greater Washington Society of CPAs (GWSCPA).

The GWSCPA Educational Foundation is a 501(c)(3) charitable organization whose mission is to: (a) strengthen the nonprofit sector through providing financial management resources and (b) educate current and future CPAs with continuing professional education programs and student scholarships.

Visit their website at the URL below. Use the web site search function to find information on specific topics:

http://www.gwscpa.org/content/about_us/nonprofit_accounting_basics.aspx

Appendix D.
Cash Flow Statement Formats

The *Cash Flow Statement* format that we have been using for Apple-Seed Enterprises' financial statements is a very simple-to-understand cash movement "in and out" presentation. We have likened it to a check register, with the "sources of cash" being deposits and the "uses of cash" being written checks.

However, most accountants would prefer to use another format for cash flow. This format (shown on the next page) is better likened to a "bridge" between the *Balance Sheet* at the start of a period and the *Balance Sheet* at the end of a period.

This bridging format specifically shows the asset, liability and equity accounts that change to provide cash, and the accounts that change when using cash.

Most of the time when you look at financial statements you will see a statement like the one on the next page. Both formats allow you to get to the same answer, *Ending Cash Balance,* but in different ways. The format introduced here focuses on cash movements divided into three major categories of interest to anyone reviewing the cash performance of a business:

1. **Cash Flows from Operations** This section shows cash sources and uses from activities such as making and selling products, the company's "operations."

2. **Cash Flows from Investing** This section shows uses of cash by the company to purchase productive assets such as property, plant and equipment.

Balance Sheet	as of T19	as of T31	T31 less T19
Assets			
CASH	$ 588,220	$ 488,462	$ (99,758)
ACCOUNTS RECEIVABLE	-	454,760	454,760
INVENTORIES	577,970	414,770	(163,200)
PREPAID EXPENSES	-	-	-
CURRENT ASSETS	1,166,190	1,357,992	191,802
OTHER ASSETS	-	-	-
FIXED ASSETS @ COST	1,750,000	1,750,000	-
ACCUMULATED DEPRECIATION	14,286	78,573	64,287
NET FIXED ASSETS	1,735,714	1,671,427	(64,287)
TOTAL ASSETS	2,901,904	3,029,419	127,515
Liabilities & Equity			
ACCOUNTS PAYABLE	$ 469,204	$ 236,297	$ (232,907)
ACCRUED EXPENSES	18,480	26,435	7,955
CURRENT PORTION OF DEBT	100,000	100,000	-
INCOME TAXES PAYABLE	-	139,804	139,804
CURRENT LIABILITIES	587,684	502,536	(85,148)
LONG-TERM DEBT	900,000	800,000	(100,000)
CAPITAL STOCK	1,550,000	1,550,000	-
RETAINED EARNINGS	(135,780)	176,883	312,663
SHAREHOLDERS' EQUITY	1,414,220	1,726,883	312,663
TOTAL LIABILITIES & EQUITY	$ 2,901,904	$ 3,029,419	$ 127,515

The figure at the left shows the computation of the difference between *Balance Sheet* T19 and T31 account values to be used in constructing the *Statement of Cash Flows* on the next page.

Statement of Cash Flows — T19 thru T31

CASH FLOWS FROM OPERATING ACTIVITIES

Net Income	**$387,662**	*(Note 1)*

Adjustments to reconsile net income to cash used in operations.

Depreciation	**64,287**	*(Note 2)*

Changes in working capital.

Accounts Receivable	**(454,760)**	*(Note 3)*
Inventories	**163,200**	*(Note 3)*
Prepaid Expenses	**$0**	*(Note 4)*
Accounts Payable	**232,907**	*(Note 4)*
Accrued Expenses	**7,955**	*(Note 4)*
Income Taxes Payable	**139,804**	*(Note 4)*
Cash Used in Operations	**$75,242**	

CASH FLOWS FROM FINANCING ACTIVITIES

PP&E Purchases	**$0**	*(Note 5)*
Cash Used in Investing Activities	**$0**	

CASH FLOWS FROM FINANCING ACTIVITIES

Sale of Stock	**$0**	*(Note 6)*
Change in Debt	**(100,000)**	*(Note 7)*
Dividends Paid	**(75,000)**	*(Note 4)*
Cash from Financing Acticvities	**$175,000**	

Net Increase (Decrease) in Cash	**(99,758)**	*(T19 thru T31)*
Beginning Cash	**588,220**	*(as of T19)*
ENDING CASH	**$488,462**	*(as of T31)*

3. **Cash Flows from Financing**
   This section shows cash received by the company from selling stock to investors, borrowing money from a bank, and uses such as paying dividends or repaying loans

   If we look on page 140 at Apple-Seed's *Cash Flow Statement* for Transaction 19, we see $588,220 as an ending cash balance. Looking at AppleSeed's *Cash Flow Statement* for Transaction 31 on page 175, we see $488,462 as an ending cash balance. Subtracting the earlier from the later cash balance, we see that in the time between these two transactions, cash has dropped by $99,758.

   Review the following notes to see how this "bridging" cash flow statement is constructed.

Note 1. Income for the period is computed from the *Income Statements* by subtracting NET INCOME as of Transaction 19 ($135,780 loss) from NET INCOME as of Transaction 31 ($251,883 profit).

Note 2. Computed as change in Accumulated Depreciation. Depreciation does not affect cash flow, but because it has been subtracted from the NET INCOME for the period, it must be added back here to get a true picture of cash movements.

Note 3. Computed as the change in these asset accounts. Note that an increase in an asset account means the company has more working capital and a positive cash flow in that account.

Note 4. Computed as the change in these liability accounts. Note that an increase in a liability account means the company has less working capital and a negative cash flow in that account.

Note 5. Computed as change in PROPERTY, PLANT & EQUIPMENT assets. An increase in PP&E takes cash.

Note 6. Computed as the change in the CAPITAL STOCK account of Shareholders' Equity.

Note 7. Computed as the change in the CURRENT PORTION OF DEBT and LONG-TERM DEBT accounts. Lowering of overall debt decreases cash. Increasing overall debt increases cash.

Note 8. Dividends paid to shareholders lowers cash.

Appendix E.
Debits and Credits

The Olden Days

Back in the olden days when systematic accounting and statement presentation was first developed, the monks would write down each and every transaction as they occurred. Literally, "the books" of a company were just that, the books containing a company's financial records!

The concept of *debits* and *credits* was invented to: (a) structure the layout of the books for everyone to understand, (b) aid the monks in classifying and recording transactions properly, and (c) catch manual transcribing errors.

The term debit comes from the Latin word *debitum*, meaning "what is due," and credit comes from the Latin *creditum*, defined as "something entrusted to another or a loan." The logic is that when you increase assets, the change in the asset account is a debit, because something must be due to pay for that increase (i.e. the cost of the asset in cash that would be entered as a credit in the cash account).

Double-Entry Bookkeeping

Debits and credits are terms first coming into used 500 years ago. Luca Pacioli, a Franciscan monk, developed the concepts underlying double entry bookkeeping. The monks would prepare books (called ledgers) with one account on each page. They would write down a description of the transaction and then put the transaction dollar amount in one of two columns at the right on the page.

The first column was labeled debit and the next column was labeled credit. Note, there was often a third column on the page with a running total for the account.

> **"Do not end your workday until your debits equal your credits."**
> **Luca Pacioli**,
> Franciscan monk, the "Father of Accounting"

Every accounting transaction had to have a credit entry on one account page and a debit entry on another account page. Hence, *double entry bookkeeping*. Thus, when a transaction is entered with these two entries, the financial statement will remain in balance according to the general equation of accounting: *Assets = Liabilities + Equity*.

Double entry and debits and credits are still used by bookkeepers when they manually record financial transactions in the company's record books. This double-entry system reduces clerical errors. Since the books must always balance, the total debits must always equal the total credits after you post the journal entries to the ledger accounts. If the amounts do not balance, you have made an error and you must find and correct it.

~

Bookkeepers and accountants still find the concept of debit and credit useful and standard accounting courses still teach this basic debit/credit structure. However, you will not find it used in this book because debit and credit nomenclature is:

1. often counterintuitive and thus confusing for nonaccountants,

2. not necessary to have a grasp of financial statement required for non-financial managers, and

3. computerization of accounting records has made catching mistakes when manually entering numbers less necessary.

Accounting is done with computer's now and database rules govern where amounts are placed in virtual ledgers. But since bookkeepers and accountants use these terms debit and credit all the time, in this appendix we will attempt to give you just enough understanding to be able to converse intelligently with the accounting types in your organization.

Transaction Entries

A double-entry bookkeeping system uses journal books (with chronological entries) and ledger books (with separate account-by-account pages), to record the transaction descriptions and associated debit and credit amounts. The so-called General Journal contains a record of all transaction in chronological order with a unique sequence number to forever remember them and tie the transaction to entries in the account ledgers. Makes finding errors easier.

Transactions are first entered in a journal and then posted to ledger accounts. These accounts show income, expenses, assets (property a business owns), liabilities (debts of a business), and net worth (excess of assets over liabilities).

In the double-entry system, each account has a left side column for debits and a right side column for credits. It is self-balancing because you record every transaction as a debit entry in one account and as a credit entry in another.

Whether a debit increases or decreases an account depends on the type of account. The basic principle is that the account receiving benefit is "debited" and the account giving benefit is "credited."

For instance, an increase in an asset account is a debit. An increase in a liability or equity account is a credit. An increase in a sales account is a debit. An increase in an expense account is a credit. As an example: paying off a debt "benefits" the liability section of the *Balance Sheet*. The entry lowers the reported numeric value. Thus, the entry is a *debit*.

Whether a DEBIT increases or decreases an account depends on the type of account. The basic principle is that the account *receiving benefit* is "debited" and the account *giving benefit* is "credited."

For instance, an increase in an asset account is a debit. An increase in a liability or equity account is a credit. An increase in a sales account is a debit. An increase in an expense account is a credit.

Effects of Debits and Credits

There are five (5) basic account types: assets, liabilities, sales/income and expense. Making account entries will either increase or decrease the account balances. Entries made on the left column (debit) in a T-Account Ledger, will either increase or decrease the balance as shown below by account type. For each debit entry there must be a compensating credit entry (made on the right column).

This debit/credit concept is easiest to remember by thinking about the:

1. *Balance Sheet* equation and keeping it in balance:

Assets = Liability + Equity

2. *Income Statement* equation and the relationship of increases in sales revenue, expenses, and income:

Sales – Costs + Expenses = Income

The table below summarizes how transaction entries effect account balances.

Effect of Debit and Credit Entries by Account Type

Account	DEBIT	CREDIT
Asset Account	*increase*	*decrease*
Liability Account	*decrease*	*increase*
Sales Revenue	*decrease*	*increase*
Expenses	*increase*	*decrease*
Income	*decrease*	*increase*
Equity	*decrease*	*increase*

Transaction Examples Following are journal entries for selected transaction examples in this book. Refer to the Transaction No. detail page earlier in the book.

Recording a Supply Purchase on Credit
(Transaction 19)

Account	DEBIT	CREDIT
Sales Expense	$103,250	
Accounts Payable		$103,250

Recording a Payment to a Vendor
(Transaction 14)

Account	DEBIT	CREDIT
Accounts Payable	$20,000	
Cash		$20,000

Recording a New Debt
(Transaction 3)

Account	DEBIT	CREDIT
Cash	$1,000,000	
LT Debt		$900,000
Current Debt		$100,000

Recording a Fixed Asset Purchase
(Transaction 4)

Account	DEBIT	CREDIT
PP&E @ Cost	$1,500,000	
Cash		$1,500,000

Recording a Sale on Credit (T20)

Account	DEBIT	CREDIT
Accts. Receivable	$15,900	
COGS	$10,200	
Selling Expense	$318	
Accrued Expense		$318
Sales Revenue		$15,900
Inventory		$10,200

Recording Sale of Stock
(Transaction 1)

Account	DEBIT	CREDIT
Capital Stock		$1,500,000
Cash	$1,500,000	

Recording Salary Payment
(Transaction 2)

Account	DEBIT	CREDIT
G&A Expense	$6,230	
Accrued Expense		$2,860
Cash		$3,370

Still Confused? Don't worry too much. You are not the bookkeeper or accountant. You can still understand financial statements and use them to run your business without being able to credit or debit!

Index

Financial Statements

current (nominal) dollars
271-273

contribution, manufacturing
145

contributions, nonprofits
275, 277

cost of capital
227

costing methods
202-203

cost elements, manufacturing
raw materials 111
direct labor 111
mfg. overhead 112-113

costs
9, 49

costs vs. expense
52

cost of goods sold (COGS)
50, T16, T20, T21, T22, T24

CPA (Certified Public
Accountant
3, 13-14

credit line
227

credits and debits
285-287

current assets
20-25, 28, 36, 190

current asset cycle,
25

current debt
31, 34

current liabilities
31-33

current ratio
190

D

dashboards, nonprofit
282

debits and credits
285-287

debt
34
current portion T3, T32
long-term T3, T26

debt ratio
196-7

debt-to-equity ratio
196-197

decision tree analysis
221-223

depreciation
27, 82, 97, 113, 125, 284,
T4, T5

dilution
226

disbursements
69

discount rate
236

discounted cash flow
178

dividends
38, 40, 278

donor restrictions
276-277

double entry bookkeeping
285

double lines in statements
14

E, F

earnings
9

elasticity of demand
246

ending cash balance
75

ending net assets, nonprofit
276, 278

equity
38, 41, 74

errors, accounting
209

estimates and judgements
12

Excel© , Microsoft
240, 243, 245

expenditures
9-10, 49, 52, 80

expense cycle
77, 80

expenses
9, 52-53

extrinsic risk
219

exchange transaction,
nonprofit
277

fair market value
254

FASB
13-14, 256, 259, 261

FIFO costing (first-in;
first-out),
203-205, 211

financial ratios by industry
198-199

finished goods
23, 121, 132, T15

fiscal period
12

fixed asset purchases
T4, T8, T33

fixed assets
26-28,

fixed asset cycle
82

fixed costs, manufacturing
114, 144

forecasting, cash flow
241-242

fraud
205-207, 263, 266

functional expenses, nonprofit
279-280

fundraising, nonprofit
276, 280

future value (FV)
235-240

G, H, I

GAAP
13-14, 203-204

general & administrative
T2, T5, T9, T24, T25, T33

gifts, nonprofit
277

goals
4, 145, 217-220, 236

going concern
11, 180

grants & contracts, nonprofit
276, 278

greater fool theory
264

gross margin (gross profit)
51, 194, 204-205

hurdle rate
236

historical cost
11

income
54,58

Further Study

Books:

Analysis for Financial Management by Robert Higgins. *2011 McGraw-Hill/Erwin* ISBN-13: 978-0078034688. This popular text is currently in its 15th edition. Expensive to buy new, but good used copies are available on-line.

Nonprofit Accounting & Financial Statements: Overview for Board, Management, and Staff, 2nd Edition by Thomas R. Ittelson, 256 pages, 2017. ISBN-13: 978-0-9971089-6-5

A Visual Guide to Financial Statements: Overview for Non-Financial Managers & Investors by Thomas R. Ittelson, *full color, 46 pages, 2019, ISBN-13: 978-0997108972*

Websites:

An excellent web site providing accounting and finance guidance is published by the Greater Washington Society of CPAs (GWSCPA). Its primary focus is nonprofit accounting but also useful for for-profit accounting information. Visit their website. Use the site search function to research specific accounting topics:

http://www.gwscpa.org/content/ about_us /nonprofit_accounting_basics.aspx

Searches:

Internet searches are an invaluable source of detailed information on accounting and financial statements. Favorites sites are information are ***investopia.com*** and ***wikipedia.org***.

To perform a search on a specific term or topic, type in the search bar the name of either site to search, "investopia" or "wikipedia," and also the term or topic of interest. Surf the results and enjoy the ride.

Other relevant books by Thomas R. Ittelson:

A Visual Guide to Financial Statements: Overview for Non-Financial Managers & Investors
full color, 46 pages, 2019, **ISBN-13:** 978-0997108972

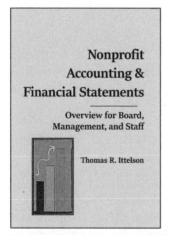

Nonprofit Accounting & Financial Statements: Overview for Board, Management, and Staff
2 edition, 256 pages, 2017, **ISBN-13:** 978-0997108965

About the Author

Thomas R. Ittelson is an expert at translating complicated financial topics in an accessible way for non-financial audiences. He is not an accountant, but rather a natural scientist by training (Harvard University in biochemistry) and an entrepreneur. His successes and challenges in both science and business helped him develop his own accounting acumen and style.

Tom shares that knowledge with non-financial managers in this new book, *Financial Statements: A Step-by-Step Guide to Understanding and Creating Financial Reports, Third Edition.* Over 200,000 copies are in print and the text is on the reading list of business and accounting courses around the country.

He first learned accounting and financial reporting "on the job" as a marketing officer and strategic planner for a large multinational corporation and then as the founder, CEO and treasurer of a venture capital backed high-technology company. Currently Tom practices with **The Mercury Group,** a Cambridge, Massachusetts-based management consulting firm specializing in marketing, financial modeling, business strategy development and fund raising for both startups and more established technology-based businesses.

Tom's recent work with nonprofits led him to recognize that non-financial nonprofit board members, managers and staff all require a simple working knowledge of accounting and financial statements to do their job. With his new book, *Nonprofit Accounting & Financial Statements: An Overview for Board, Management, and Staff, Second Edition,* Tom's audacious nonprofit "mission" is to significantly improve the efficiency and effectiveness of U.S. public charities by improving financial literacy within those organizations. He is available to speak at Board of Director's meetings and with senior staff.

Contact Thomas Ittelson at:

The Mercury Group
Harvard Square Station
PO Box 381350
Cambridge, MA 02238-1350

617-285-1168

ittelson@mercurygroup.com

https://www.mercurygrouppress.com/

Notes